AF594468

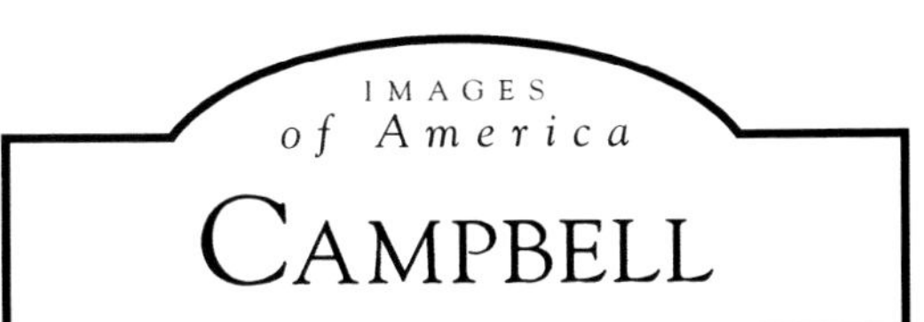
IMAGES
of America
CAMPBELL

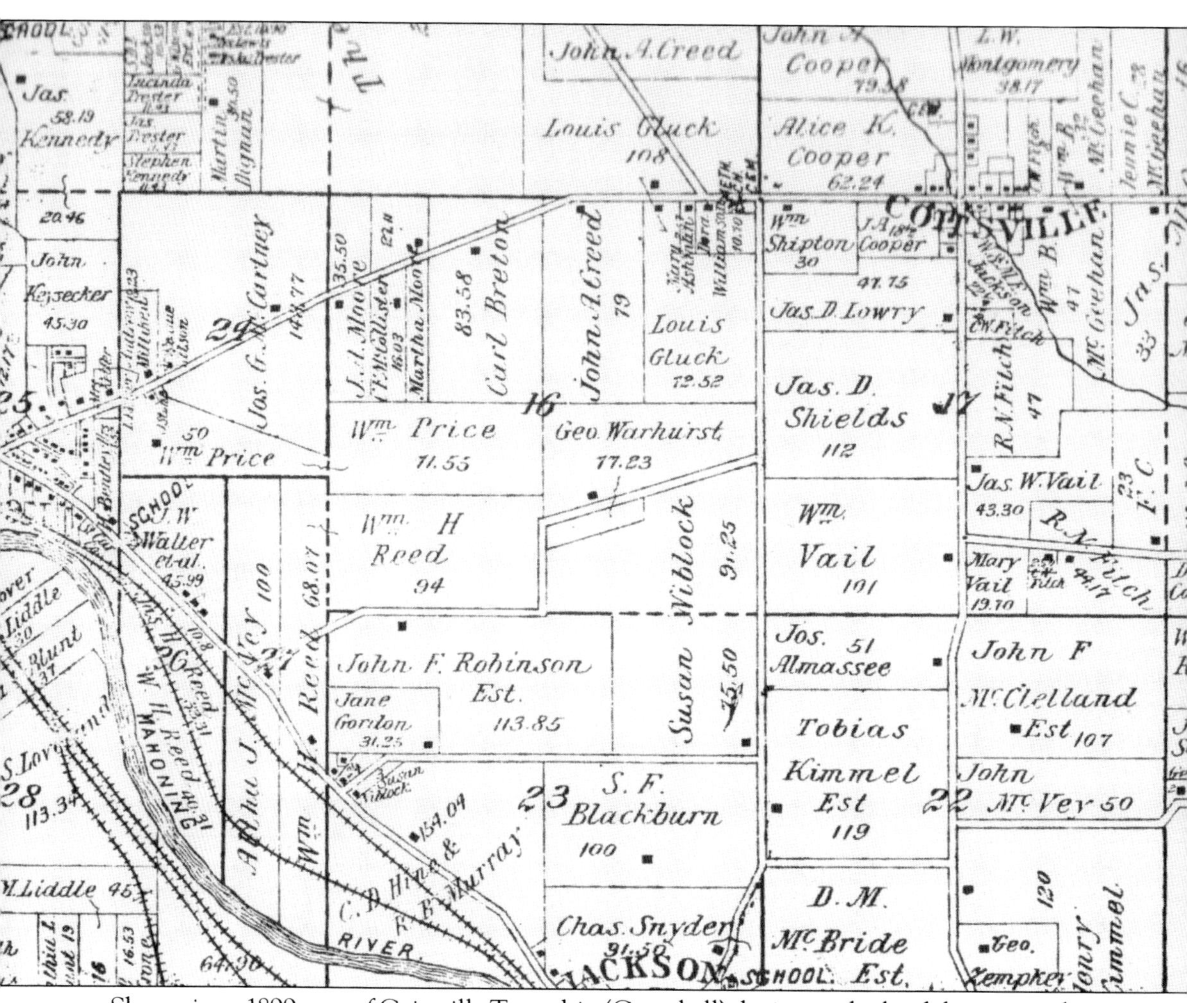

Shown is an 1899 map of Coitsville Township (Campbell) depicting the land division and owner of each lot. A vast majority of early settlers have been immortalized through city street names, such as Robinson, Blackburn, Creed, and Moore. The Mahoning River, which is located in the bottom left corner, was reformed during the formation of the steel mills. Before the industrial sector was built, the river had been much closer to present-day Coitsville Road at Wilson Avenue. (Courtesy of Florence Galida.)

On the Cover: Campbell pride is alive and well in 1946 with these Memorial High School cheerleaders. From left to right are Mary Ann Matosky, Betty Carney, Mary Ann Perno, and Alma Vrable. Whether on the gridiron or on the court, the cheerleaders have always added a fighting spirit to the football and basketball teams. (Courtesy of Florence Galida.)

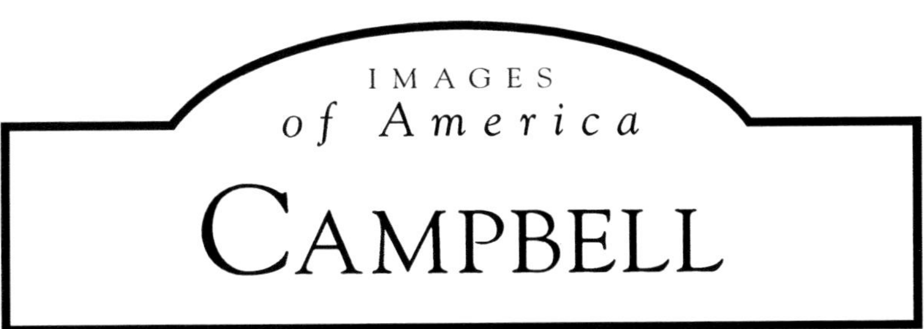

Joseph Pavlansky

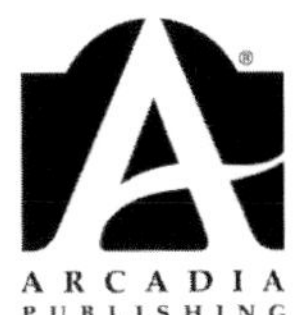

Copyright © 2016 by Joseph Pavlansky
ISBN 978-1-4671-1698-5

Published by Arcadia Publishing
Charleston, South Carolina

Printed in the United States of America

Library of Congress Control Number: 2015960789

For all general information, please contact Arcadia Publishing:
Telephone 843-853-2070
Fax 843-853-0044
E-mail sales@arcadiapublishing.com
For customer service and orders:
Toll-Free 1-888-313-2665

Visit us on the Internet at www.arcadiapublishing.com

To all the past, present, and future generations of Campbell, Ohio

Contents

Acknowledgments 6

Introduction 7

1. Soup City 9
2. The Mills and Company Homes 39
3. City of Churches 55
4. School Days 63
5. Home of the Red Devils 83
6. The City's Finest 97
7. The Bicentennial and Beyond 115

Acknowledgments

This photographic history of the city of Campbell is meant to stimulate our sense of pride in past generations who, through their blood, sweat, and tears, created a prosperous city from a land of swamps, forests, and hills. Most of the images were acquired from the collection that makes up the Campbell Historical Society, while other images came from private collections. These images were selected to give you a sense of how Campbell rose from the ashes of the steel mills and continued on through thick and thin. Every effort was made to ensure that dates, names, places, and information are correct. During my research, I consulted many people who were more than enthusiastic to assist with information and picture gathering.

This book never would have begun if it were not for the constant encouragement of my girlfriend, Antonietta "Toni" Iacobacci, and her unending faith in me. Thank you for your love and continual support through all my endeavors. I would also like to express my deepest, deepest gratitude to Florence Galida and her husband, John Galida, for opening up their home and the Campbell Historical Society's vast collection of photographs and references for my research. Through the many months of research, the Galidas endured my constant knocking at their door and popping in unexpectedly, just to get a few pictures. Thank you again for your love, friendship, and assistance.

I extend a special thanks to Mike Parise for his support and information and for being a great friend. Many years, we sat over coffee and cakes discussing the city's history, looking at old photographs, and reminiscing about the good old days. Finally, I got moving and put something together that will hopefully inspire many more years of Campbell historical talks.

My grateful thanks are also extended to Lorraine Sabol for her continuous e-mails and for taking time to meet with me to review photographs and talk about Campbell's past. Many more thanks to Uncle Edward Zamets, Irene Moylan, Aunt Carol Dolan, Eugene Skelley, Karen Repasky, Lynette Hardman, Nancy Johngrass from the *Hometown Journal*, and anyone else I might have missed. Also a special thank you to Sarah Gottlieb from Arcadia Publishing for keeping me on track and answering my many questions.

Thank you to my mother, Bonnie; my father, Dennis; my sister, Shannon; and the rest of my family and friends for giving me a lifetime of love and support. And last, but most important, thank you God for giving me the opportunity and ability to put this book together for the benefit of all who read it.

I sincerely mean this when I say Campbell people are the greatest!

INTRODUCTION

Tucked away on a small area of land in northeastern Ohio, the city of Campbell and its citizens enjoy a rich history that began at the dawn of the steel industry and continues to this very day. Even before the mills sprung up along the Mahoning River, the occupants of the land worked for a better and brighter future.

Native Americans vastly used the lands of Campbell as hunting and fishing grounds, with the Mahoning River providing easy transportation in and out of the region. In 1630, the area's earliest recorded history began when King James I of England granted the Northwest Territory lands to the Plymouth Company of Massachusetts. Since that time, the land grants changed many hands until finding an owner with the Connecticut Western Reserve in 1662. Owners of the land held on to the rights until members of the Connecticut Land Company purchased three million acres for $1.2 million. With many of the original members of the company purchasing their own plots of land, Daniel Lathrop Coit purchased lots No. 1 through No. 28 in Township No. 2 located in the First Range, which eventually became Coitsville Township. During the early 1800s, much of the southwestern parts of Coitsville Township, namely land plots No. 16, half of No. 17 and No. 22, and No. 23 to No. 27 were sold to various settlers of Irish, Scotch, and English ancestry. These plots of land in the southwestern section eventually became the boundaries for East Youngstown and, later, the city of Campbell.

In 1835, the State of Ohio began construction on an 86-mile Pennsylvania-Ohio canal that ran along the Mahoning River near what is now Wilson Avenue. The canal ended the isolation of the local farmers and brought businesses and jobs to the area. With the expansion and efficiency of the railroad system, however, the canal was abandoned in 1877. As the area began to expand rapidly, the Youngstown Sheet and Tube Company decided to settle along 300 acres near the Mahoning River in 1900, with operations starting in 1902. With such an expansion, people were needed to fill the employment slots left open by a sparse population. As word quickly spread of a new steel mill looking for employees, those seeking opportunity from the area and from Europe began to flood the east side of Youngstown looking for work. The area of East Youngstown became so inundated with people living in crude shacks and anywhere they could have a roof over their head that the section became its own entity. On November 19, 1908, the geographical location on the east side of Youngstown was incorporated as the village of East Youngstown. Elections were held on April 24, 1909, with David C. Hamilton as the first mayor, J.V. Murphay as solicitor, and Jerry Dailey, O.G. DeForgarossy, William Gordon, Joseph Maust, William H. Reed, and Isaac M. Fink as councilmen.

The village of East Youngstown was growing exponentially with people and businesses, and with that came the problems. Overcrowding, mill hazards, pollution, and the homesickness of the immigrants in a foreign land led to a difficult life in this compact locale. Knowing that they were stuck here for good, the men and women decided to make the best of their new opportunities. Soon, ideas were put into action, and the residents established a police department, fire department, education centers, and general stores to fit the needs of the families and workers. The village started to take shape and began to grow into a thriving community with everyone working together to survive and make a better life for themselves and future generations. Although the new community had suffered through mill workers rioting for higher pay, fires that destroyed several buildings, and a general outburst of violence during the strike of 1916, villagers rebuilt. By 1919, the steel workers had arranged for another strike, but this time without all the violence. The men, and even many of their wives, joined the picket line and held fast to their union beliefs. Not wanting to budge on the issue, the steel companies instead hired 5,000 blacks to replace those on strike. Eventually, the strike failed, and those who had strongly supported the unions were not hired back by the companies.

Even with such calamities occurring in the small village, the population had been increasing so much that, on January 1, 1922, the village became a city. But the damage had already been done, and East Youngstown kept its bad reputation, both locally and nationally. Local political, religious, and respected citizen leaders gathered to figure out a way to put the past behind them. After years of trying new ideas and names, the committee and a majority of the populace agreed that the city should be named after James Anson Campbell, the president of Youngstown Sheet and Tube Company, so on April 26, 1926, an official proclamation changed East Youngstown to Campbell. By now, the city had settled down and began to focus on the future and transforming a little boomtown into a thriving American city. The decades to come would present trying times for the little city through Prohibition, the Great Depression, war, floods, flu epidemics, fires, and more. However, sports, academics, entrepreneurship, cultural and religious activities, and community pride would conquer any hardships that the people faced.

Things were looking good for the city as all the pieces started coming together and the rough lands were transformed into a beautiful place to live and visit. The mills had provided all the revenue Campbell could have needed and more. Along with all the businesses and tax base, Campbell became one of the richest little cities in the nation. But all the years of enjoying a comfortable living would come to an end on September 19, 1977, when the Youngstown Sheet and Tube Company Campbell Works suddenly, and without warning to the locals, closed its doors and laid off over 5,000 workers. This was an extreme and unexpected blow to the people who relied on the mill for employment and city revenue. With the mills now closed, local businesses soon followed as many of the people started to leave the area in search of new jobs. Campbell would thrive for another few years but quickly found itself struggling without the revenue it had been used to. The little boomtown that rose from the rough lands, endured harsh disasters, and emerged as a diamond in the rough was now spiraling toward the same bottom it had come from.

Today, the proud citizens do what they can to keep traditions alive and show their love for a city that still has so much potential to offer. Memorial Red Devils from all across the city, and even those who have moved away, will always hold a special place in their heart for Campbell. By embracing the past, Campbell can truly move forward and hope to thrive once more as a strong and prosperous little city.

One

Soup City

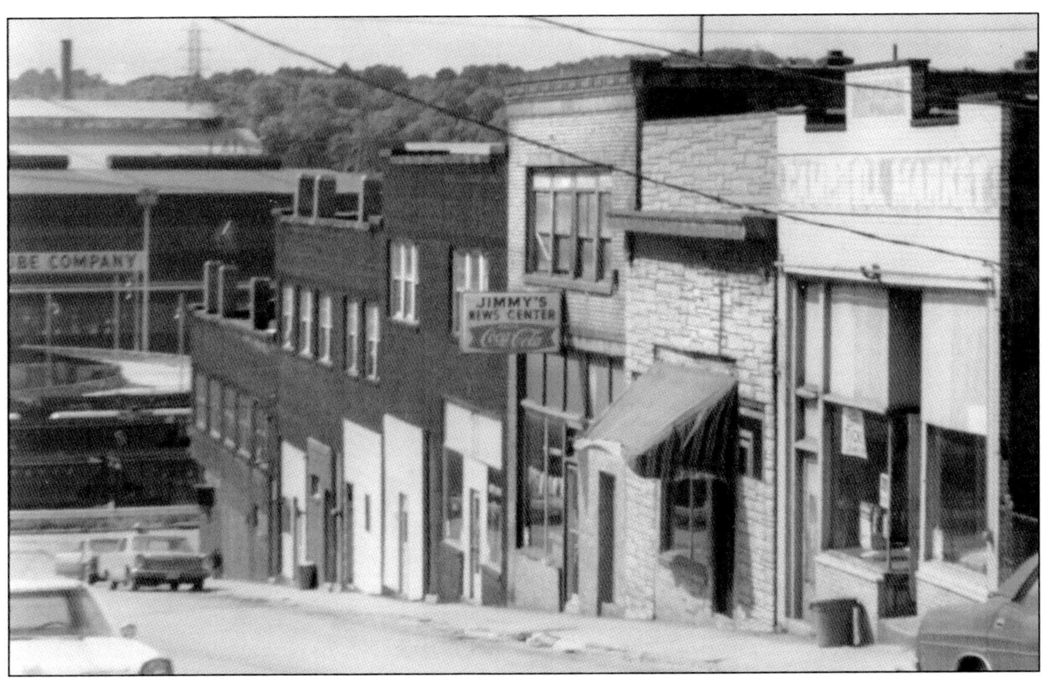

This is an undated photograph looking down Robinson Road toward Wilson Avenue showing the various taverns and markets available to mill workers as they crossed the Short Street Bridge. The buildings have been home to food markets, taverns, doctor's offices, apartments, a movie theater, and more. The Youngstown Sheet and Tube Company plant can be seen in the background. Today, many of the buildings pictured are no longer standing. After the steel mills closed in 1977, small businesses began to decline as jobs and money became scarce. Buildings were abandoned and left vacant until demolished by a new owner or the city. Today, Mother Nature has reclaimed some lots, while private companies have purchased the others. (Courtesy of Florence Galida.)

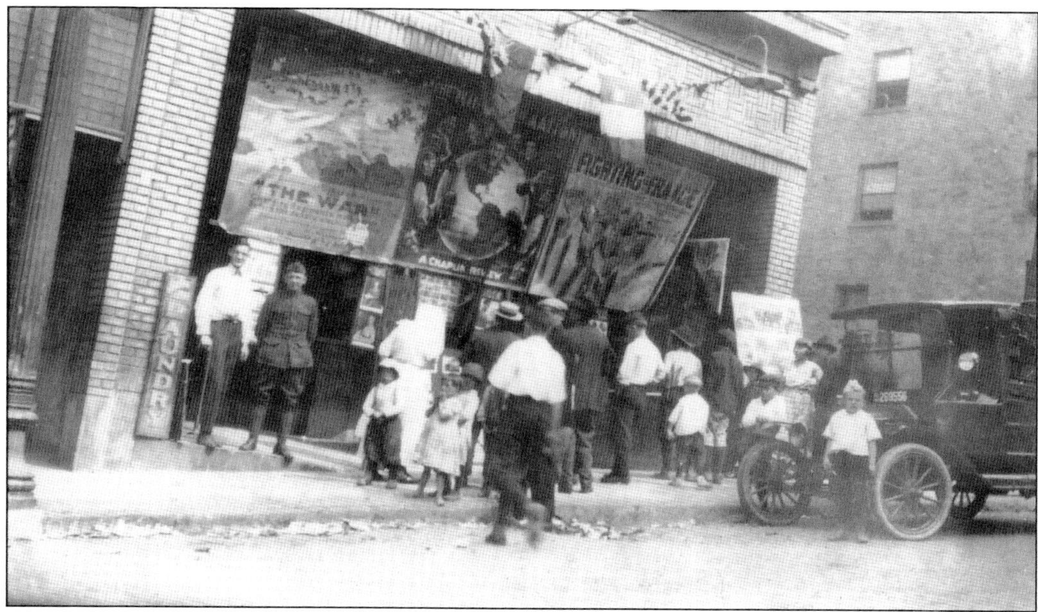

This photograph of the Hodgekin's Home Theater, located on Robinson Road and Short Street, was taken in 1919. Robinson Road and Short Street was a central location for many Campbell residents looking for entertainment after work and on the weekends. This area of the city was also filled with businesses to accommodate employees returning from work across the Short Street Bridge. (Courtesy of Mike Parise.)

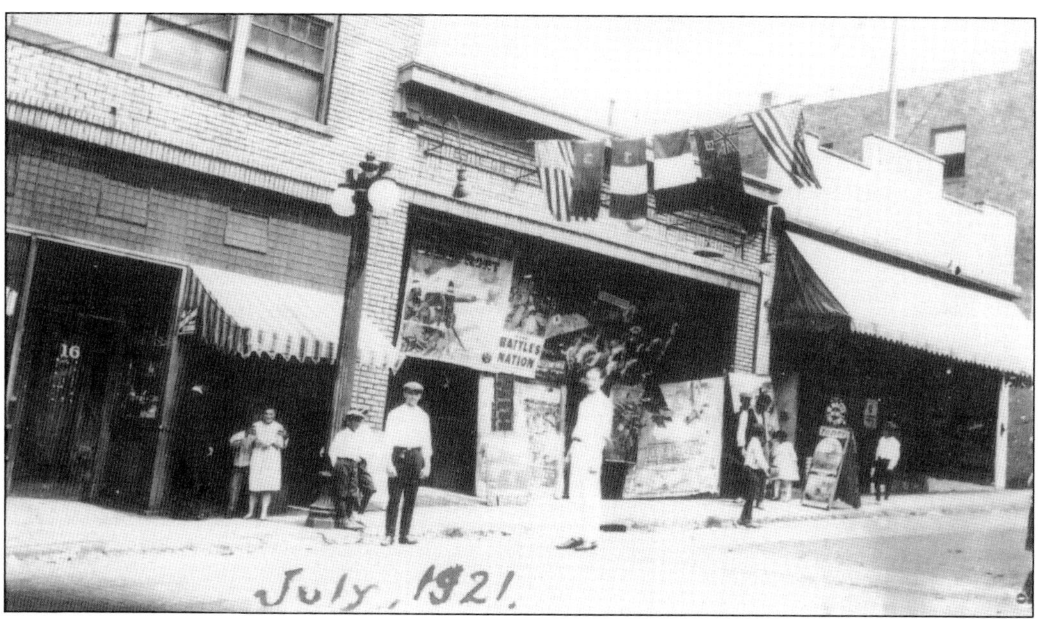

The Hodgekin's Home Theater, pictured here in July 1921, played movies and serial cliff-hangers for kids and adults. Various promotional war movie posters can be seen hanging in front of the building. Several multinational flags are hanging from the building and across Robinson Road in recognition of the many different immigrants in the city. The theater was the earliest to open in East Youngstown (Campbell) and closed down at an unknown date. (Courtesy of Mike Parise.)

Not all immigrants found work at the steel mills; some took more desirable positions on the railroads. Shown in this photograph from July 28, 1913, are railroad workers with electric streetcars in the background. The streetcars and trolleys were housed at the Haselton Car Barns location along Wilson Avenue near Coitsville Road. The barns shut down in 1944 and later became the site for the Calex Corporation. (Courtesy of Florence Galida.)

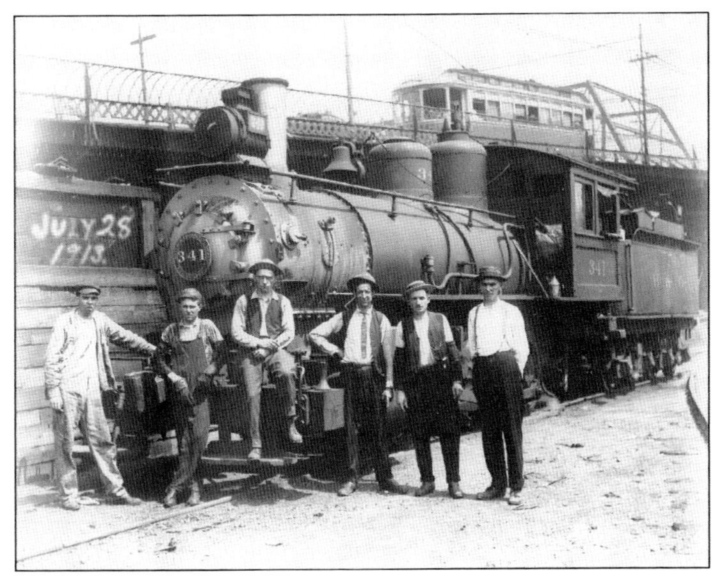

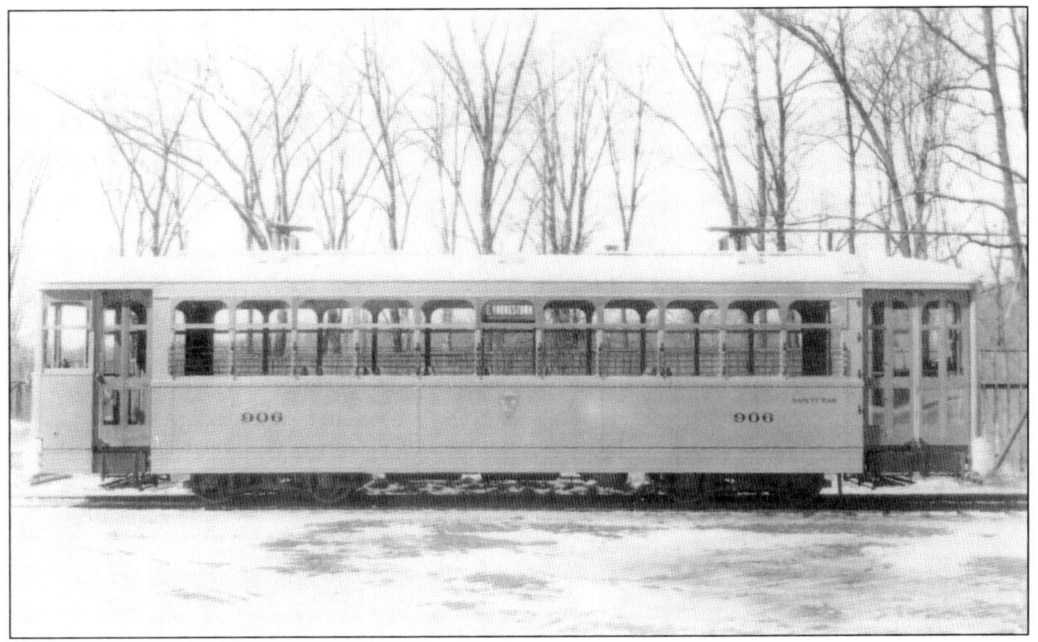

In the early 1890s, electric streetcars ran from Youngstown to East Youngstown at Stop One (Wilson Avenue at Coitsville Road). By 1899, a single track had been established through East Youngstown to Struthers and later into Lowellville. Operated by the Mahoning Valley Electric Railroad Company, the tracks ran from Stop One to behind the homes on the south side of Wilson Avenue and then behind the residences on the riverbank before continuing north on Eighth Street, where they ran parallel to Wilson Avenue all the way into Lowellville. The electric streetcars operated until 1940, when they were replaced by the electric trolley buses. (Courtesy of Mike Parise.)

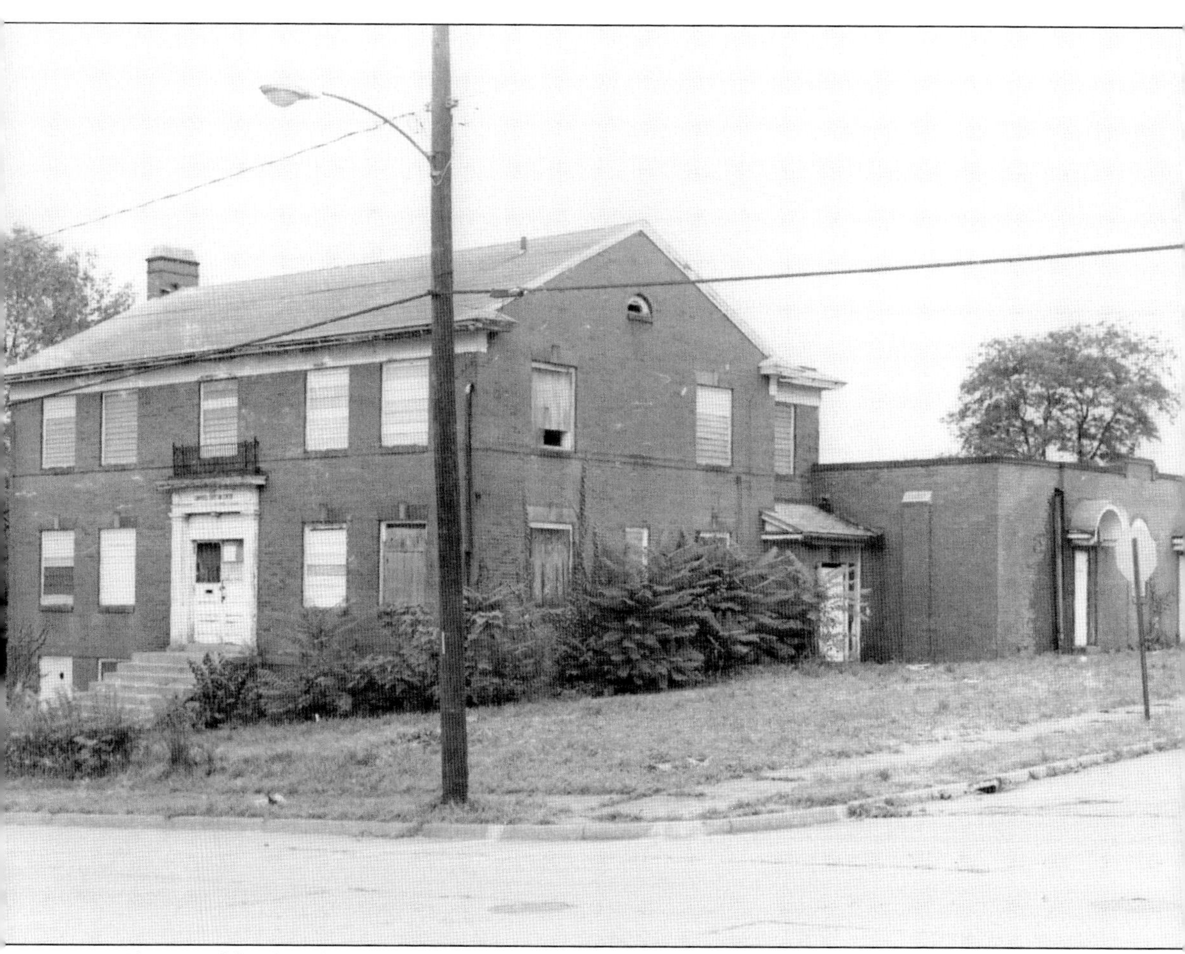

The Neighborhood House Campbell Christian Center on the corner of Gordon Avenue and Fifteenth Street is pictured as it appeared in 1980. After the closure of Hamrock Hall on Wilson Avenue at Washington Street in 1923, various Presbyterian churches in Youngstown became concerned with the drastic increase in the immigrant population. In 1927, these churches raised approximately $12,000 and constructed the Neighborhood House the same year. The Neighborhood House, along with the Bethal House, played a major role in assisting the citizens of Campbell during the Great Depression and throughout World War II. (Courtesy of Florence Galida.)

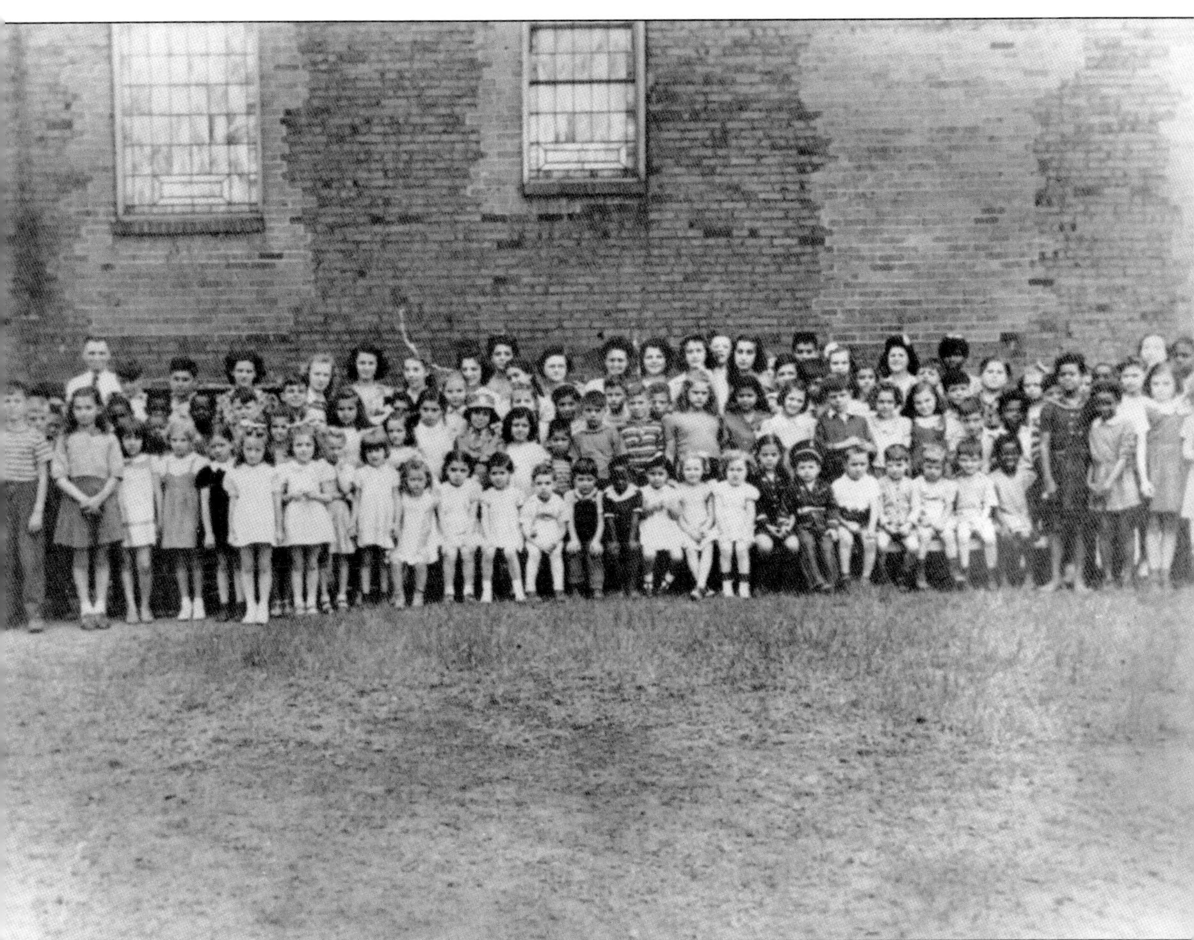

This 1943 photograph shows the children of the Bethal House, which was located on Murray Avenue at Washington Street. The origins of the Bethal House began in 1919 when Rev. Robert Hughes of the Hazeltine Baptist Church began a missionary Sunday school in a small storeroom located on Ninth Street. With the immigrant population of the area growing, Hughes moved to a hall on Reed Avenue before finally settling at the Bethal House. (Courtesy of Florence Galida.)

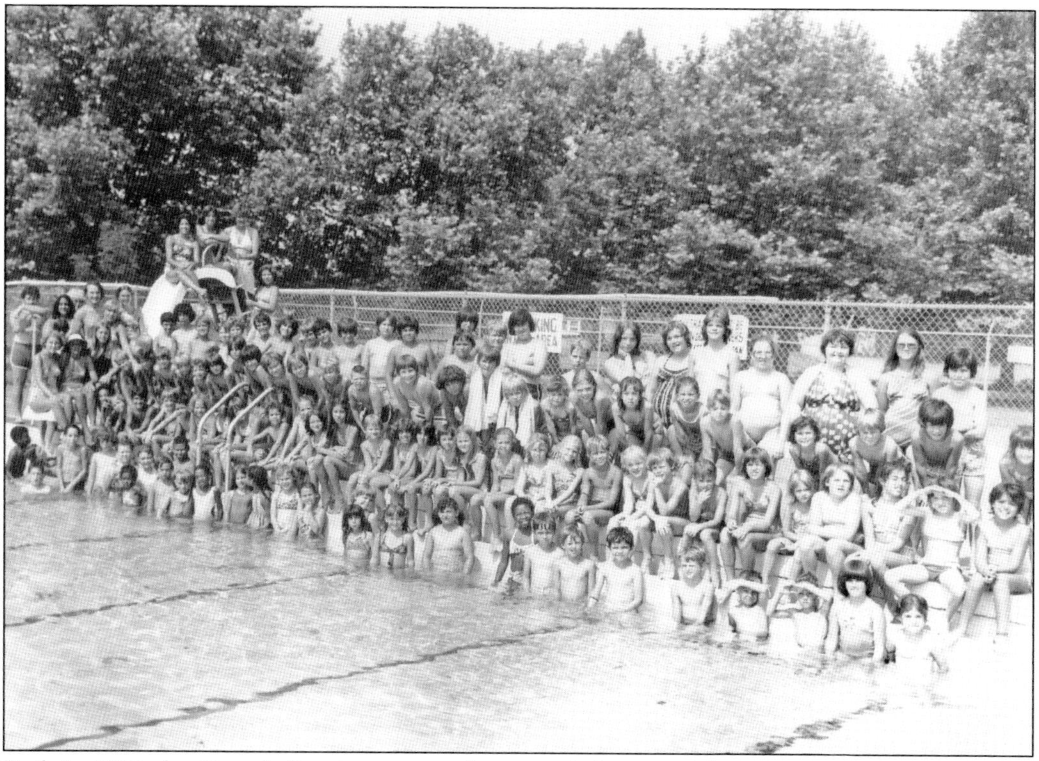

Built in 1950, the Campbell swimming pool occupied the site of the current community center. During its operation, the pool's water supply was provided solely from well water and was more than likely the only city pool in the state that did so. Children and adults alike flocked from the city and from Youngstown to enjoy not only the refreshing pool water but also the beautiful scenery of Roosevelt Park. (Courtesy of Florence Galida.)

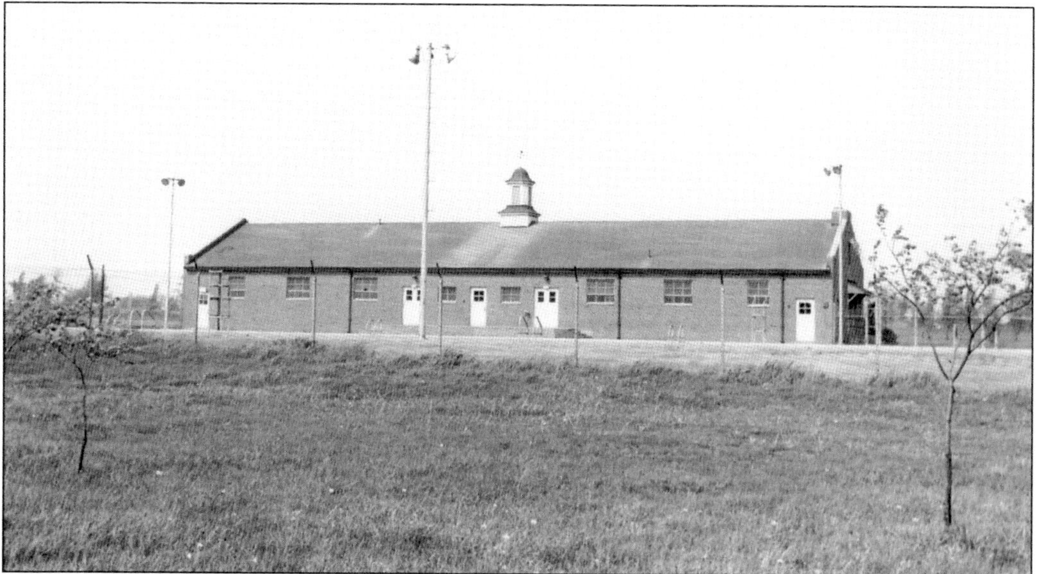

Here is an undated photograph of the Roosevelt Park pool house. The Campbell Community Center and gazebo currently occupy the land, and the pool has since been filled in with dirt.

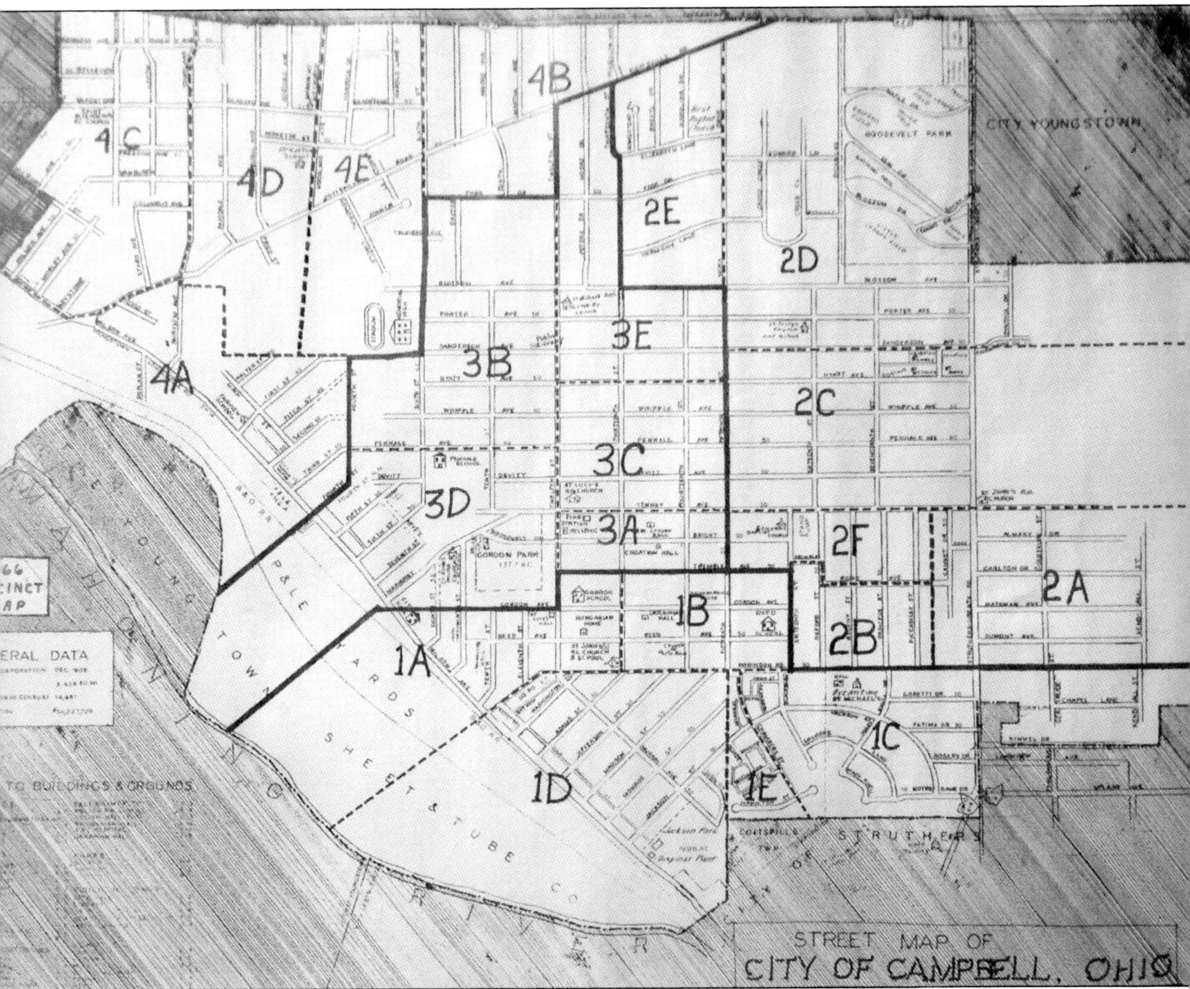

This precinct map from 1966 shows the jurisdictional borders of the city and the region that each of the four wards encompassed. Each ward was broken into four to six smaller zones. City police officers used this map for an easier recognition of their area of responsibility during foot or car patrols. Many of the city churches, businesses, or other prominent establishments are also marked on the map. (Courtesy of Joseph Pavlansky.)

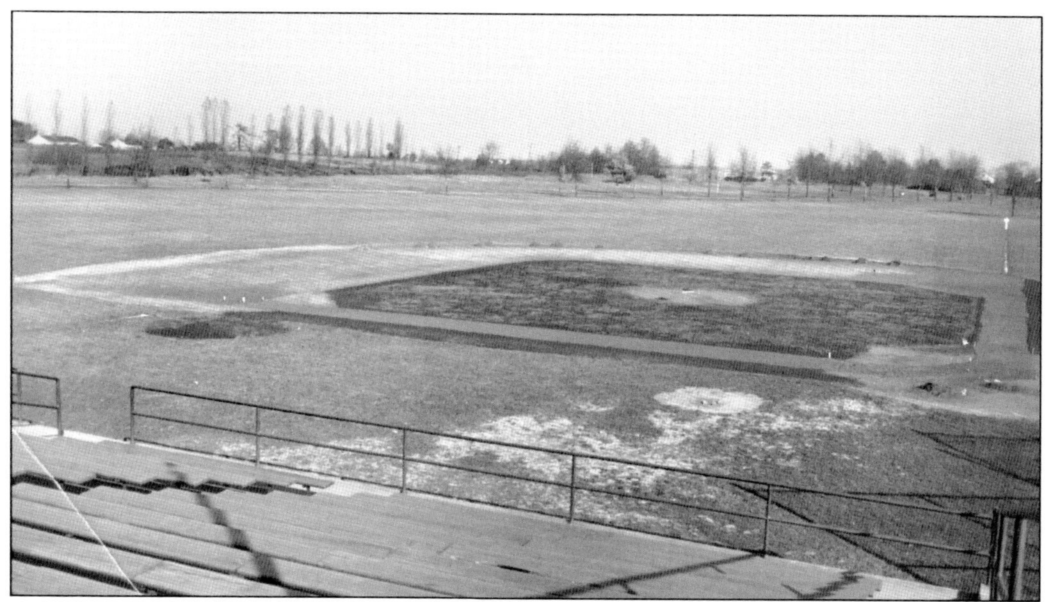

In 1937, under the recommendation of the Hazelton Slovak City Improvement Club, Mayor John Borak purchased the 64.5-acre Gluck farm for $6,250 in order to provide a large enough area for a city park. Most of the land at the time was swamp, and through the combined effort of extensive programs, it was drained and improved upon over the next several years. (Courtesy of F. Galida.)

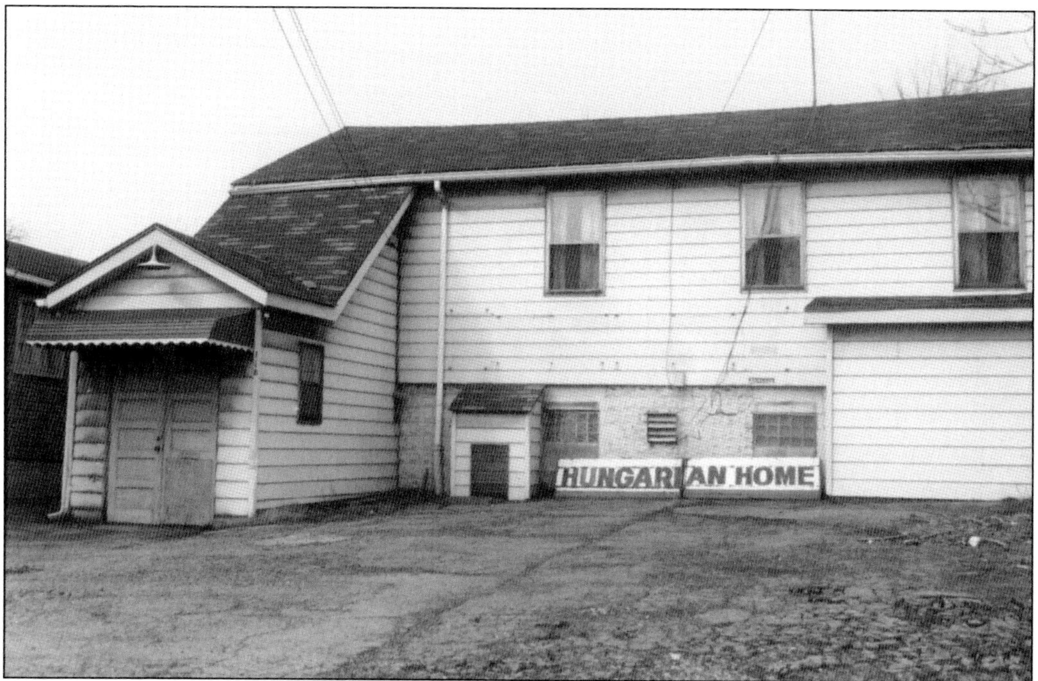

Local immigrants established various social halls according to their nationality to provide a venue for special events, political meetings, weddings, and other gatherings. Some halls even played host to boxing and wrestling matches. The Hungarian Home, pictured here, was formerly called the Hungarian American Citizens Club. (Courtesy of Florence Galida.)

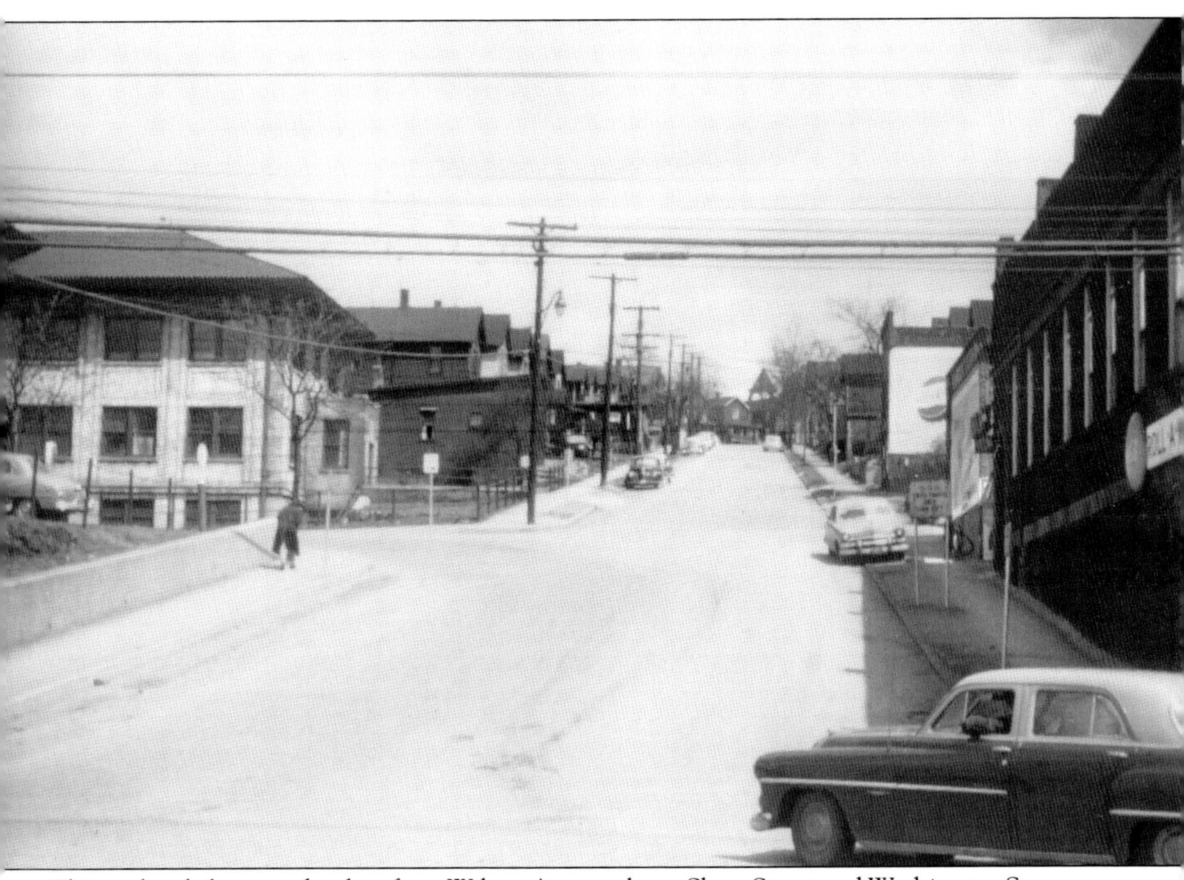

This undated photograph taken from Wilson Avenue shows Short Street and Washington Street as they appeared during the heyday of the mills. Several businesses can be seen on the right, along with the Youngstown Sheet and Tube Company hospital on the left. Houses line both sides of Washington Street all the way up to Murray Avenue. These houses and businesses are no longer present, as the land is now privately owned. (Courtesy of F. Galida.)

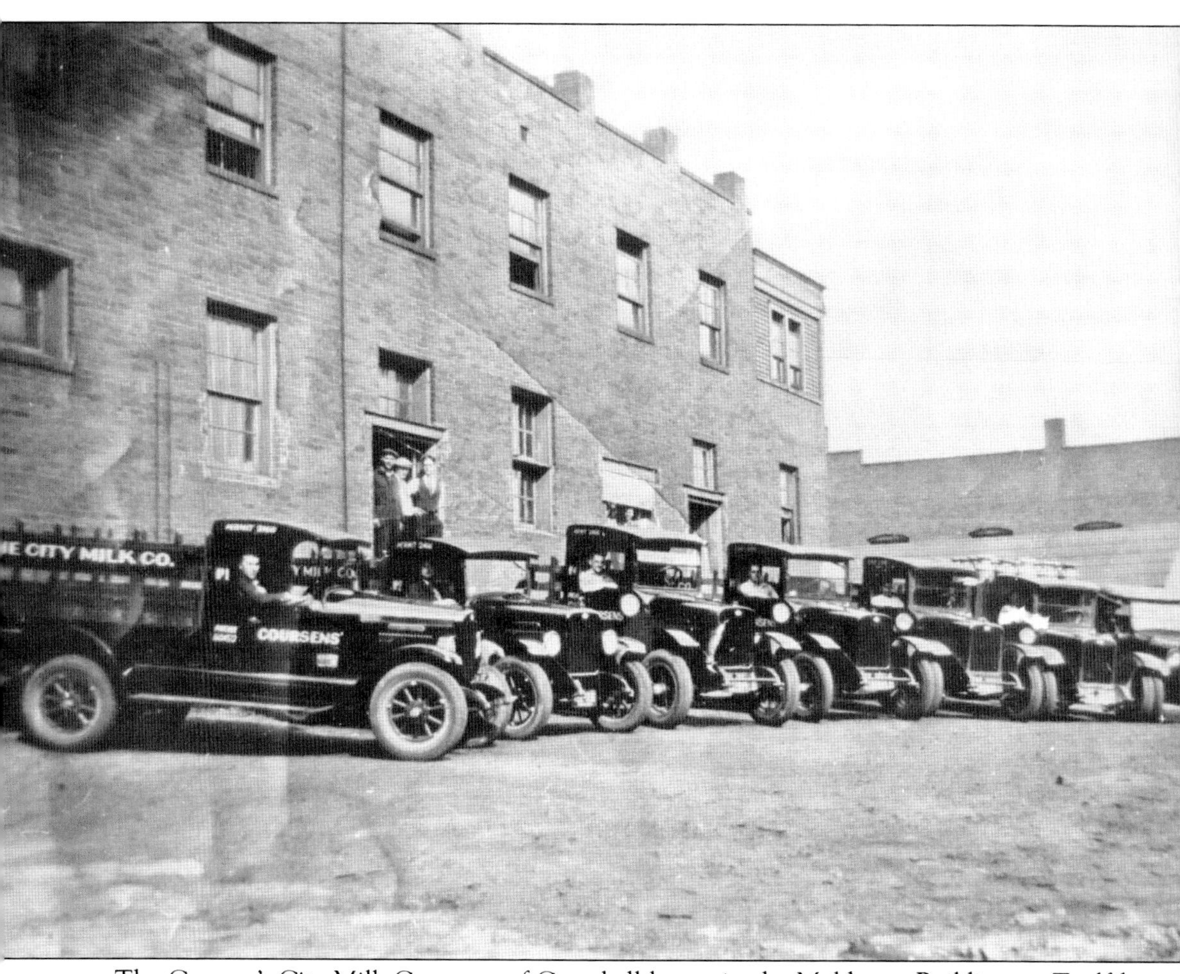

The Coursen's City Milk Company of Campbell began in the Moldovan Building on Twelfth Street in 1926. Owned and operated by Richard and Kenneth Coursen, the business moved to Washington Street at Murray Avenue in 1928. It remained at this location until the Coursens left the city in the early 1930s. Pictured in this 1928 photograph are, from left to right, (drivers) Steve Zetts, Elmer Davis, George Ducat, Frank Horvath, and Nick Stephens; (doorway) Fred Zamary, Charles McQuillan, and Ken Coursen. Although this photograph is not of the best quality, it is the only known image of the Coursen City Milk Company of Campbell to exist. (Courtesy of Florence Galida.)

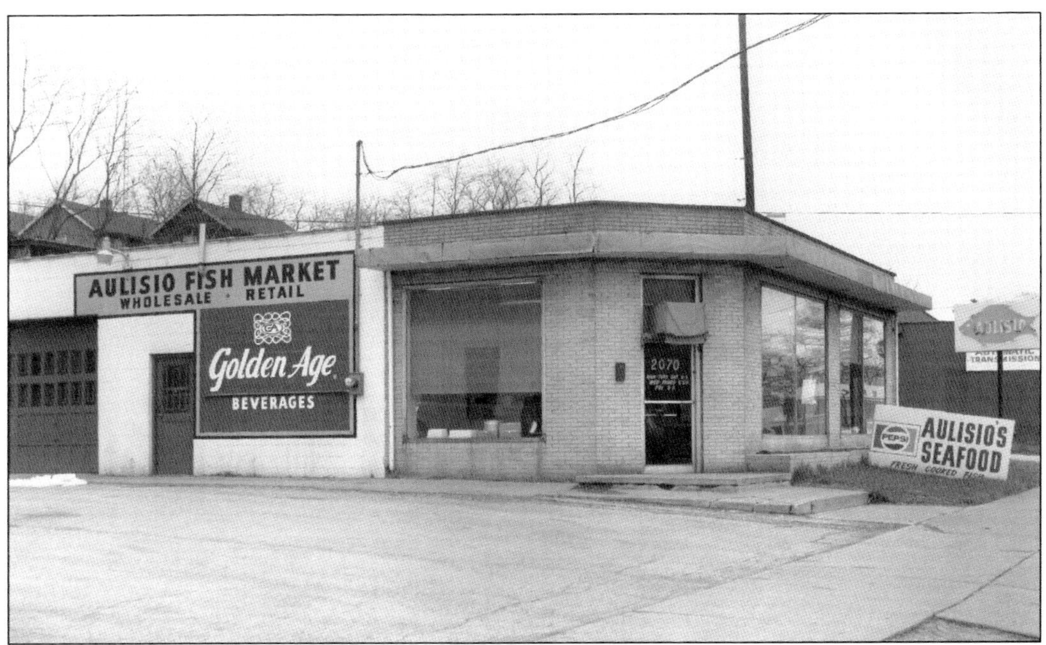

This 1970s photograph shows Aulisio Fish Market, located on the corner of Wilson Avenue at Morley Avenue. Anthony Aulisio owned the market from 1930 until his passing in 1994. (Courtesy of Florence Galida.)

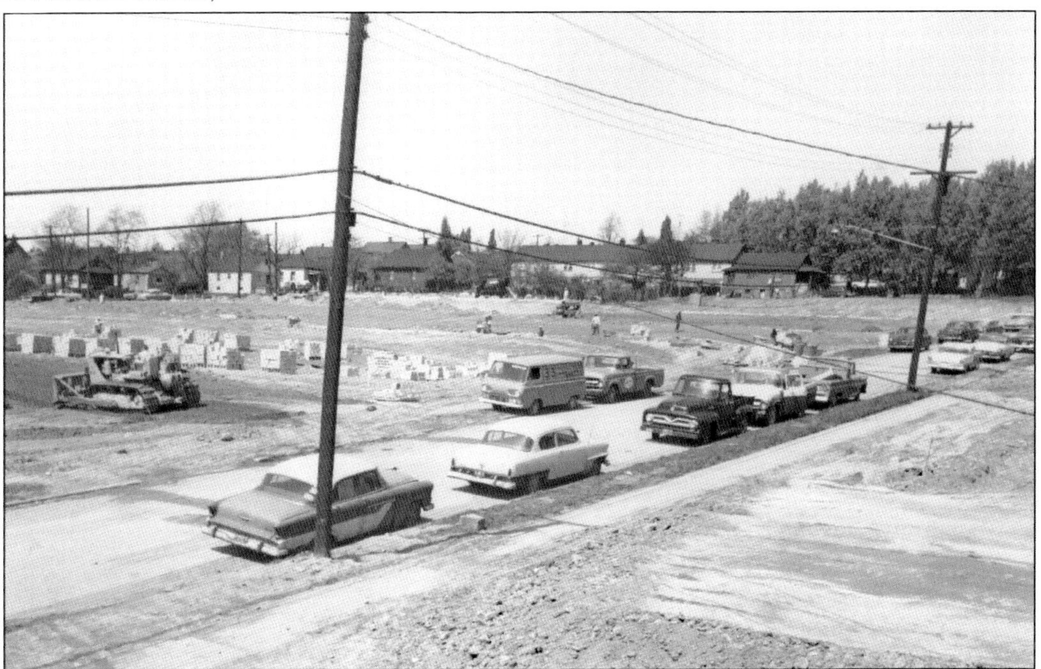

Construction began on the Kirwan Homes in the early part of 1962 and finished in the latter half of 1963. The housing complex, operating under the Youngstown Metropolitan Housing Authority, was developed for low-income families and named after Congressman Michael J. Kirwan. This view looking north shows the construction in progress with Jackson Street in the foreground. (Courtesy of Florence Galida.)

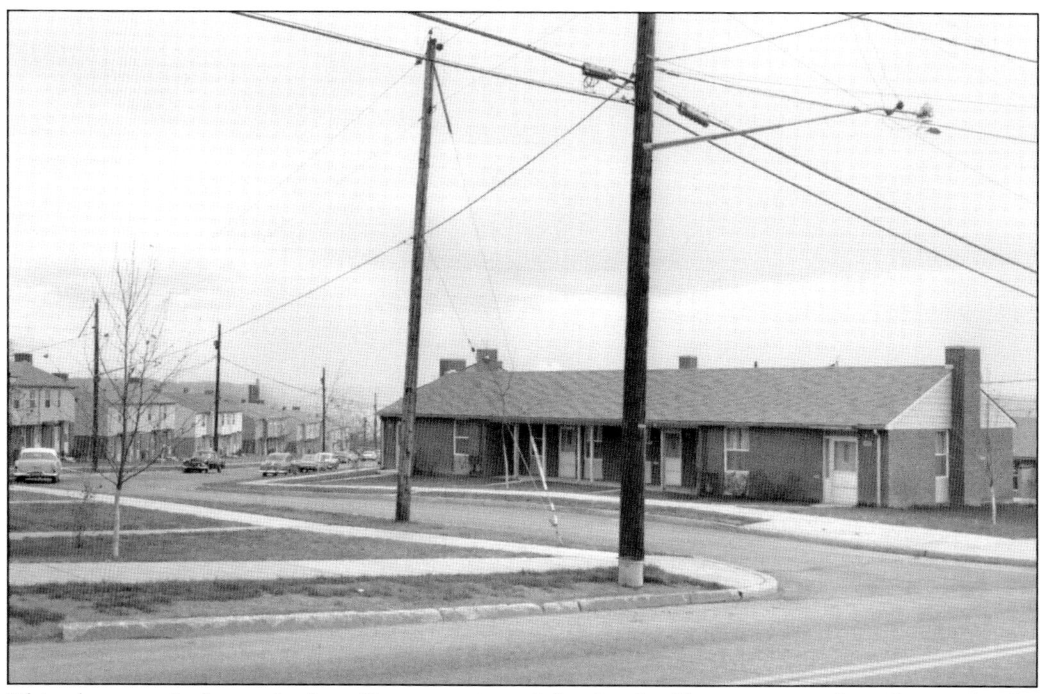

This photograph shows the Jean Street section of the finished housing complex. Currently, the Kirwan Homes occupy Jean Street and sections of Jackson Street, Murray Avenue, and Monroe Street. (Courtesy of Florence Galida.)

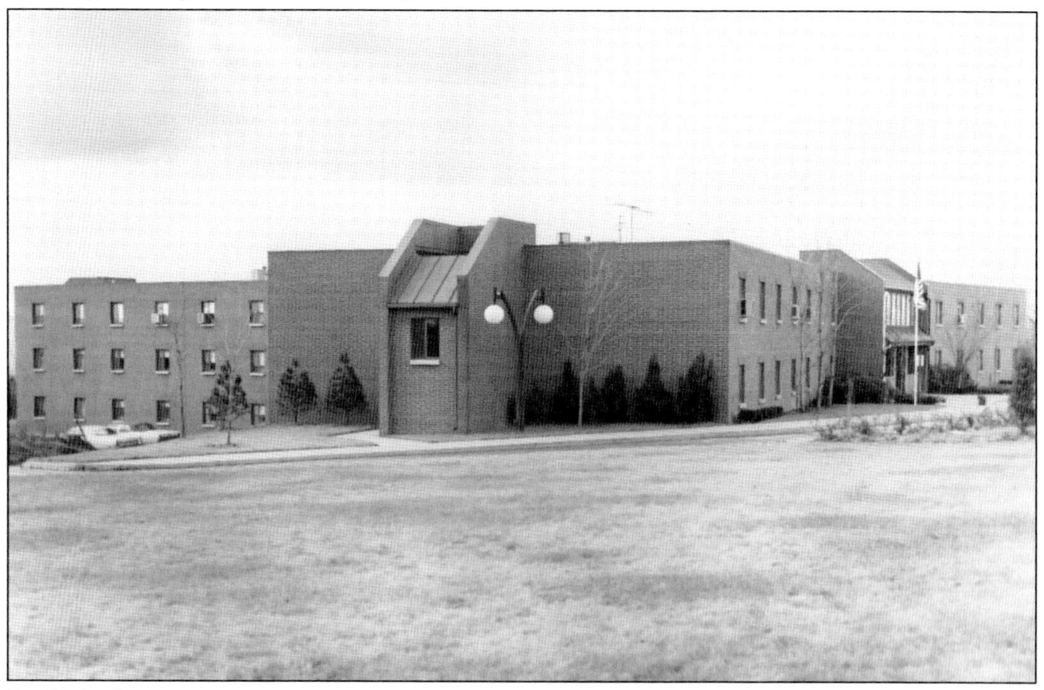

Established in 1973, Vasu Manor is named after Romulus G. Vasu, a board member of the Youngstown Metropolitan Housing Authority. The apartment complex, located on Roosevelt Drive at Twelfth Street, is used to house handicapped or elderly citizens. (Courtesy of Florence Galida.)

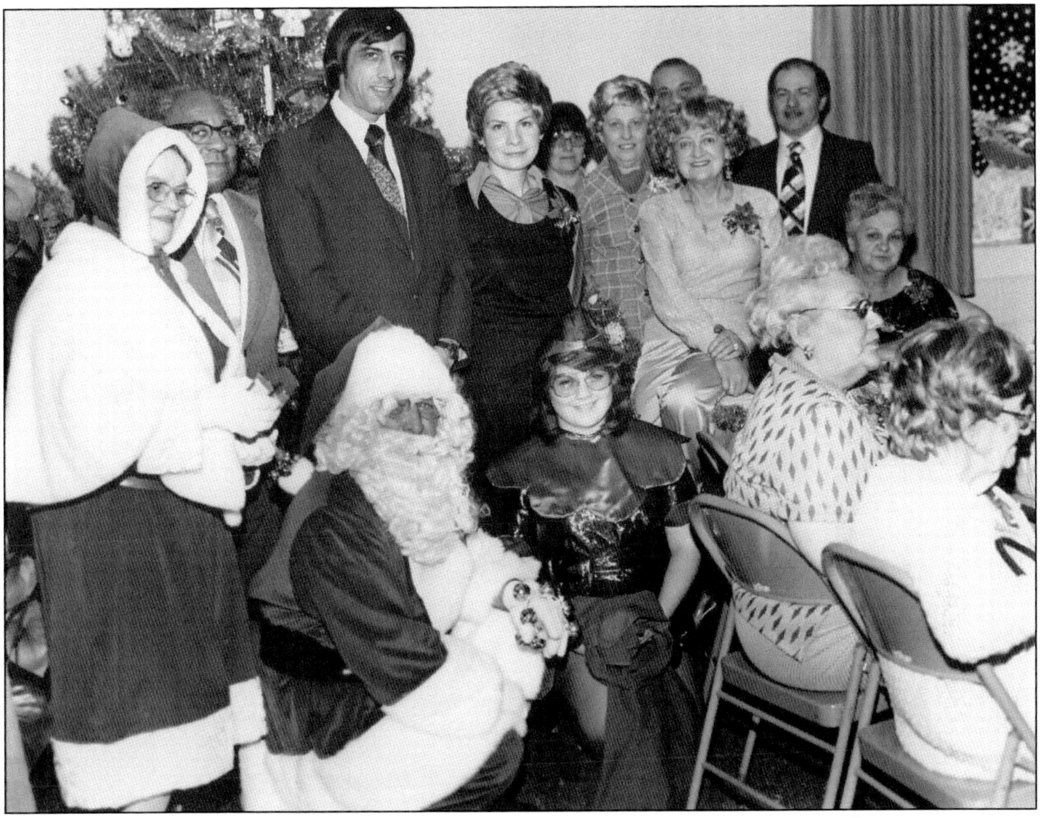

This 1977 photograph shows Mayor Michael J. Katula Jr. participating in a Christmas party at Vasu Manor. Several activities and events take place each week, including holiday celebrations, birthday parties, bingo, cultural dinners and dances, arts and crafts, and various other social gatherings. (Courtesy of Florence Galida.)

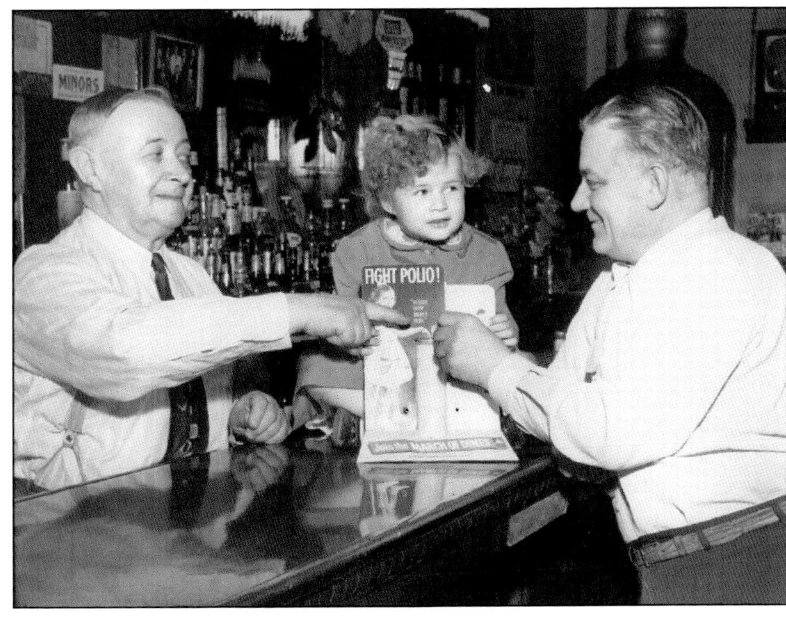

Shown in this undated photograph taken at Cvengros Bar are, from left to right, owner Michael Cvengros, unknown poster child, and Frank Brayer. Michael Cvengros served as a primary witness to the 1916 riots and fire that destroyed a majority of the city, as well as a councilman-at-large from 1938 to 1947. (Courtesy of Florence Galida.)

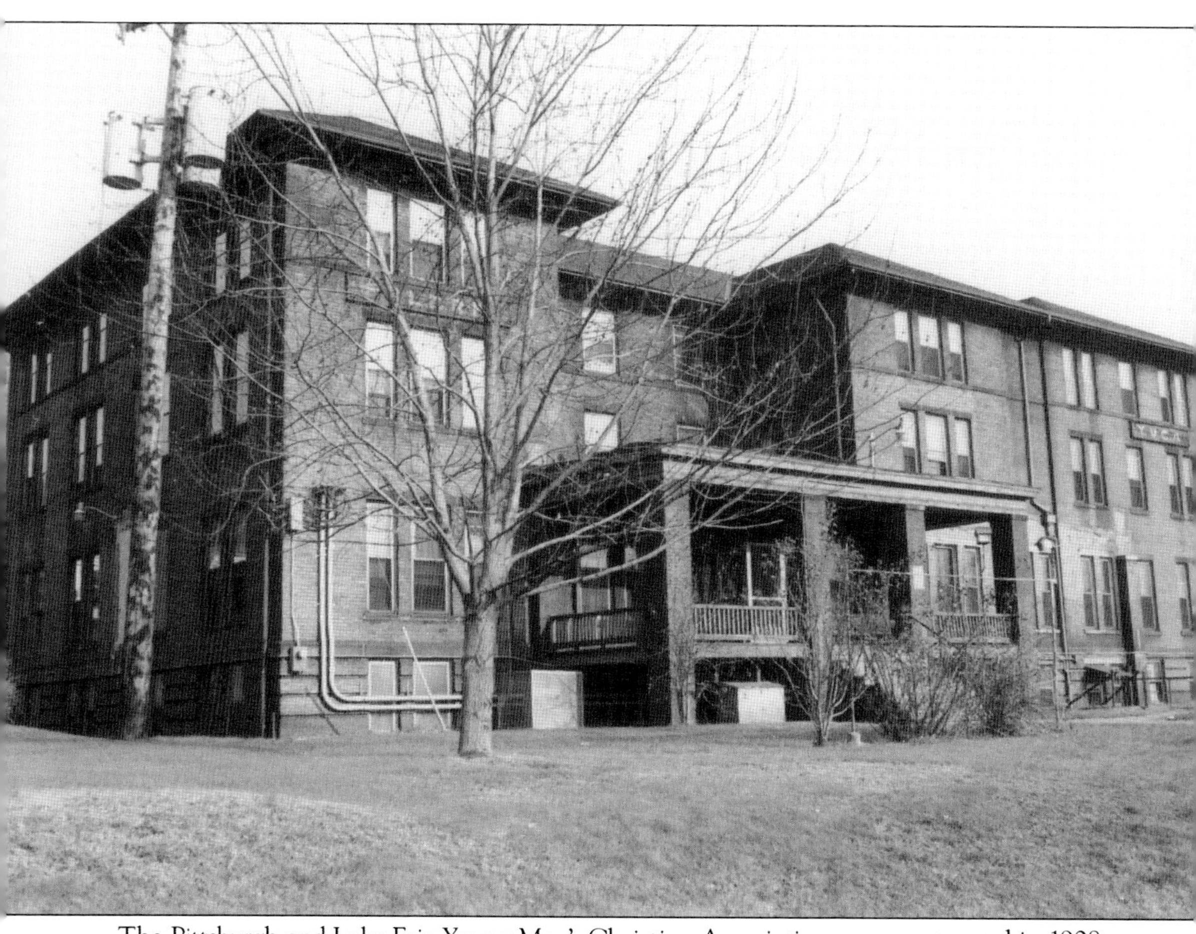

The Pittsburgh and Lake Erie Young Men's Christian Association was constructed in 1908 as a place of rest and recreation for railroaders, followed by an addition in 1917 to meet the demands of increased workers and that of a growing village. The building stood just south of Wilson Avenue, near Third Street. (Courtesy of Florence Galida.)

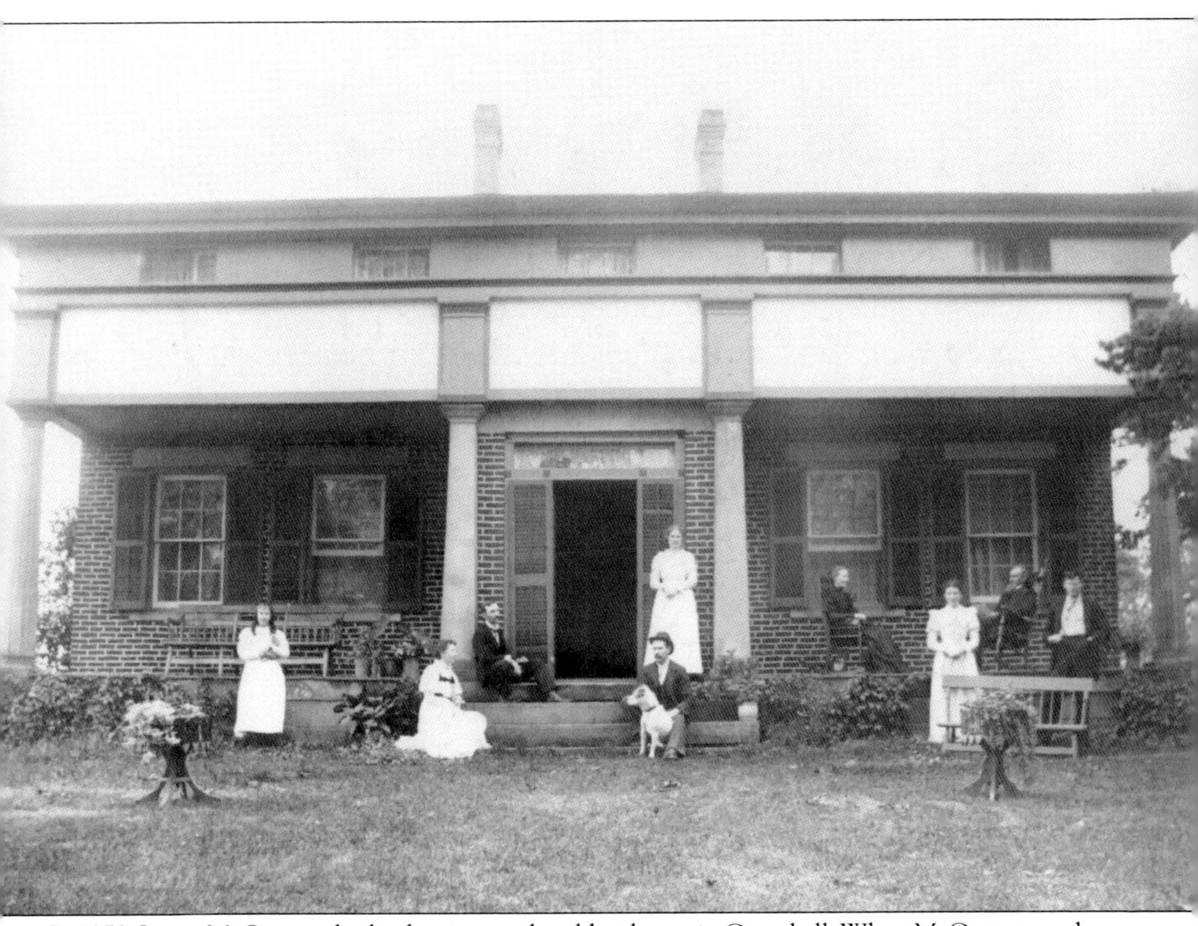

In 1850, James McCartney built what is now the oldest home in Campbell. When McCartney and his family settled in Section 24 of Coitsville Township, they had done so in a previously built log cabin. Using his background as a bricklayer, McCartney and his sons created bricks from nearby soil to build the durable redbrick house that still stands today. The McCartney family is pictured here in the late 1880s. (Courtesy of Florence Galida.)

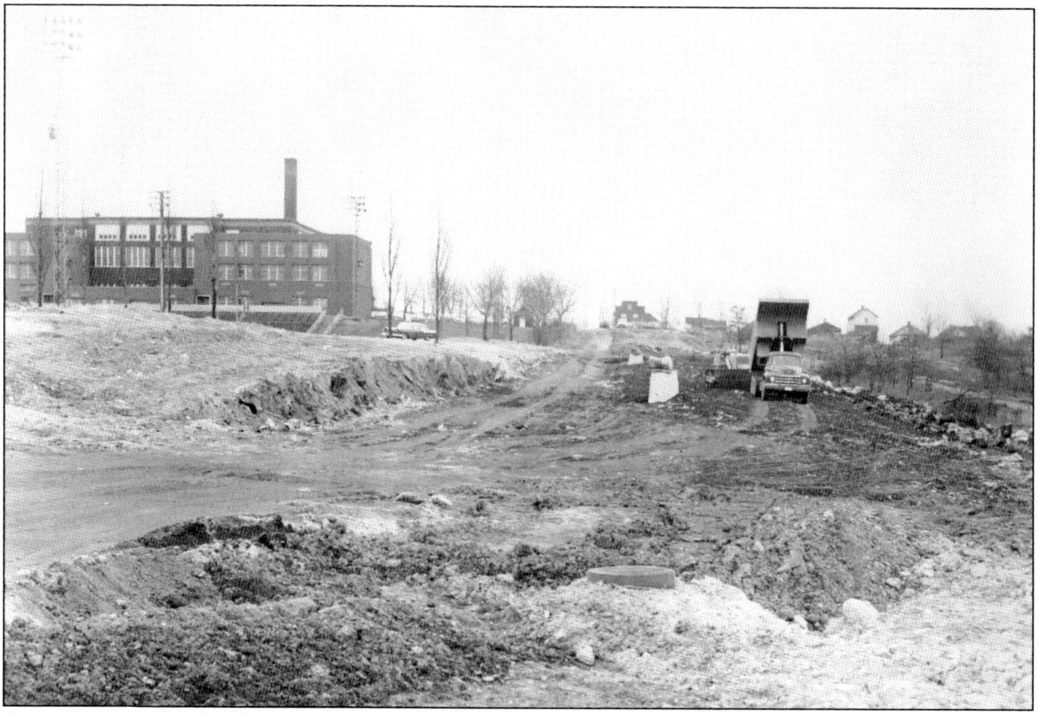

During Mayor Michael J. Kovach's term in office, Sanderson Avenue was expanded to connect to First Street, running along the south end of the high school and stadium. Memorial High School can be seen in the background of this 1950s photograph. (Courtesy of Florence Galida.)

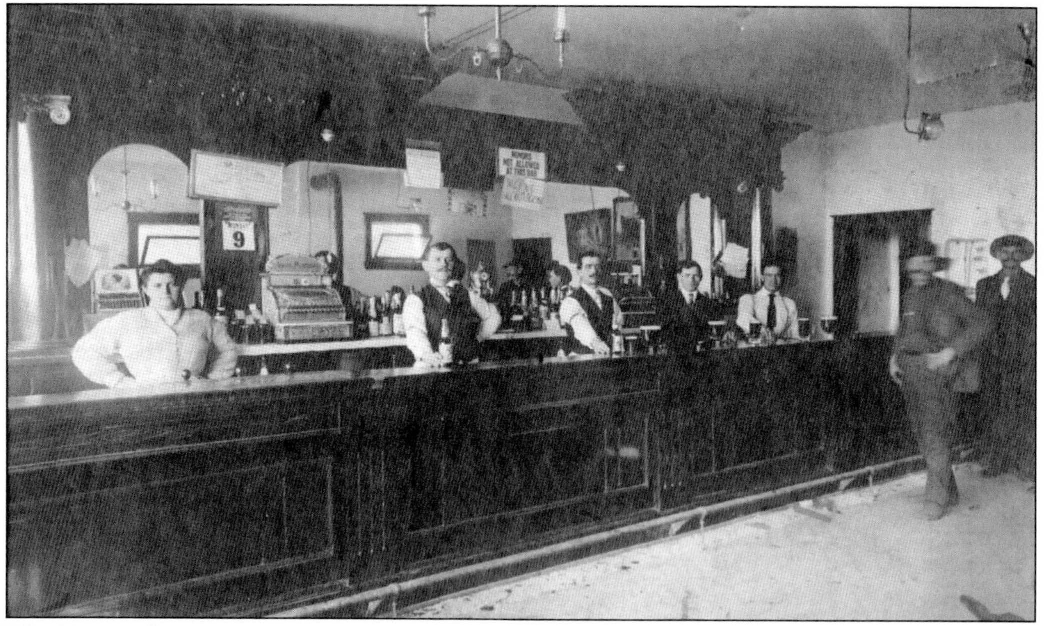

The Hamrock Tavern, pictured here sometime before the Great Fire of 1916, was located on Broad Street near the corner of Robinson Road. When East Youngstown was changed to the city of Campbell in April 1926, Broad Street was renamed Wilson Avenue after Pres. Woodrow Wilson. (Courtesy of Florence Galida.)

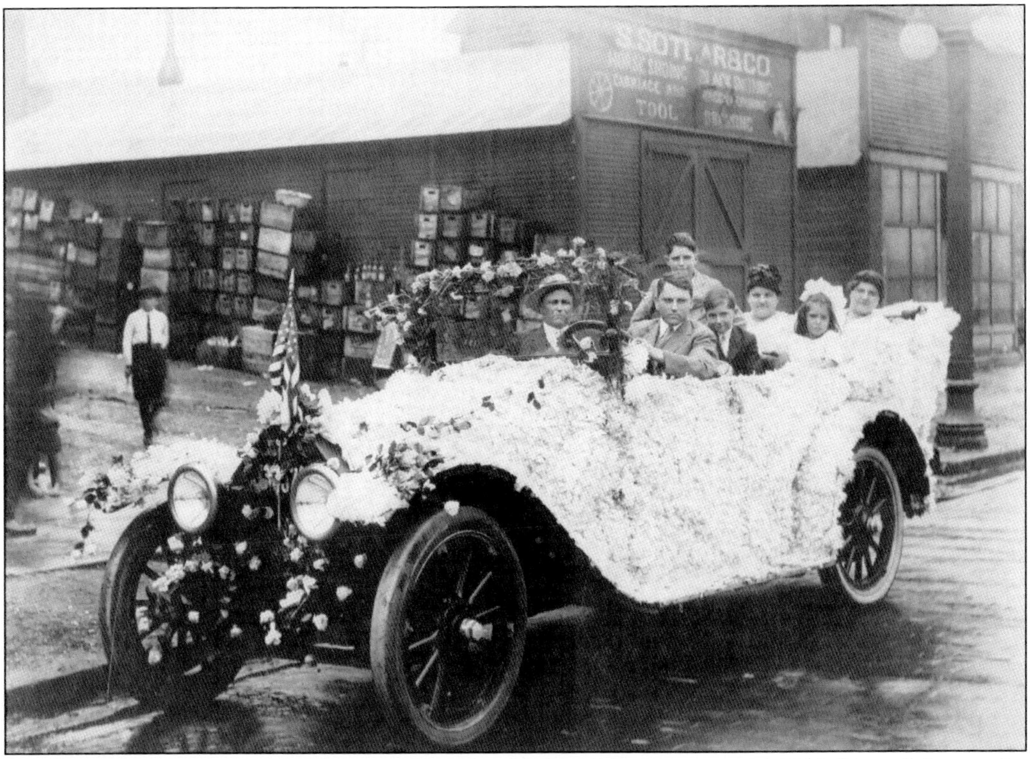

The Copp family is pictured during a Fourth of July celebration around 1916. From left to right are (front seat) Joseph Copp and Anthony Copp; (behind driver) Harry Copp; (back row) Joseph Copp, Frances Copp, Emma Copp, and Amelia Copp. (Courtesy of Florence Galida.)

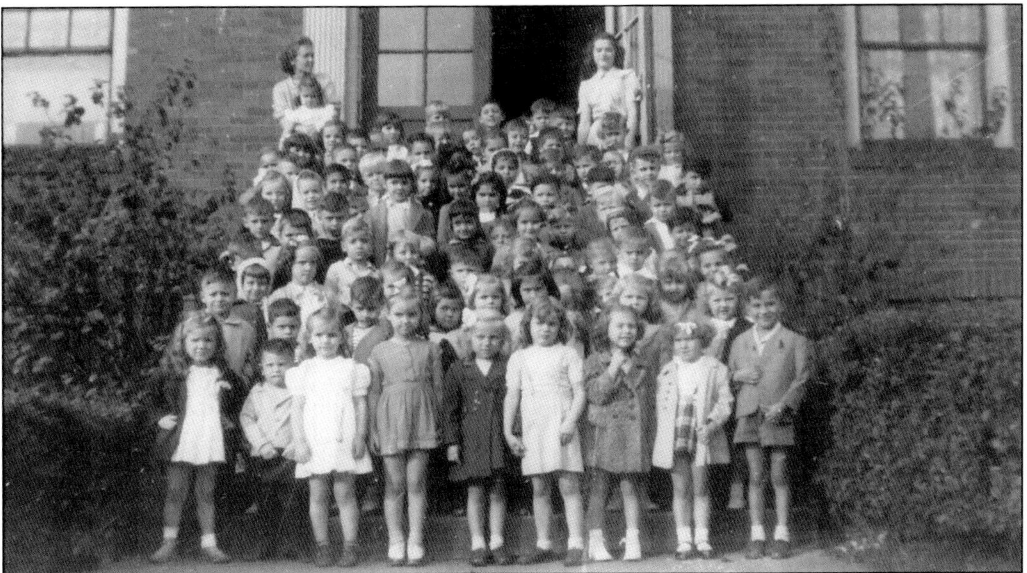

A 1947 kindergarten class takes a trip to the Neighborhood House for a fun day of crafts, sports, and other exciting events. Although the Neighborhood House closed its doors in 1971, its work continues today with the Kirwan Homes Community Center, located on the corner of Murray Avenue and Jackson Street. (Courtesy of Lorraine Sabol.)

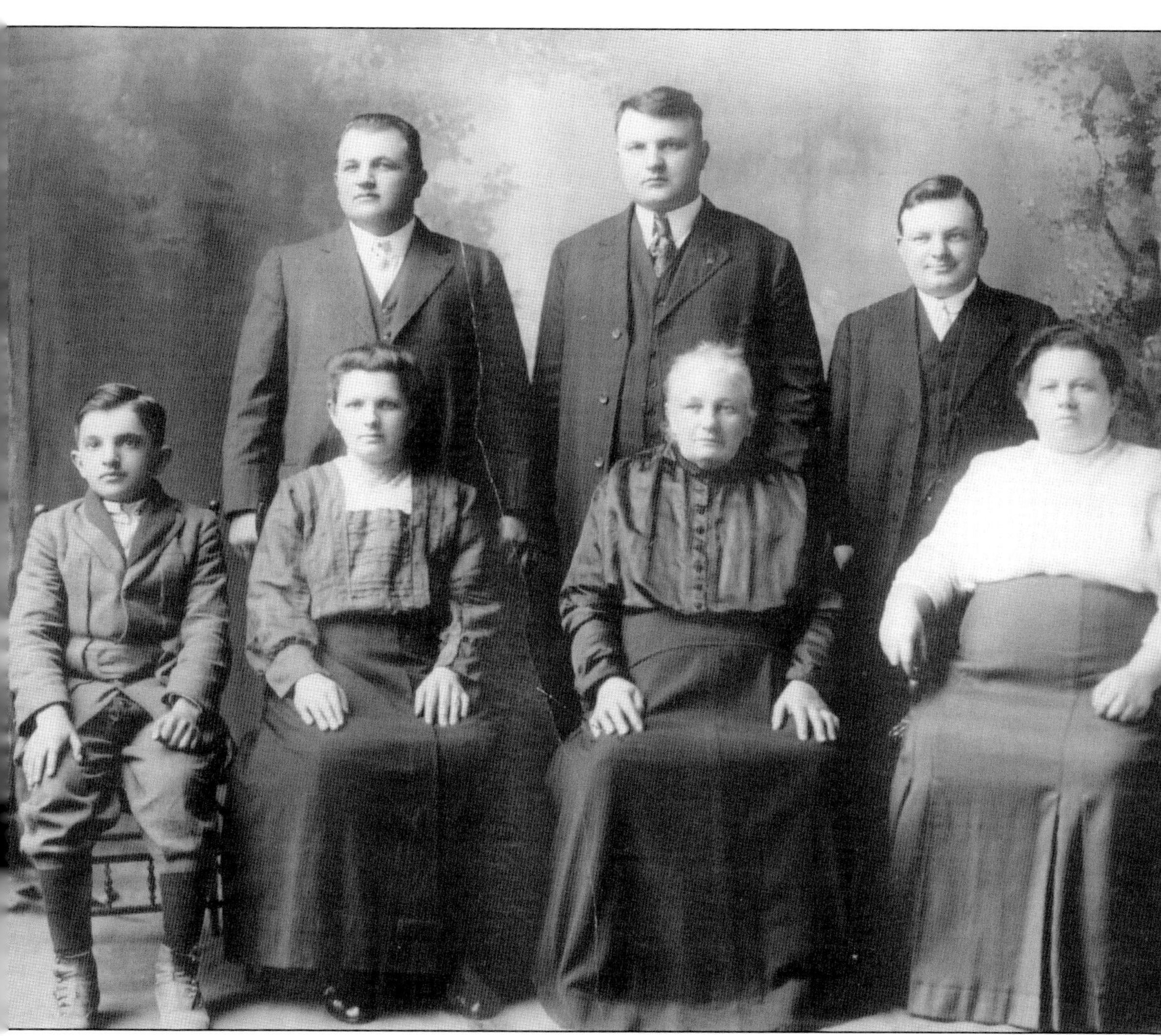

The Hamrock family is pictured in this undated photograph. From left to right are (first row) John Hamrock Jr., Mary Hamrock Salata, Agnes Richnovska Hamrock Yavorsky, and Elizabeth Hamrock Waschak; (second row) John M. Hamrock, Aloyious Hamrock, and Andrew Hamrock. (Courtesy of Florence Galida.)

Pictured outside the company homes are, from left to right, Patricia Malys, Adele Malys, and Mary Ellen Turocy. Each little girl is dressed in traditional Eastern European fashion, which they often meshed with the current American trends of the time. (Courtesy of Lorraine Sabol.)

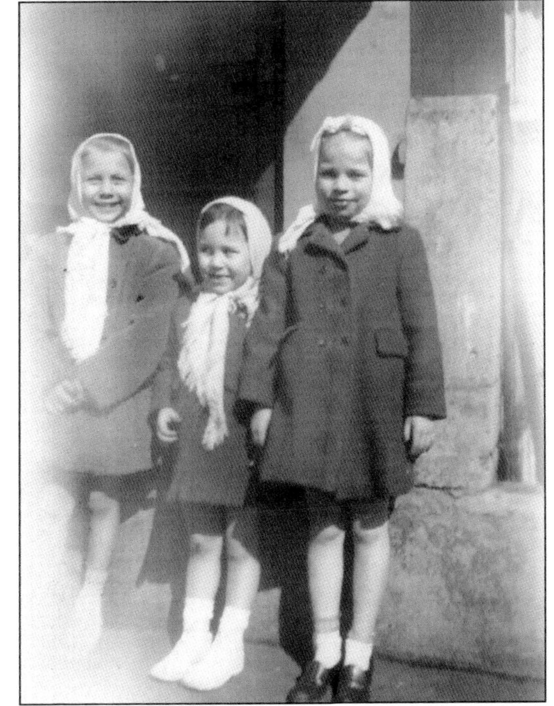

Born in Campbell, Betty Allen was a famous operatic mezzo-soprano. In 1971, she was given the key to the city to add to her already outstanding list of awards. From left to right are Councilman Robert Miles Wilson, Betty Allen, an unidentified male, and Mayor Joseph Vrabel. (Courtesy of Florence Galida.)

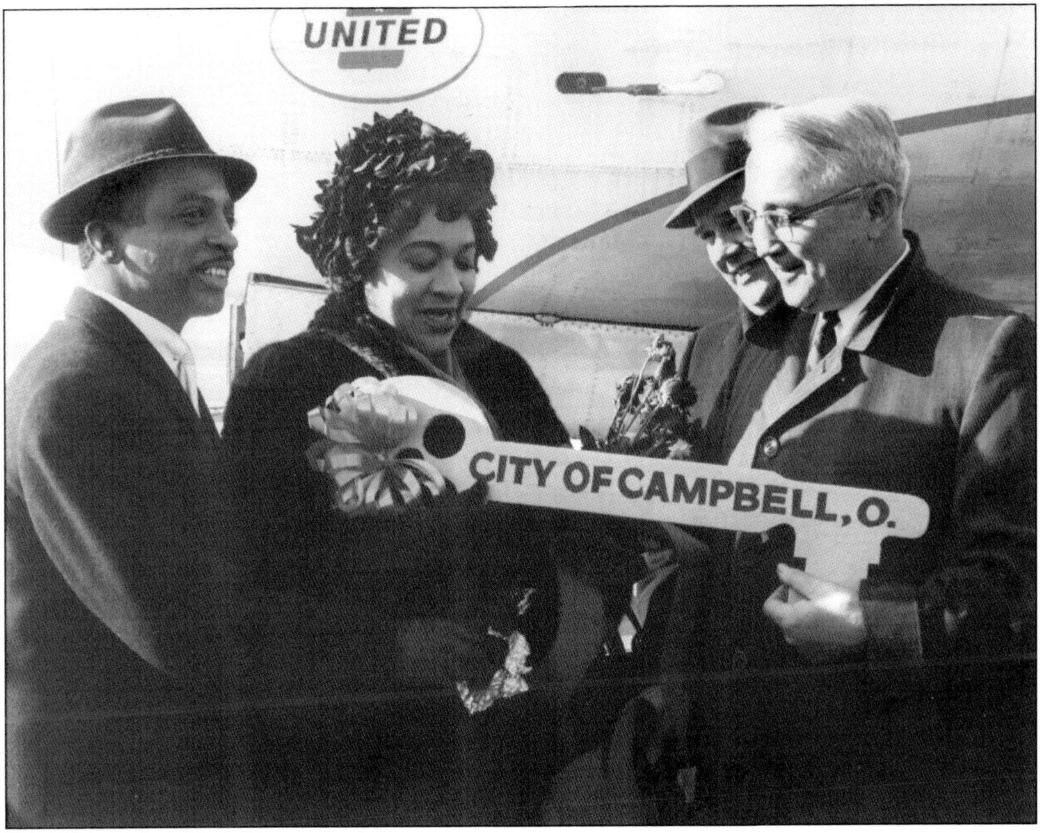

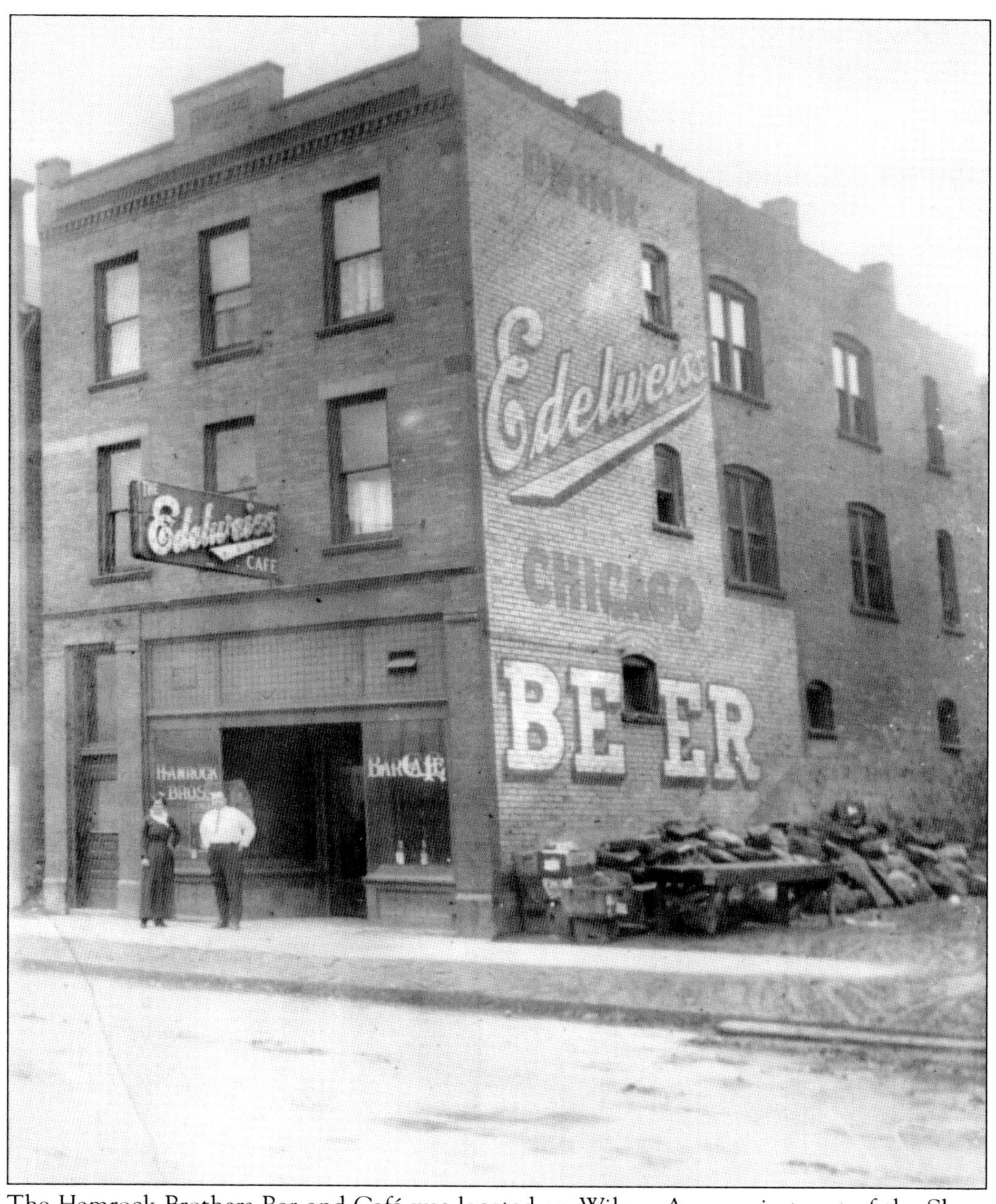

The Hamrock Brothers Bar and Café was located on Wilson Avenue, just east of the Short Street Bridge. During the Great Fire of 1916, the bar fell victim to rioting steel workers and was subsequently damaged. Helen Waschak Hamrock and John M. Hamrock Sr. are pictured just after their wedding. (Courtesy of Florence Galida.)

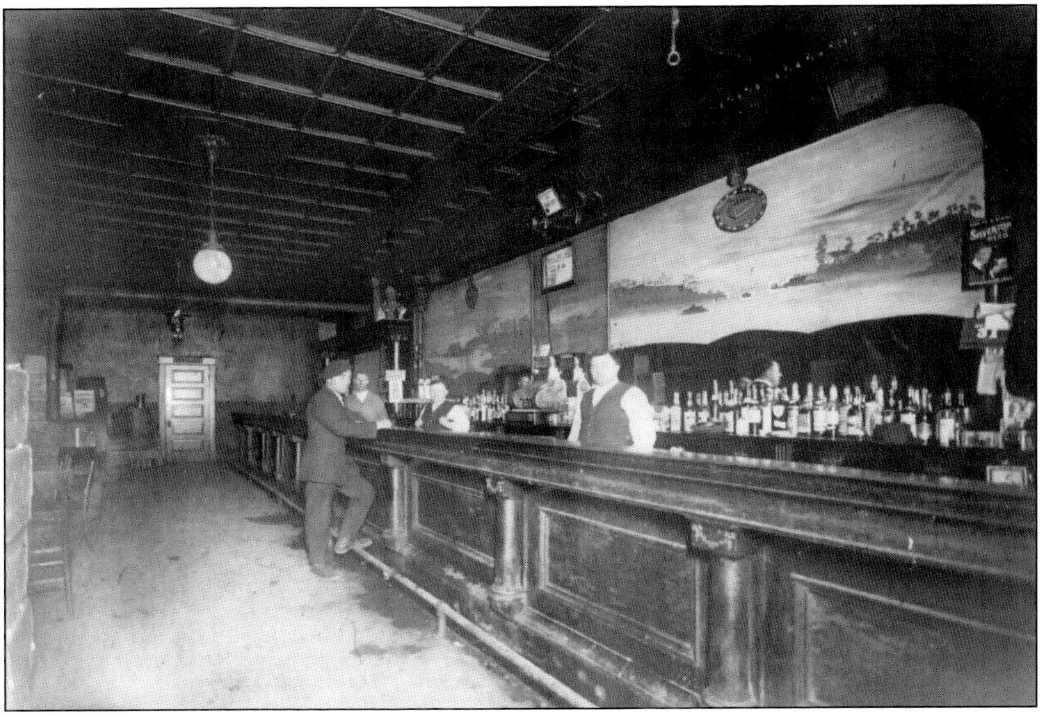

During the early 1900s, taverns and bars occupied many of the lots near the Short Street Bridge. Oftentimes, mill workers would cash their paychecks at the bar and enjoy a few drinks before going home. This c. 1918 photograph of the interior of the Hamrock Brothers Bar and Café illustrates the simplicity of its design, with only a few tables and chairs for relaxing. The two vested bartenders are Andrew Hamrock (left) and John Hamrock (right). (Courtesy of Florence Galida.)

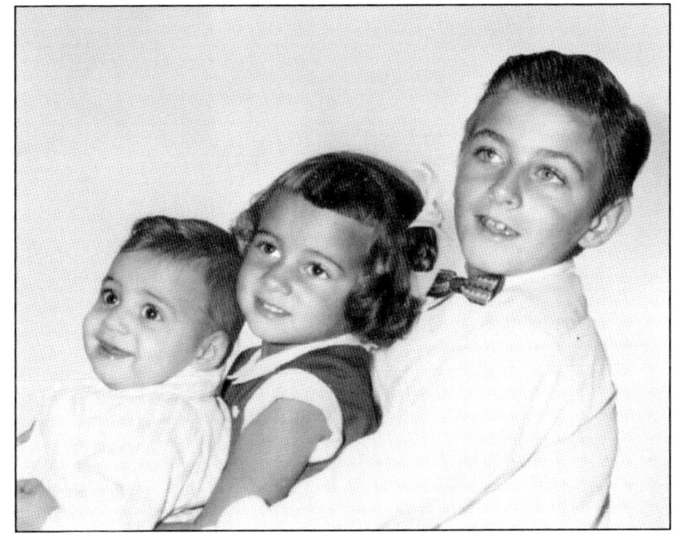

Photographers often visited residents to capture their family portraits. Bonnie Zayac remembers the day when the photographer came to the house and her mother would not let him in because she did not know why he was there and forgot that she had an appointment with him. So the man left and came back the next day; they all had a good laugh over the incident. The Zayac family is pictured at 154 Camvet Drive. From left to right are Dennis Zayac, Bonnie Zayac (Pavlansky), and Gary Zayac. (Courtesy of Edward Zamets.)

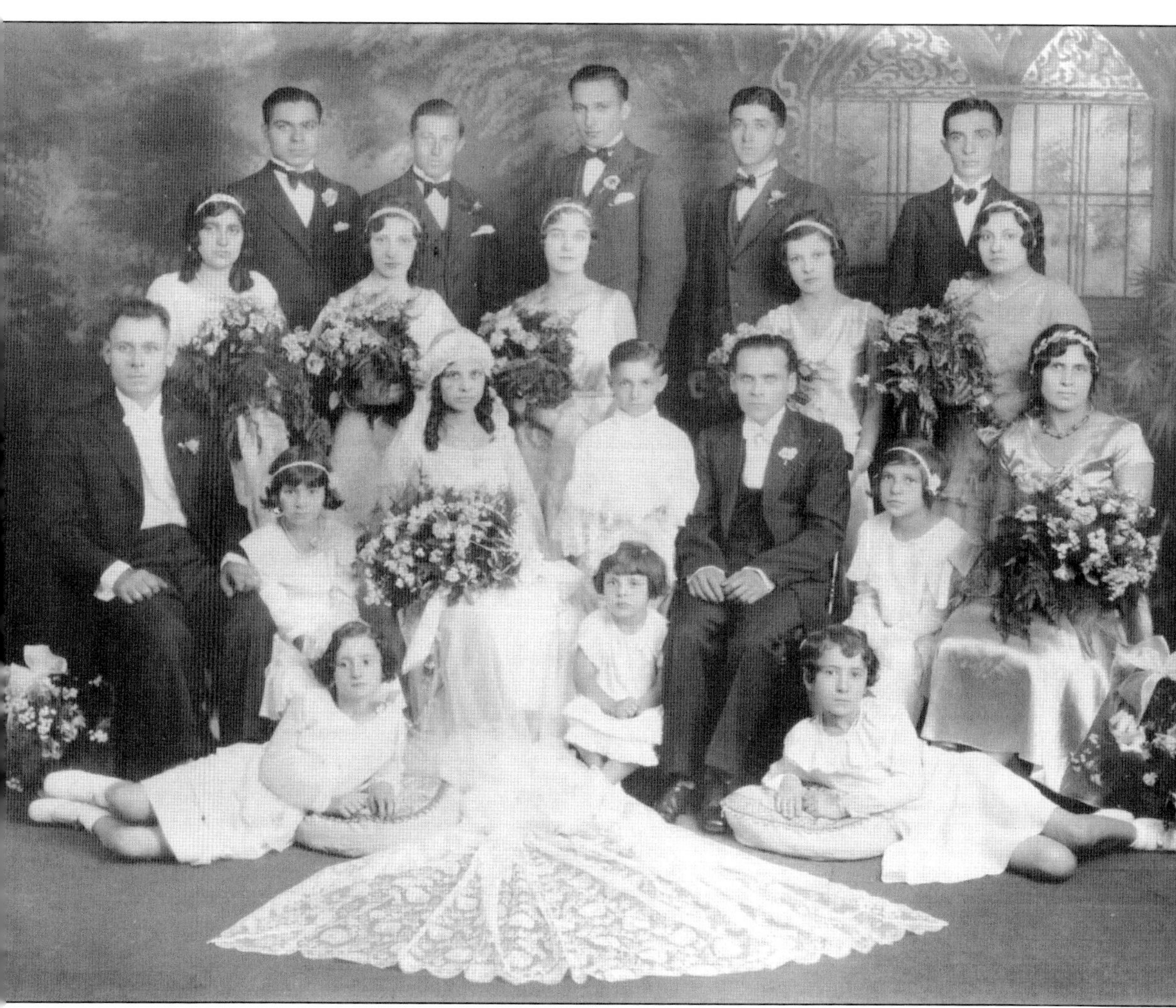

Mary Cuva and Manuel Castro are pictured with family at their wedding on July 25, 1931. From left to right are (first row) Yolanda Trombacco, Josephine Cuteri, and Mary Trombacco; (second row) Mike Trombacco, unidentified child, bride Mary Cuva, Rocky Galleta, groom Manuel Castro, Florence Myers, and Sylvia Armeni; (third row) Mary Galetta, Sophie Rotz, Jeanette Diorio, Mary Roscoe, and Antionette DeMart; (fourth row) Tony Yeropoli, unidentified, Carmine Crina, Ben Tucci, and John DeMart. (Courtesy of Florence Galida.)

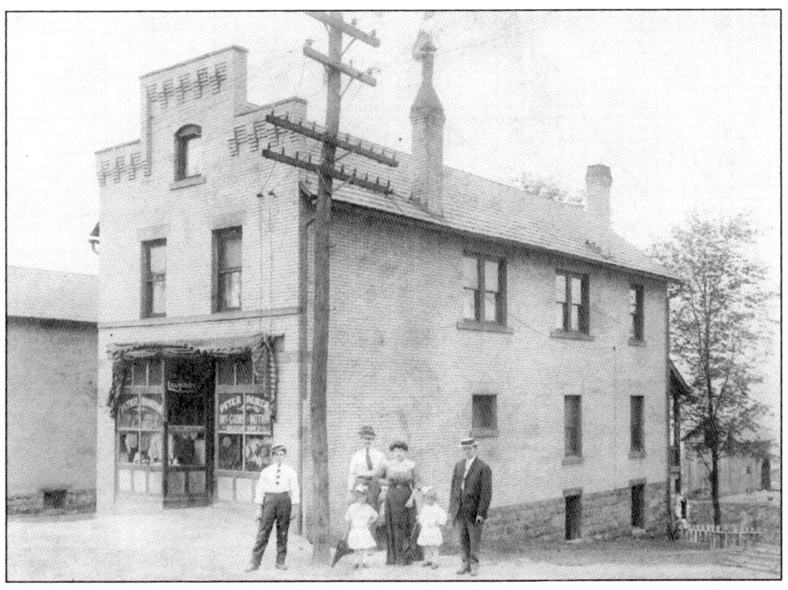

The Resetar family is pictured in front of their store at 28 Twelfth Street in the early 1900s. Peter Resetar Dry Goods Store and Notary was located near the intersection of Twelfth Street and Reed Avenue. (Courtesy of Florence Galida.)

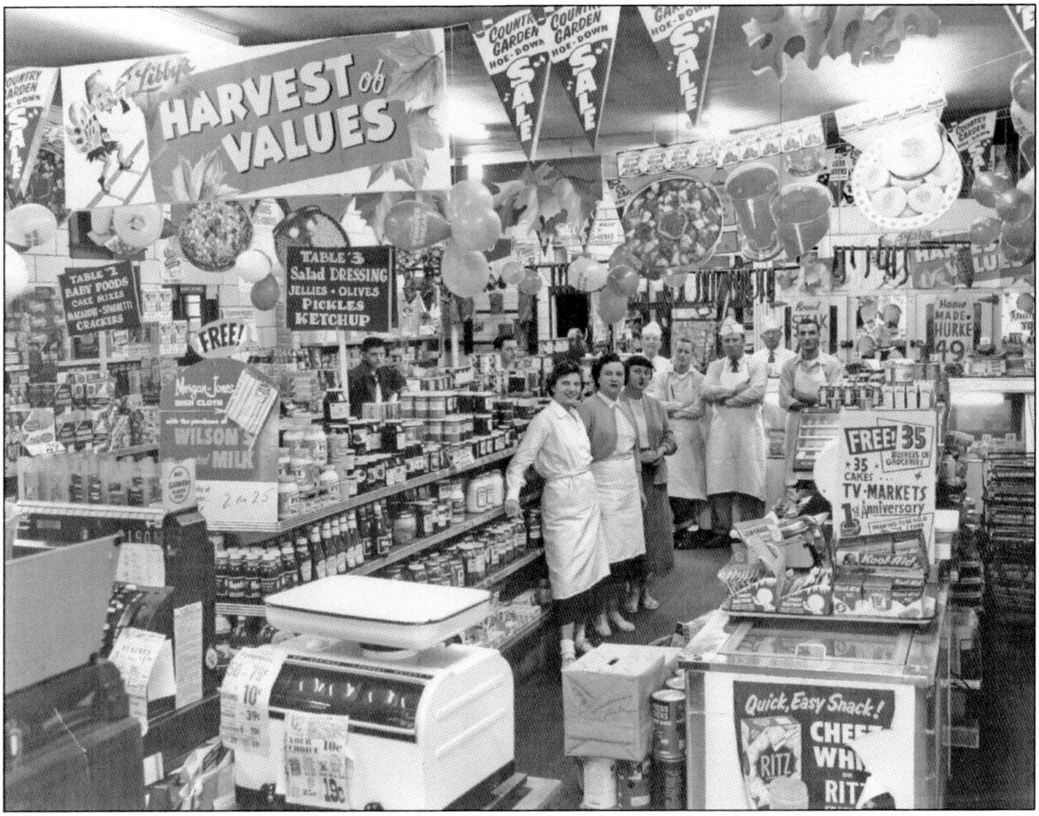

From the 1920s through the 1970s, Campbell had many grocery stores throughout the city to meet the needs of an ever-increasing population. Most stores carried general goods, while others catered to a particular ethnicity to make the immigrants feel more at home and to better adjust to the American lifestyle. Kornyak's Food Market, pictured here in the 1950s, provided general goods to the people on Reed Avenue and nearby streets. (Courtesy of Florence Galida.)

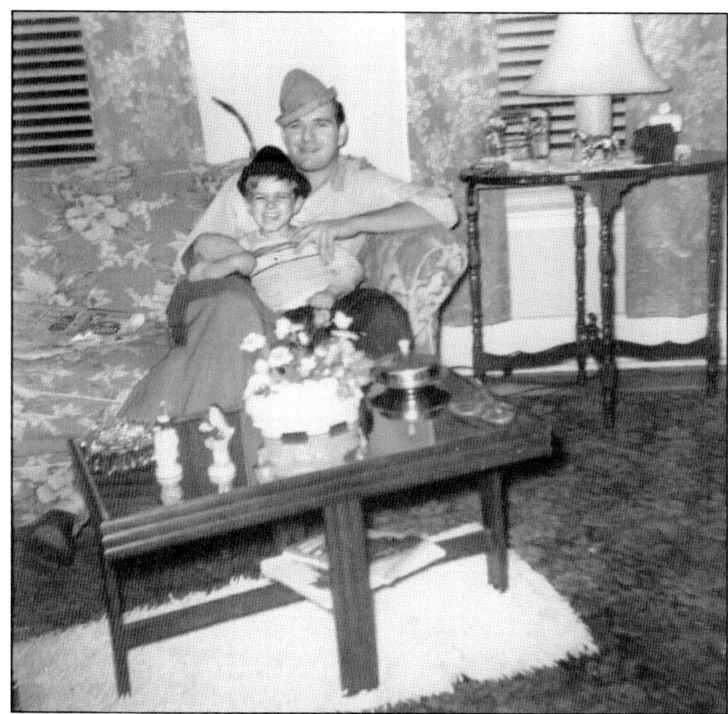

Samuel Fitch and his family settled into Coitsville Township in 1801 and later became the owner of Section 26 along the Mahoning River, which extended to the present-day area of Sixth Street and Blossom Avenue. In 1875, this land was passed on to the Walter family, then was sold to the Reeds, and finally to the Youngstown Sheet and Tube Company in 1899. Other parts of the land were sold to the Fairview School or as private lots. Edward Zamets (rear) and Gary Zayac (front) are pictured at 26 Walter Street around 1951. (Courtesy of Edward Zamets.)

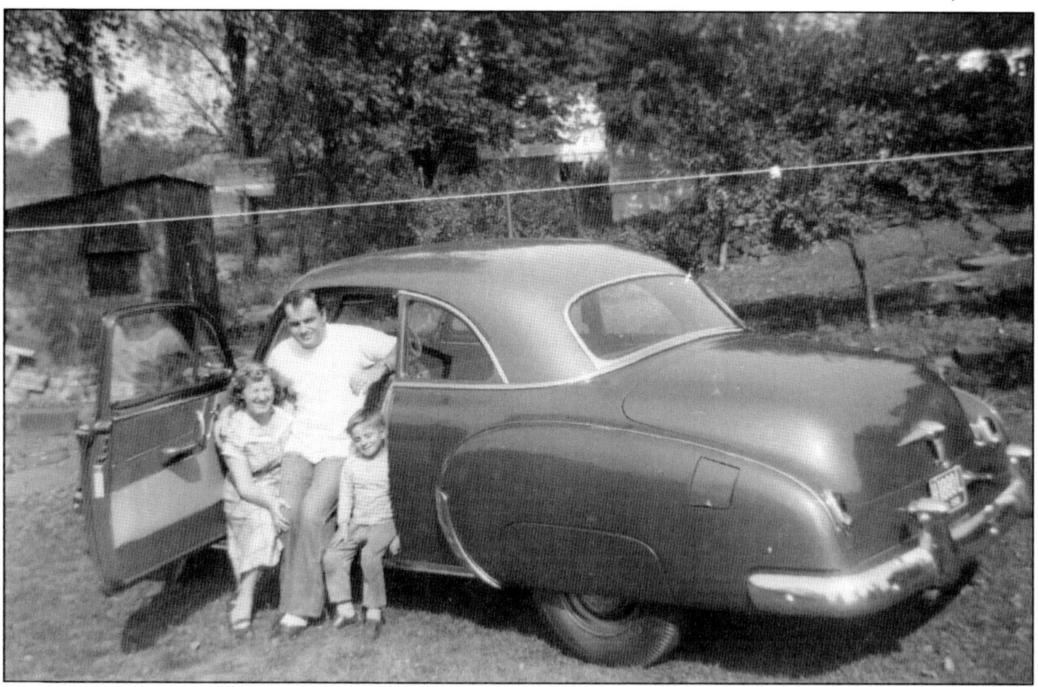

The Zayac family is pictured with their new car in the yard of 26 Walter Street in the early 1950s. From left to right are Violet Zayac, George Zayac, and Dennis Zayac. The vehicle was later sold to Stephan Zamets so that the Zayacs could purchase a house on Camvet Drive. At the time, only Campbell military veterans could purchase a house on Camvet Drive. (Courtesy of Edward Zamets.)

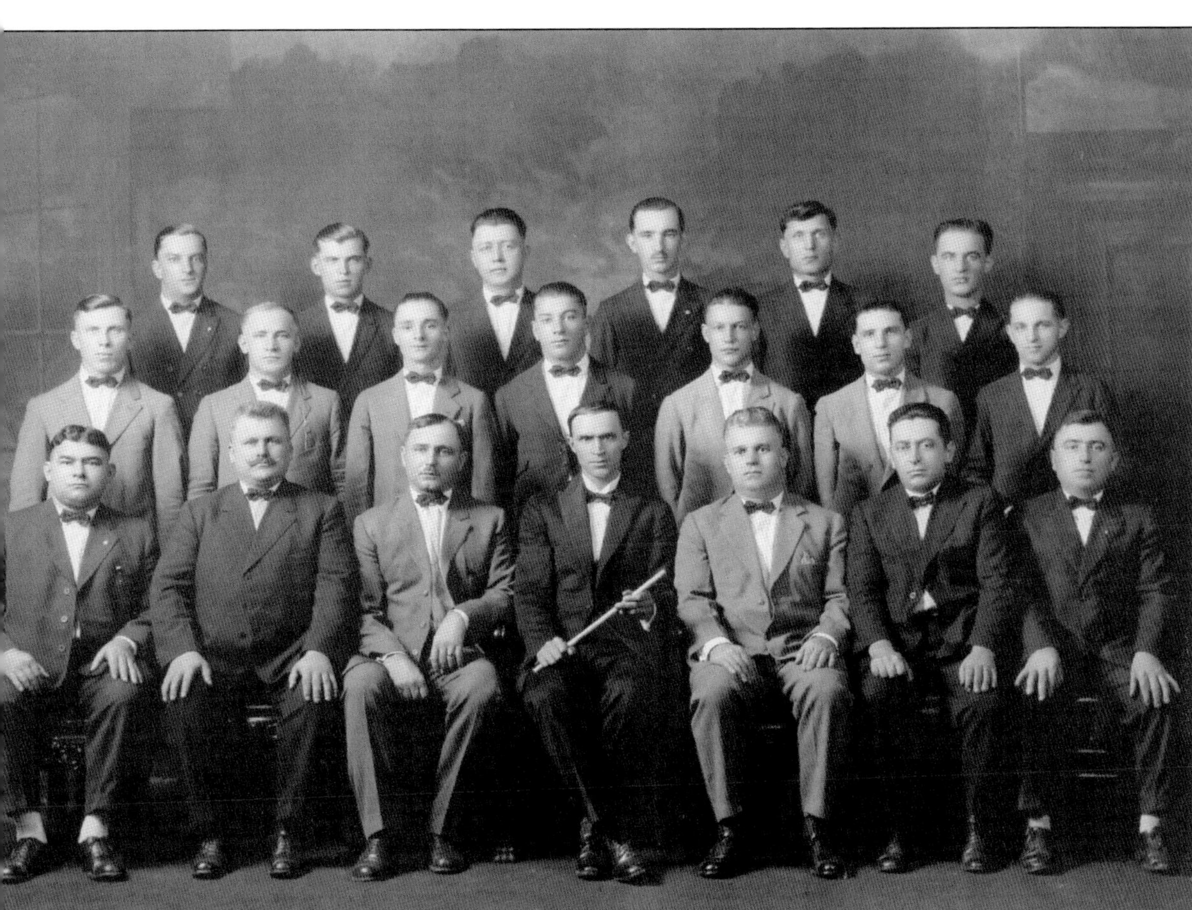

Members of the East Youngstown (Campbell) Croatian Glee Club are pictured here in 1920. From left to right are (first row) Matt Yankovich, Nick Paradizk, George Pavicic, Ed Belovich, John Bachan, George Patrusha, and Pete Horvatavich; (second row) Tony Lazar, Paul Wilk, George Marshall, Joe Lubonovich, M. Mrakovich, Steve Milekovic, and Mike Milenic; (third row) John Lubonovich, John Evanusha, Yovo Voynovich, Pat Muratic, Mike Busonec, and Frank Bogdan. (Courtesy of Florence Galida.)

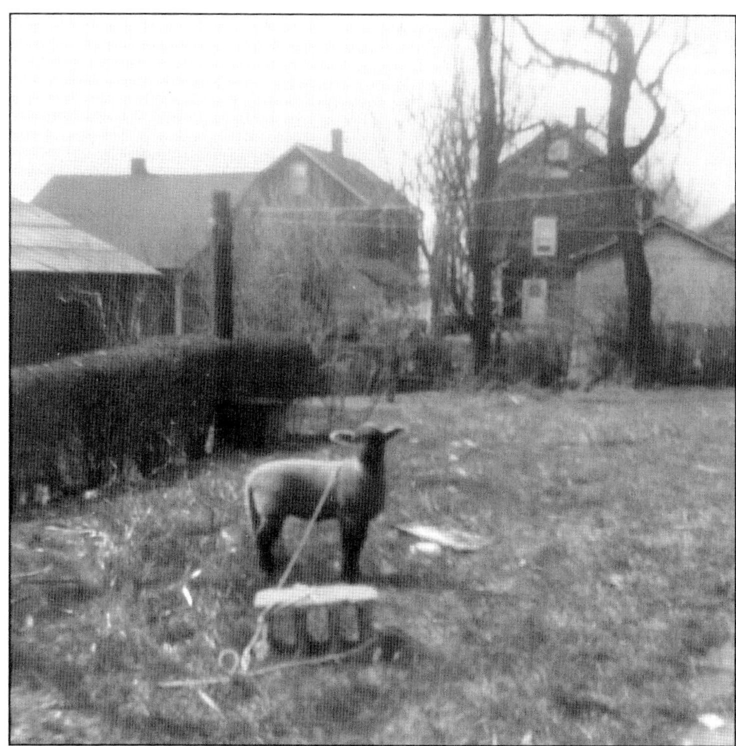

This photograph taken in late May 1969 shows a lamb tied to a cinder block in the backyard of a Greek Orthodox household. Although Easter Sunday occurs days and sometimes weeks before the Greek Orthodox Easter celebration, many Greek families carry on the tradition of slaughtering a lamb on Easter morning and cooking the meat for family and friends. (Courtesy of Irene Moylan.)

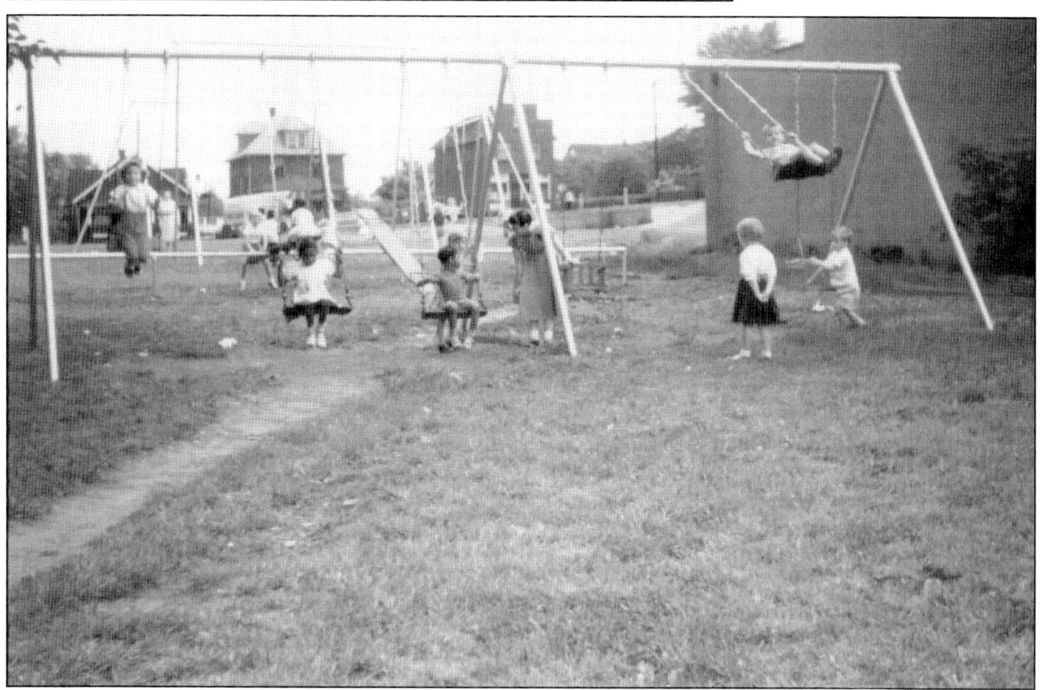

When not busy with schoolwork or daily chores, local children often visited the Neighborhood House to participate in organized activities or just to play in the outdoor recreation area. Such facilities offered children the opportunity to meet new people and learn different cultures and traditions. (Courtesy of Florence Galida.)

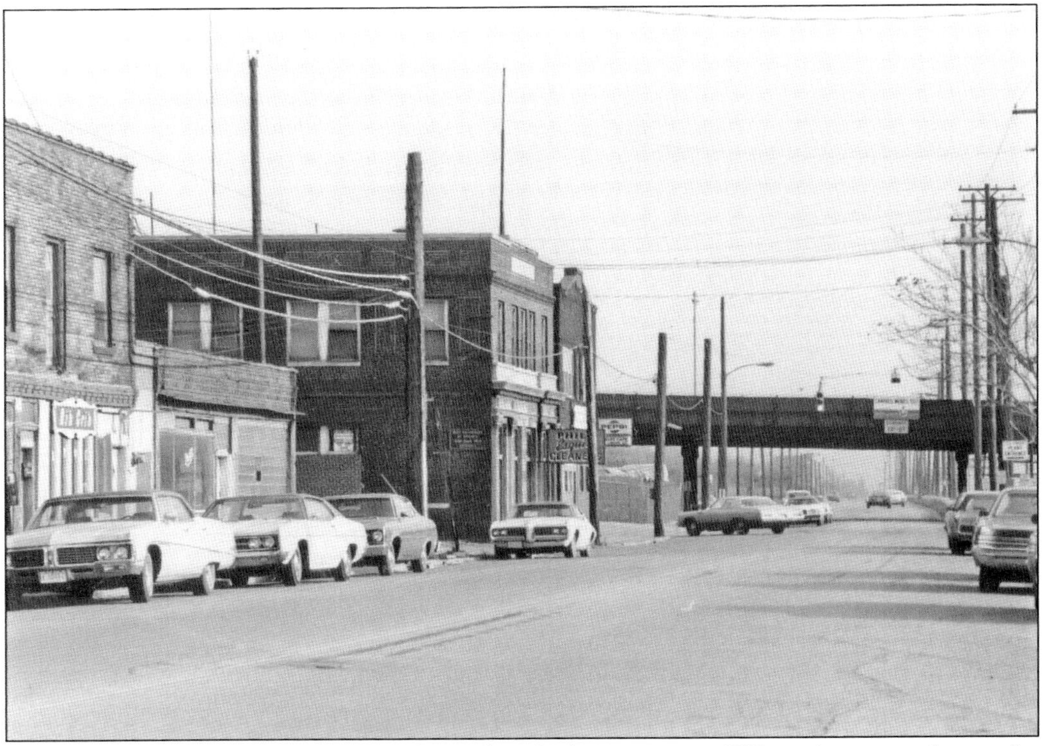

The Short Street Bridge entrance to the mills, which went across Wilson Avenue and onto the mill property, was originally erected over the Monongahela River in the 1880s. As the number of immigrants drastically increased during the early 1900s, employees needed a quick way to get to work, so the bridge was brought to East Youngstown in several sections and subsequently reconstructed over Wilson Avenue. (Courtesy of Florence Galida.)

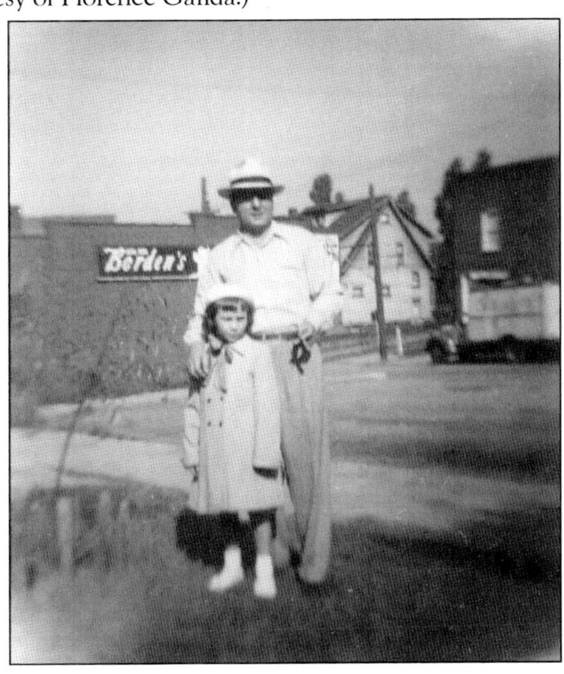

With the population of East Youngstown (Campbell) containing such a large amount of immigrants from all different locations throughout Europe, various social centers were established to Americanize the citizens. Not only were these immigrants taught American culture and language, but they also had the opportunity to meet different people and learn about their ethnic traditions. Adolph Malys and Adele Malys are pictured at right. (Courtesy of Lorraine Sabol.)

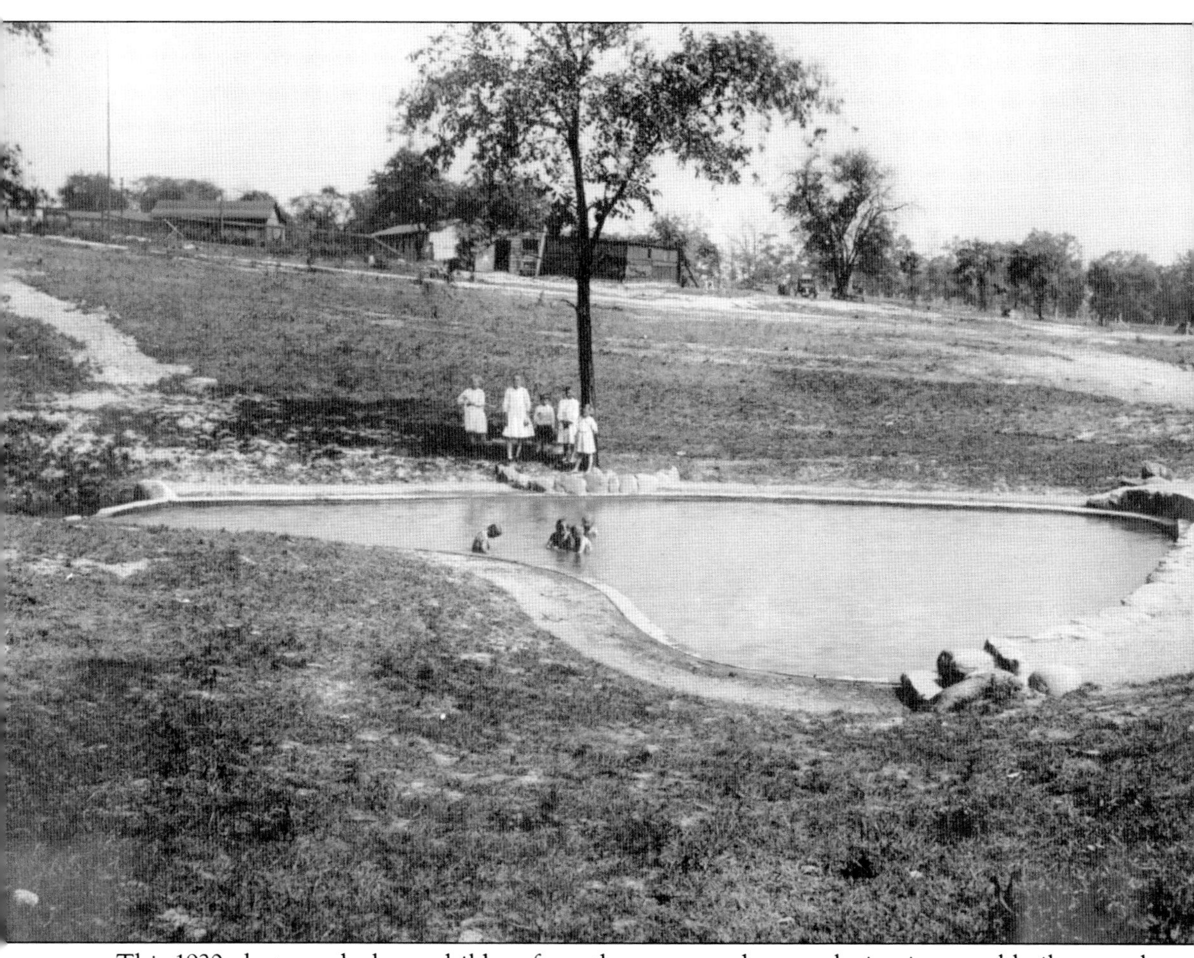

This 1920 photograph shows children from the company homes playing in a pool built to cool off people during the hot summer days. The area would later play host to more company homes and houses as the population increased. (Courtesy of Florence Galida.)

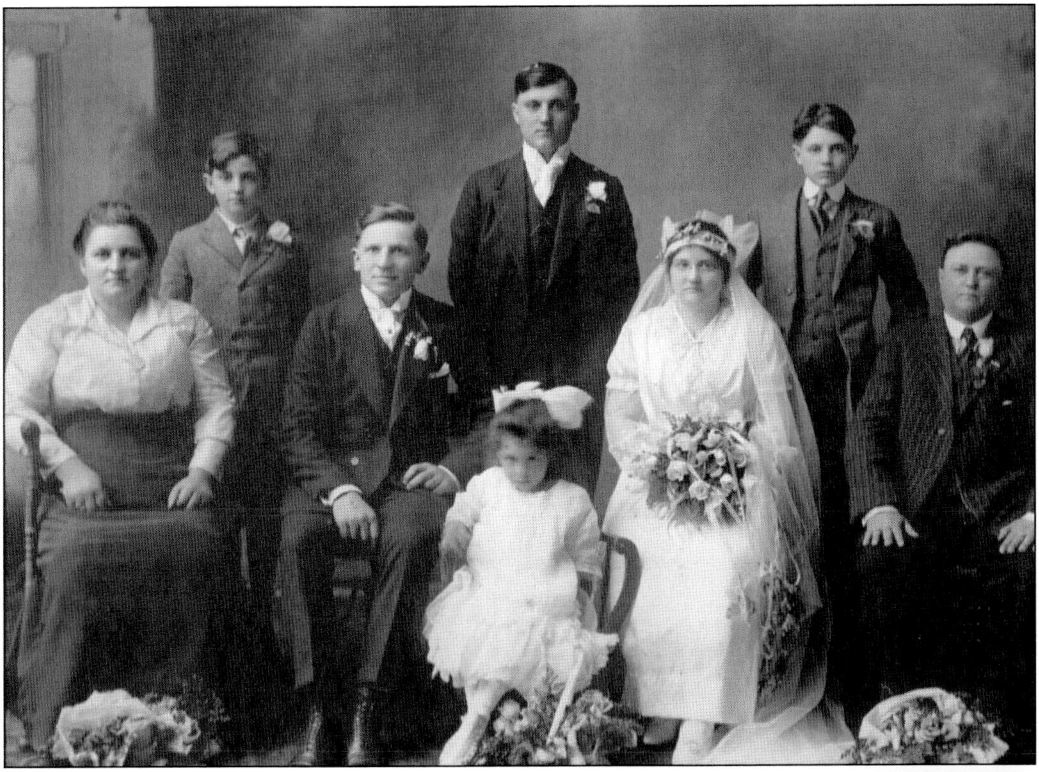

Shown is the 1917 marriage of future Campbell mayor John K. Borak and Amelia Copp. From left to right are (first row) sister of the bride Emma Copp; (second row) mother of the bride Frances Resetar Copp, groom John J. Borak, bride Amelia Copp, and father of the bride Joseph Copp; (third row) brothers of the bride Hary Copp, Anthony Copp, and Joe Copp. (Courtesy of Florence Galida.)

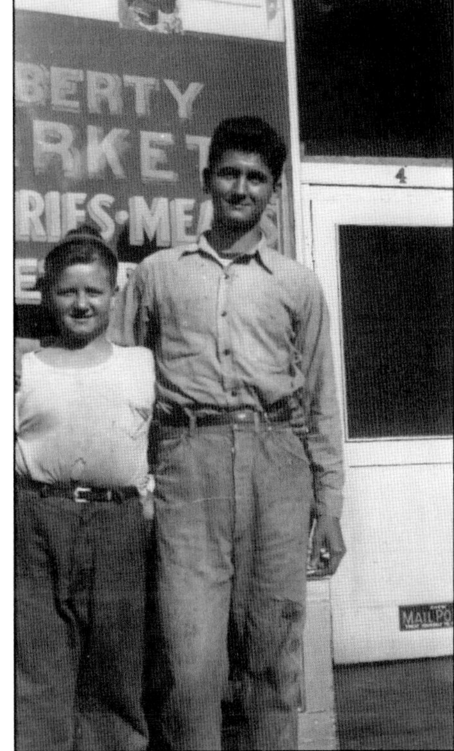

The Liberty Market at 4 Short Street served as a local grocery store specializing in meats and fresh vegetables. Christ Kust (left) and Gust Kust (right) are pictured in front of the market in the 1950s. (Courtesy of Carol and Bob Dolan.)

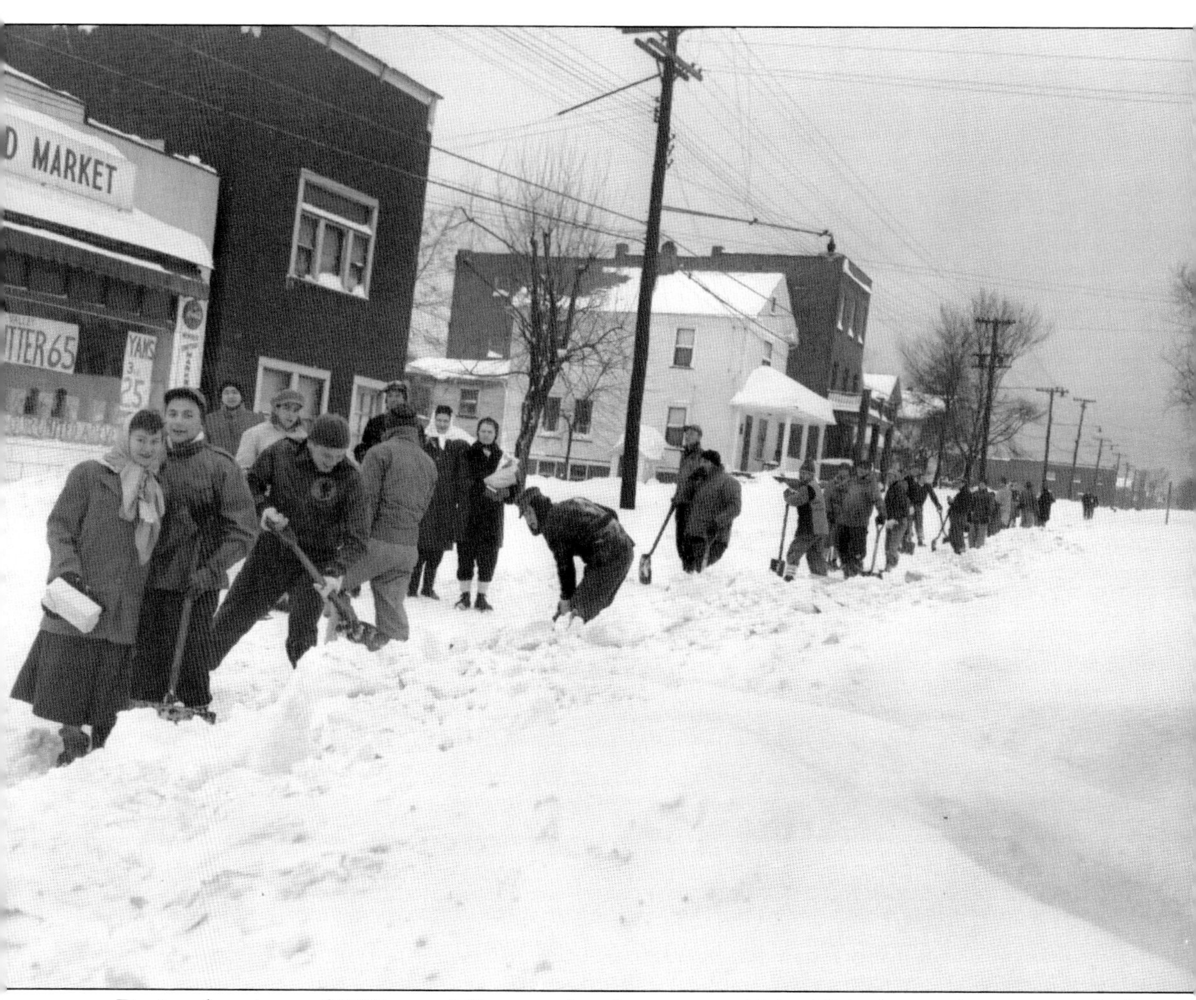

During the winter of 1950, snowfall accumulated to an astonishing 29 inches, with some snowdrifts reaching six to seven feet. This calamity brought the city together, however, as men, women, and children all pitched in to clear paths to the grocery stores until the National Guard could be called out to assist with large machinery. Not only was the city of Campbell affected, but the entire Mahoning Valley remained at a standstill for days. (Courtesy of Florence Galida.)

Two

THE MILLS AND COMPANY HOMES

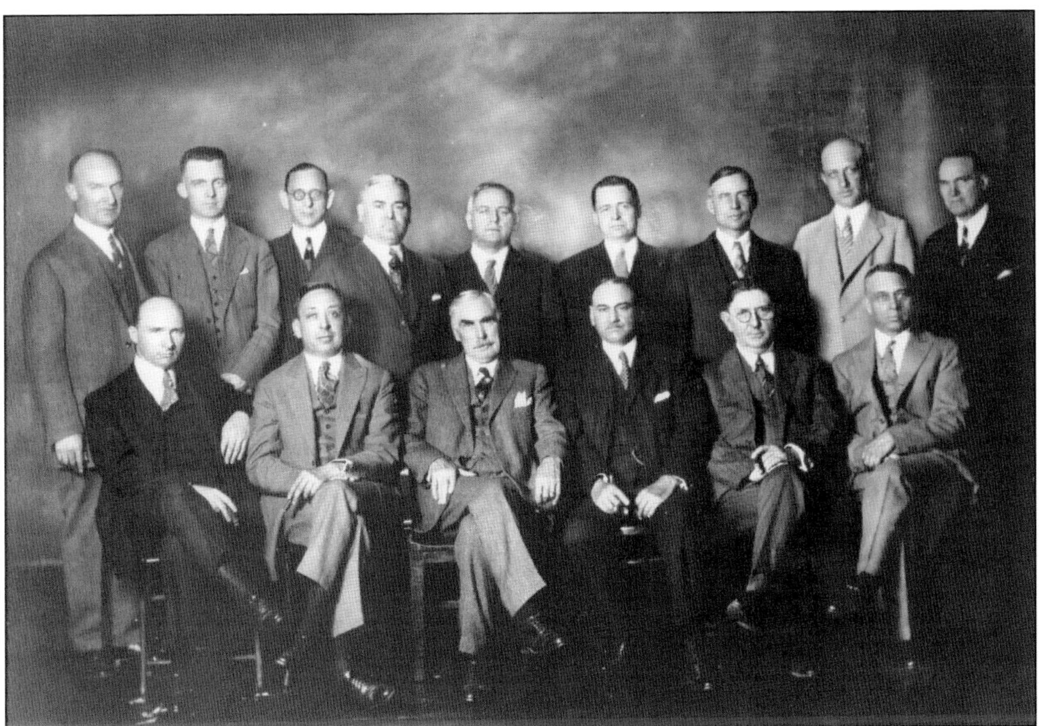

James Anson Campbell was an original owner of the Youngstown Sheet and Tube Company and served as its president from 1904 to 1929. So beloved was this man that the people of East Youngstown, along with the chamber of commerce, chose his name for this new city. On April 26, 1926, an official proclamation changed East Youngstown to Campbell. James Anson Campbell is shown in the first row, third from the left. (Courtesy of Florence Galida.)

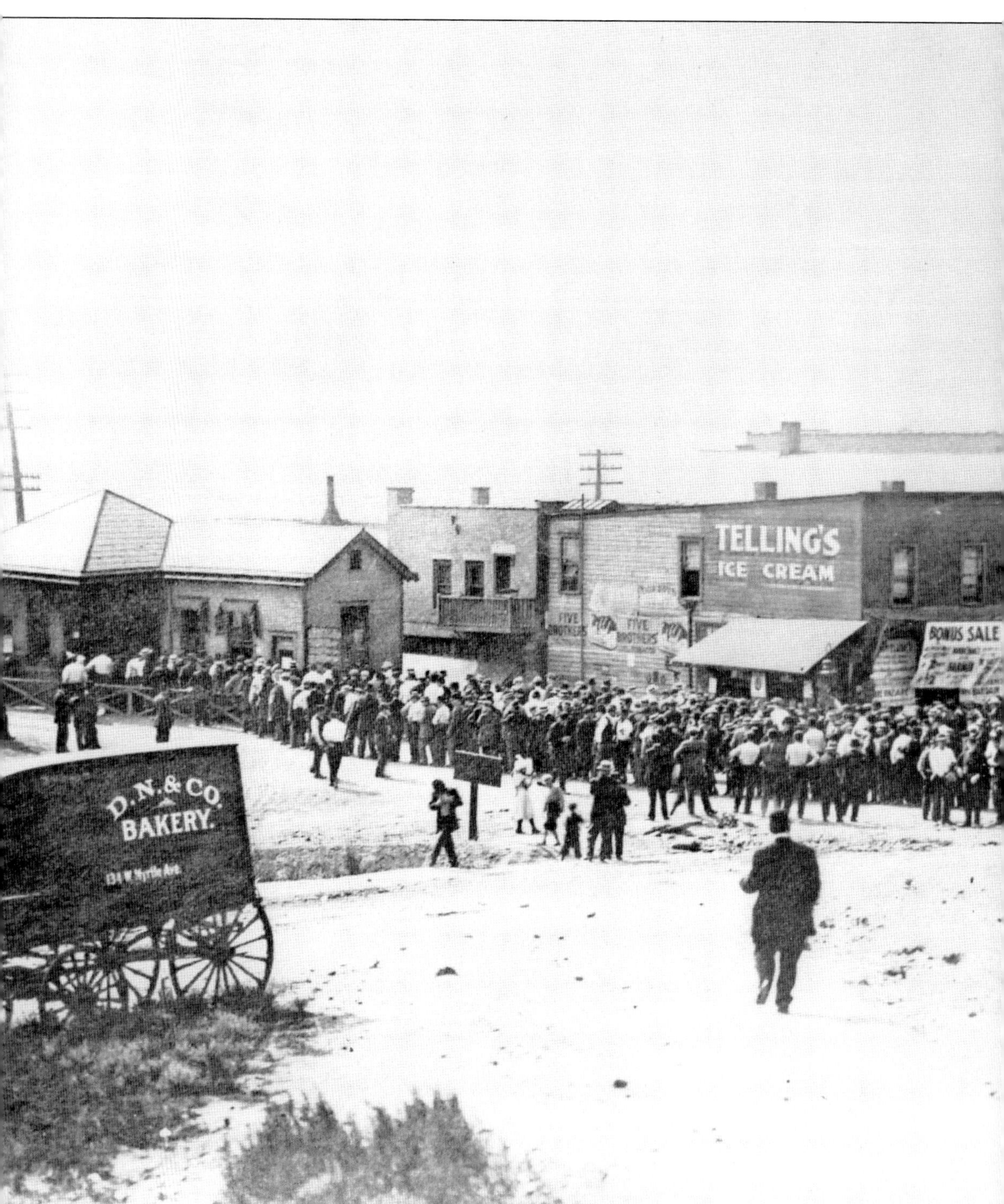

One of the busiest days of the week was payday at the Youngstown Sheet and Tube Company Campbell Works. Thousands would flock to the employment office near the Short Street Bridge to pick up their paychecks. During the 1920s, the annual payroll of Youngstown Sheet and Tube Company was over $22 million, with a majority coming from the Campbell Works plant. However,

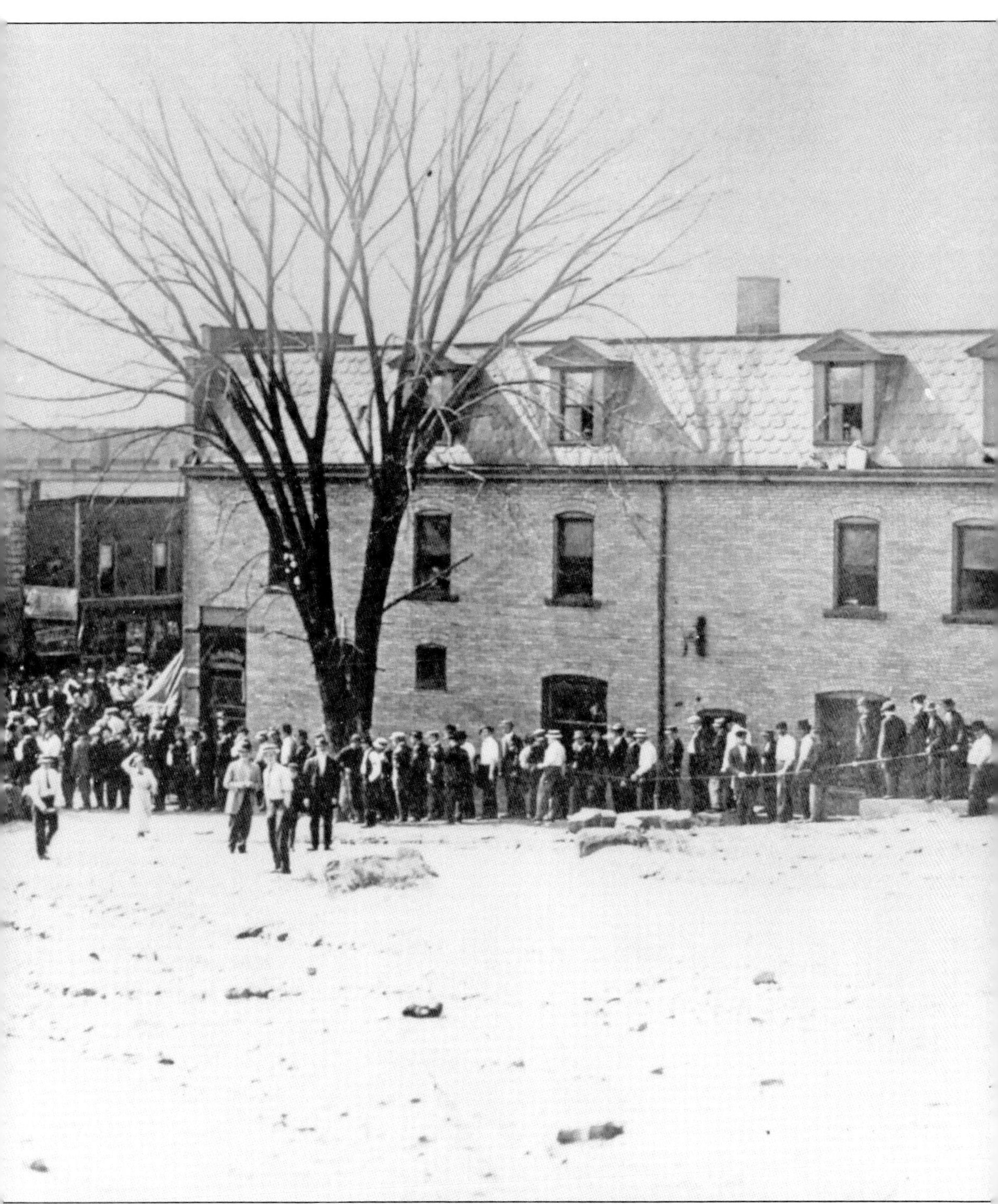

a majority of this money was spent in Youngstown rather than East Youngstown (Campbell). But East Youngstown collected enough taxes to transform the area into an industrial powerhouse, attracting more residents and small businesses alike. The employment office can be seen at the far left. (Courtesy of Florence Galida.)

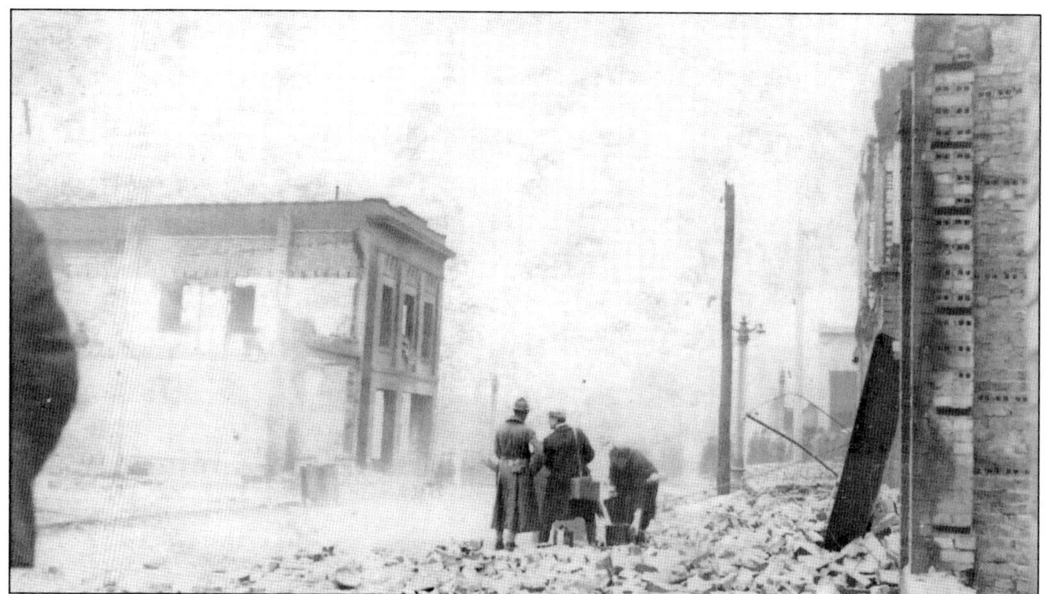

In January 1916, more than 1,000 Youngstown Sheet and Tube Company employees went on strike for higher pay when they knew that the company had begun to receive an increase in war orders for steel. Unable to come to a mutual agreement between the union and steel officials, what ensued were riots that gained national attention, as well as that of the state militia. This view looking west on Short Street toward Robinson Road shows the destruction of the city. (Courtesy of Mike Parise.)

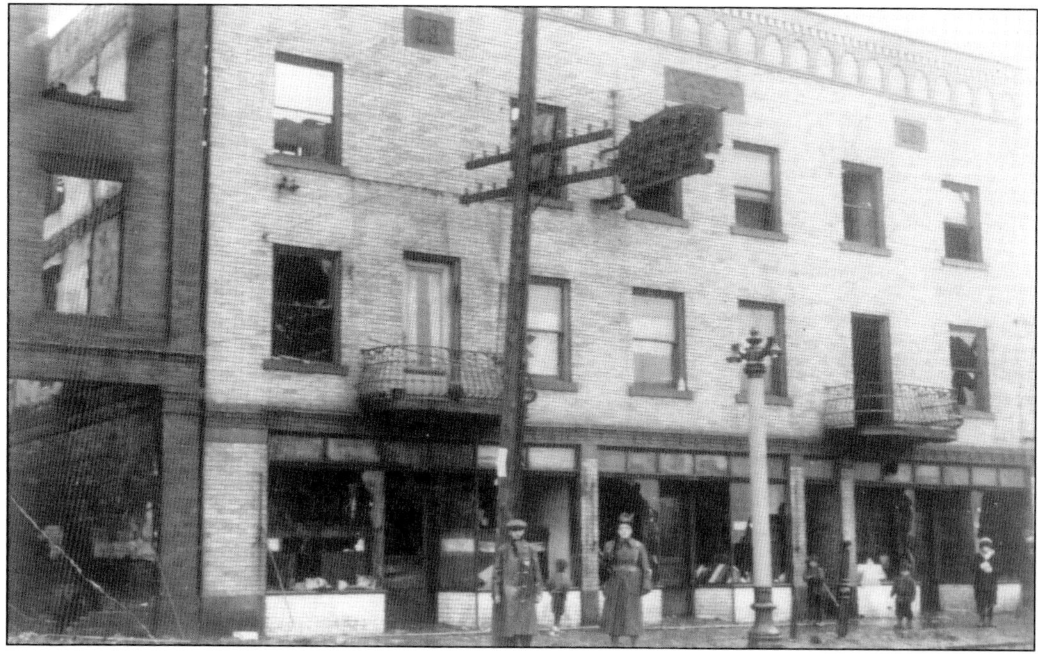

Thomas Skelley leans against a telephone pole while a National Guard soldier stands by keeping order during the early days of the 1916 steel mill riots. Massive fire damage can be seen at the Vacca Building on Broad Street (Wilson Avenue). Damages reached from Wilson Avenue to Twelfth Street, with claims reaching $1.5 million. (Courtesy of Florence Galida.)

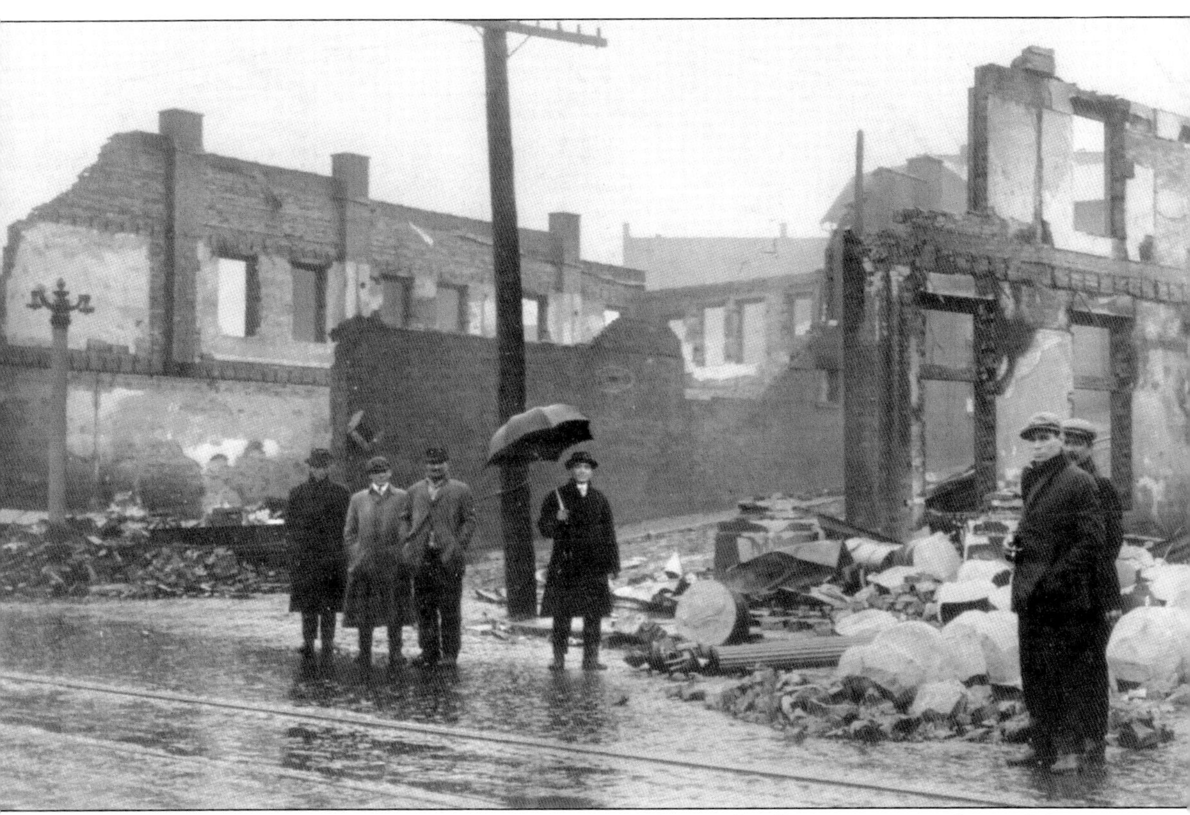

The rioting from over 1,000 steel workers took its toll on the small village just in its infancy. After order was restored, the National Guard handed over the village to reputable elders and officials. While many buildings at the time were not insured against rioting, this did not deter the owners. New mortgages were acquired so that the merchants could rebuild larger and stronger businesses. (Courtesy of Mike Parise.)

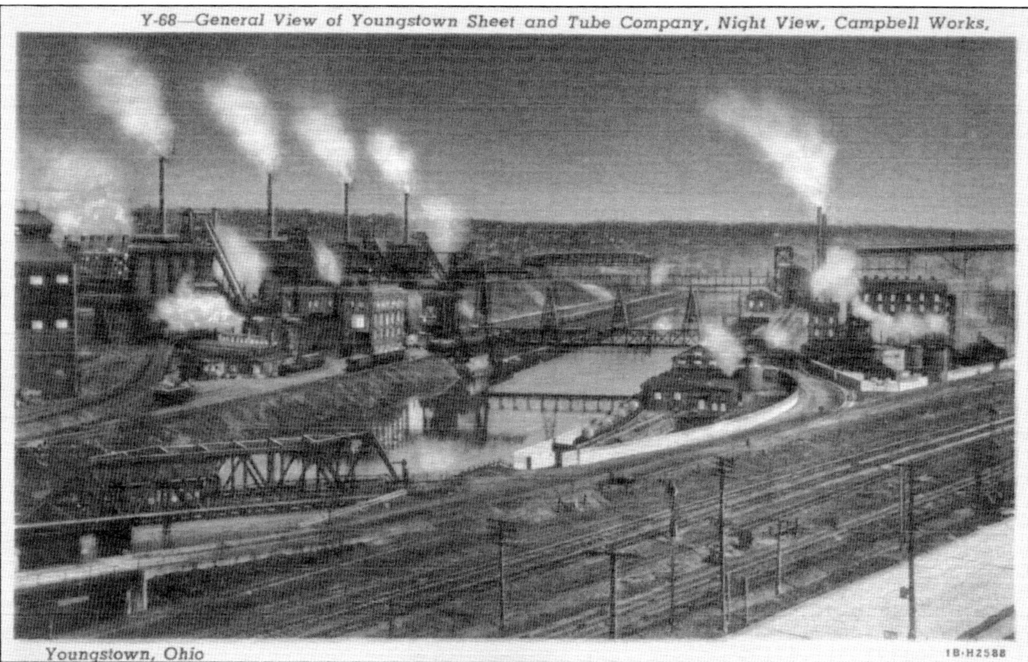

This postcard portrays a general view of the Youngstown Sheet and Tube Company Campbell Works, seen at night from Wilson Avenue. The Youngstown Sheet and Tube Company mills were constantly active and rarely saw time for a break in production. (Courtesy of Mike Parise.)

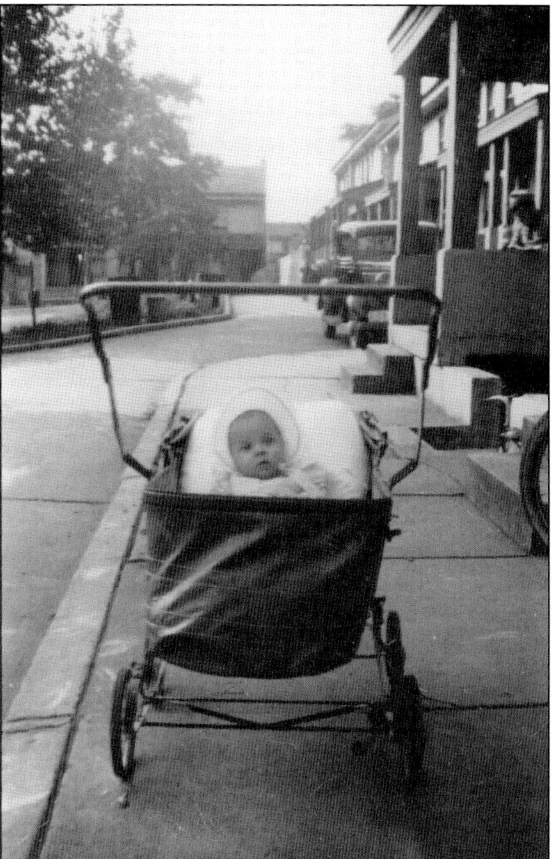

The Youngstown Sheet and Tube Company homes are nestled in a small area of Campbell in relative walking or biking distance to the mills. Nearly 300 apartments consisting of mostly immigrant families were packed into that small area. Living in such close proximity afforded the families the opportunity to become close friends and learn various cultural traditions. (Courtesy of Lorraine Sabol.)

During the 1930s and 1940s, many families who immigrated into the city moved into small concrete apartments known as the Youngstown Sheet and Tube Company homes. These homes, which were built between 1918 and 1920, were the world's first prefabricated concrete estates. The size of the house was constructed to be small in order to reduce the amount of people living in each one. (Courtesy of Lorraine Sabol.)

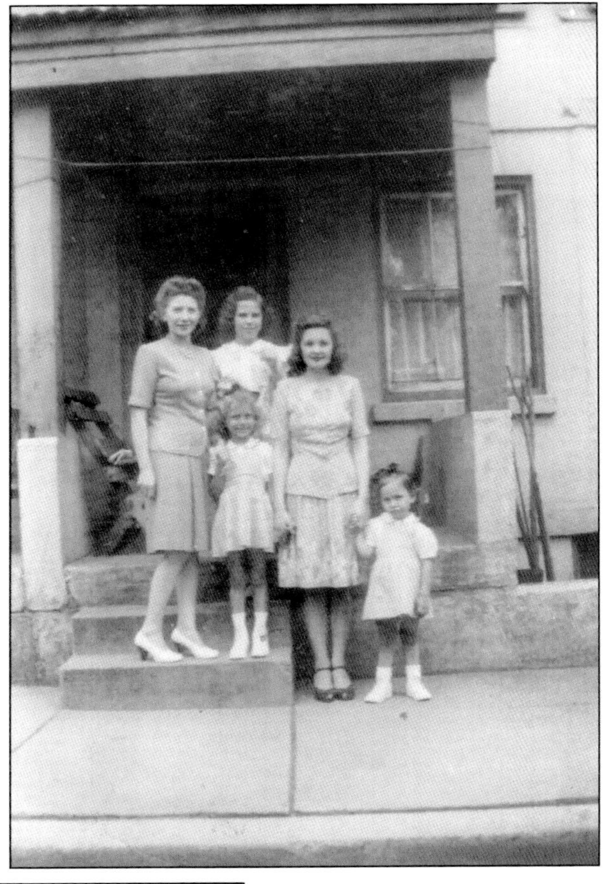

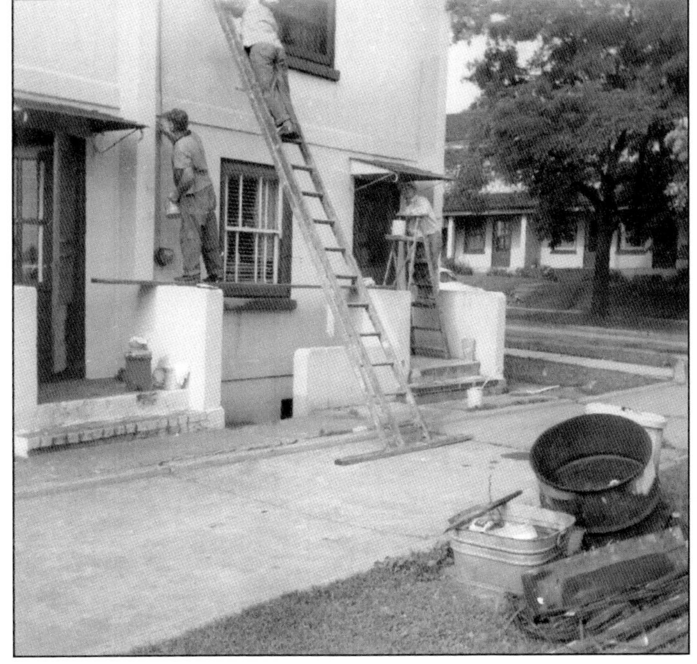

This photograph shows the Youngstown Sheet and Tube Company homes being painted by the residents during the summer of 1956. When the Youngstown Sheet and Tube Company sold the houses to the families, many would pitch in to restore and paint the apartments to keep them looking new. (Courtesy of Lorraine Sabol.)

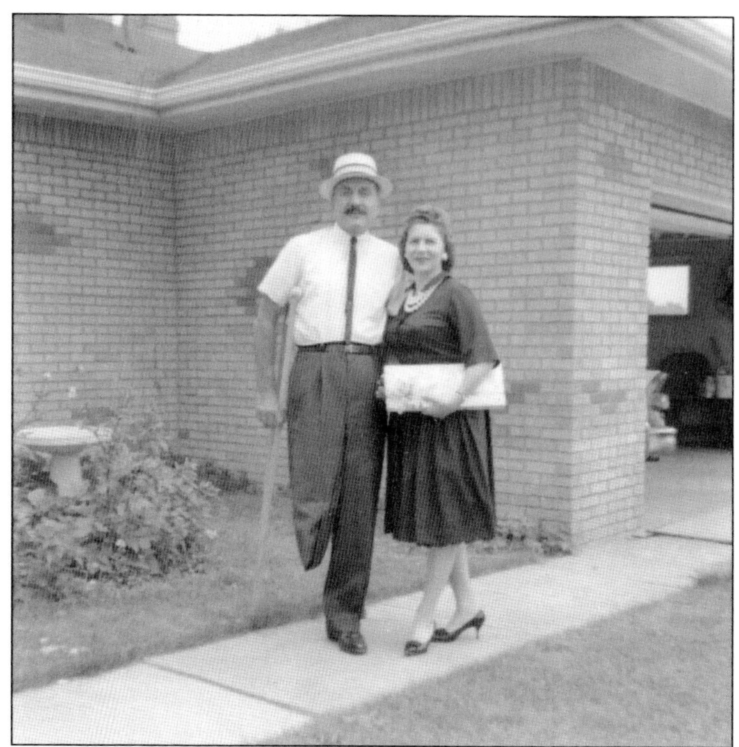

This photograph of mill worker Adolph Malys illustrates the hazards of working at the plants. A 1,000-pound roller crushed Adolph's leg before he was taken to the emergency room at the Youngstown Sheet and Tube Company hospital. The on-call surgeon arrived at the hospital, from a poker game, wearing a baseball cap and chewing tobacco. (Courtesy of Lorraine Sabol.)

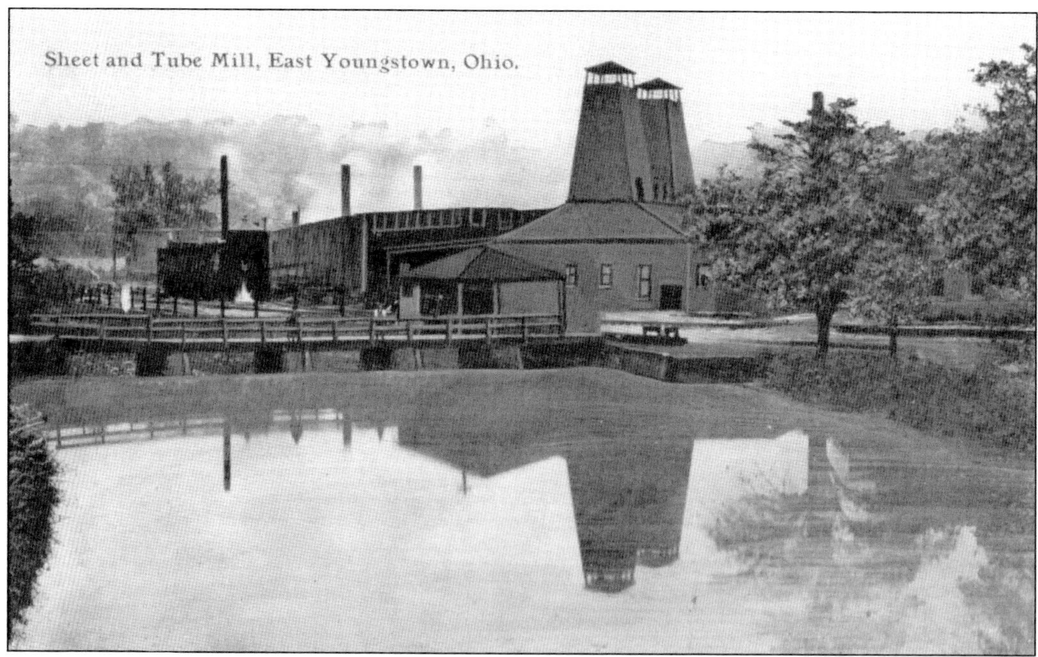

This c. 1911 postcard is an artist's rendition of the Youngstown Sheet and Tube Company mill in what was then East Youngstown, Ohio. Due to the chaos from a labor strike in January 1916, the city took on the reputation of violence and lawlessness. With a steady increase of population, the village of East Youngstown became a city on January 1, 1922, and its name was changed to Campbell on April 26, 1926. (Courtesy of Mike Parise.)

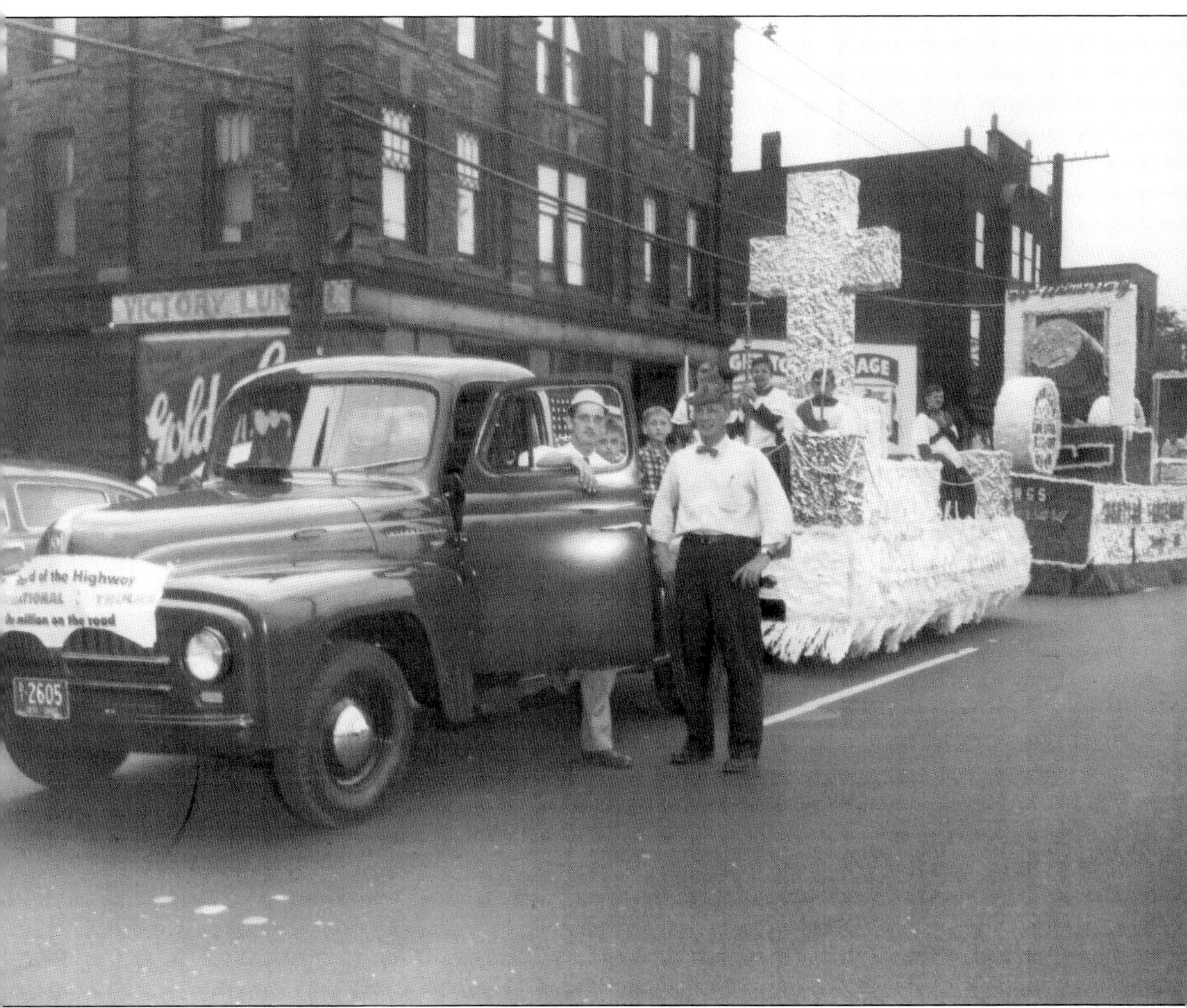

This float for St. John the Baptist Slovak Catholic Church appeared in the Youngstown Sheet and Tube Company's 50th Jubilee parade in 1951. Steve Zetts (left) and John Zimmerman (right) are pictured in front. The altar boys can be seen holding crosses and candles on the float behind them. (Courtesy of Florence Galida.)

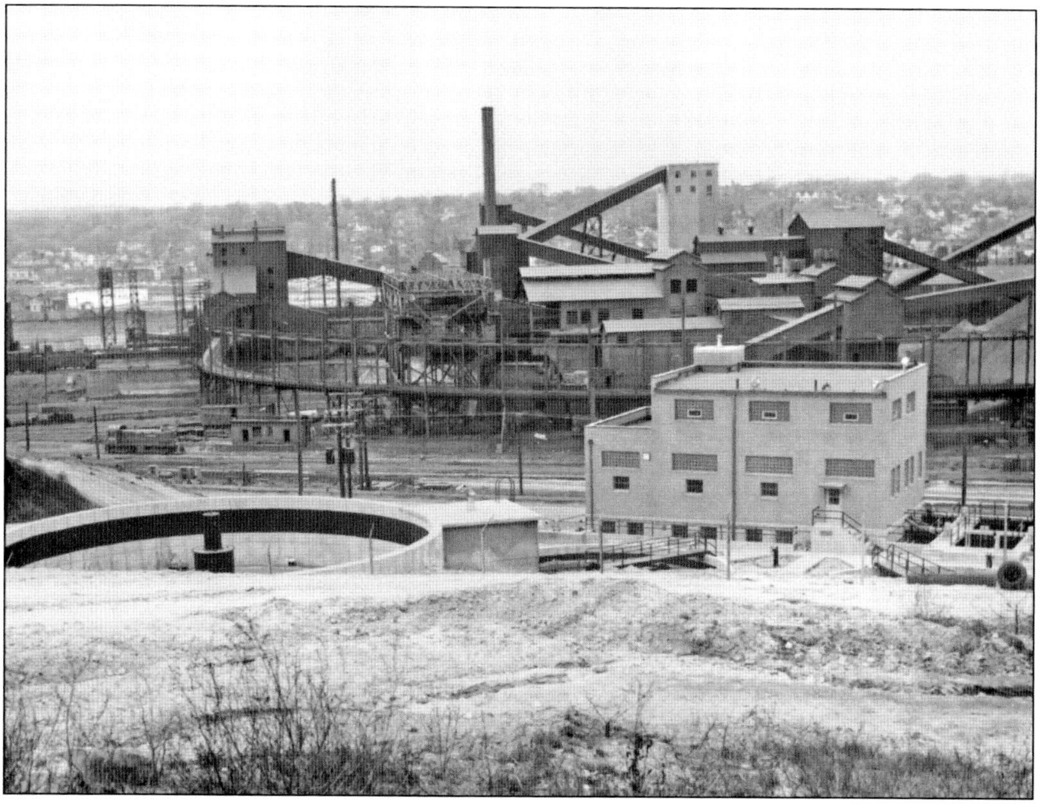

The Youngstown Sheet and Tube Company Campbell Works is perfectly encapsulated in this view from behind the Wastewater Treatment Plant taken around 1958. Out of all the mill plants in the Youngstown District, the Campbell Works was the largest, with 381 choke vents, 12 furnace open-hearth shops, and 4 blast furnaces, along with several other buildings to assist with production. (Courtesy of Florence Galida.)

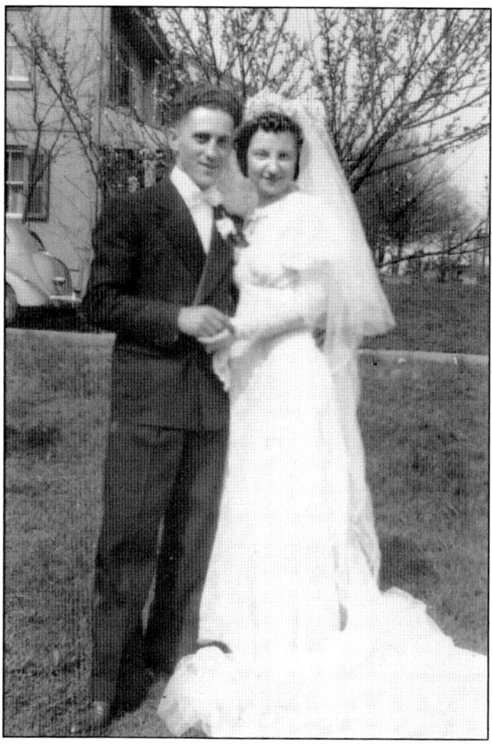

Frank Sabol and Stella Wyrobek Sabol are pictured in the company homes after their wedding on May 18, 1939. When World War II broke out, Frank desperately wanted to go fight for America. As an immigrant, he truly appreciated how great this country was and felt a strong desire to serve. But because of his boxing injuries, he could not breathe through his nose, and the Army would not take him. In an even more desperate attempt to serve, Frank tried to have an operation to open his nasal passages, but it did not work and the military still would not accept him. (Courtesy of Lorraine Sabol.)

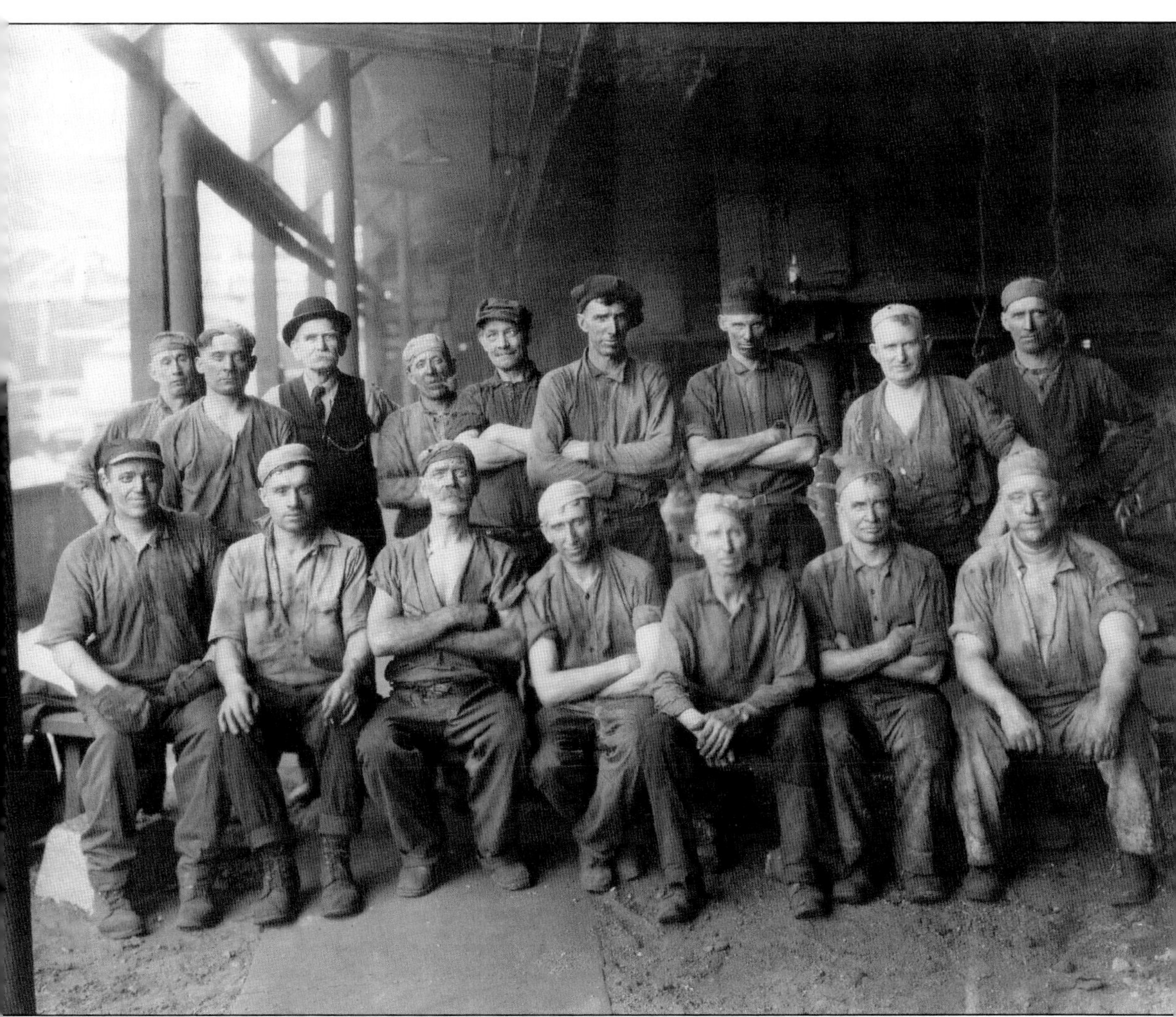

Shown in this undated photograph are iron puddlers from the Youngstown Sheet and Tube Company. Their boss John Nestor is pictured wearing the derby hat and suit. The Youngstown Sheet and Tube Company closed its Campbell Works on September 19, 1977, to the surprise and dismay of an entire city. This date will forever be known as "Black Monday," as some 5,000 workers lost their jobs at the Youngstown Sheet and Tube Company. (Courtesy of Florence Galida.)

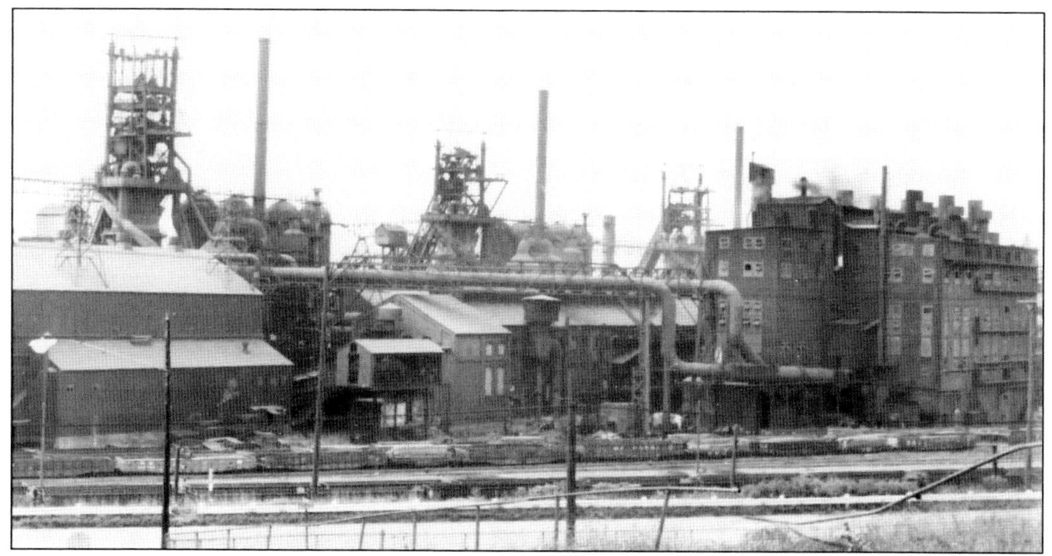

In 1856, the Cleveland & Mahoning Railroad was established as the first of its kind in the Mahoning Valley. By 1878, tracks had been installed in the old bed of the Ohio-Pennsylvania canal, which ran through the Mahoning Valley and continued eastward. The Pittsburgh & Lake Erie (P&LE), the Baltimore & Ohio (B&O), and the Pennsylvania & New York Central Railroad (Penn-Central) all operated on their respective tracks, which are shown in the foreground, along with the Youngstown Sheet and Tube Company plant in the background. (Courtesy of Florence Galida.)

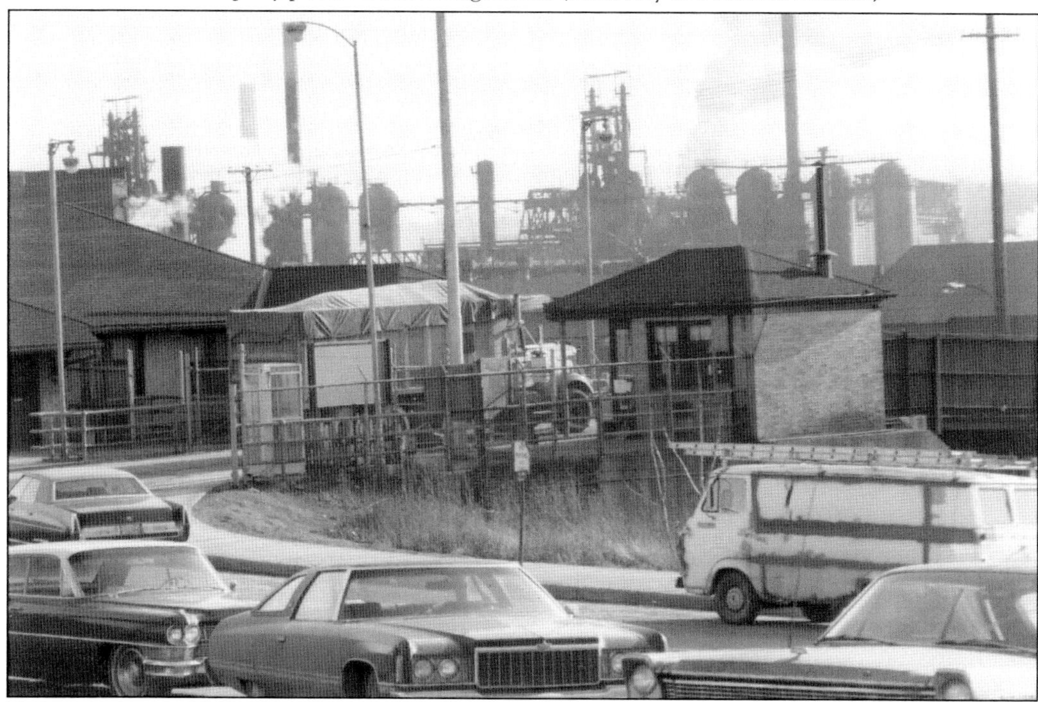

Leading over Wilson Avenue, the Short Street Bridge took workers to and from the mill yards. The small building on the right was used as a guard booth, and the building on the left was office space. This bridge allowed for a high fraction of the 13,000 mill workers to travel back and forth to Campbell. (Courtesy of Florence Galida.)

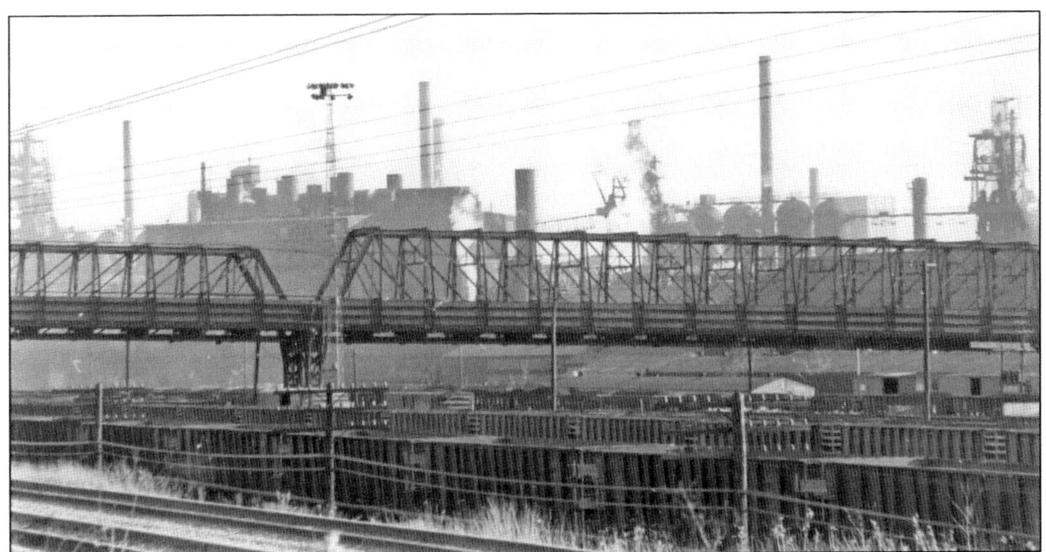

Although the Youngstown Sheet and Tube Company comprised many areas along the Mahoning River, the Campbell Works remained the largest plant in the Youngstown District. During the early days of its operation, the Youngstown Sheet and Tube Company had an annual payroll of over $22 million. The city of Campbell emerged from the needs of the plant, and it has been said that the city could have lined its streets in gold during the days of the mill operations. (Courtesy of Florence Galida.)

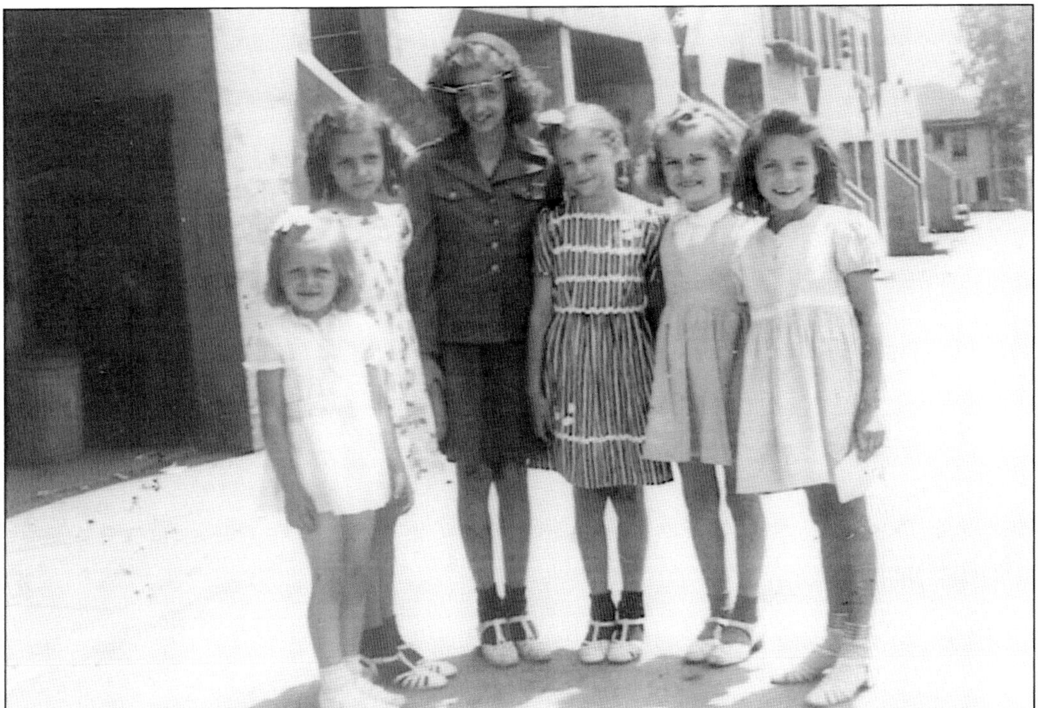

These girls stopped for a photograph before heading off to their last day of school in 1943. From left to right are Elaine Sokol, Florence Katula, Carol Katula, Ann Marie Solic, Mary Ann Sokol, and Gloria Katula. (Courtesy of Florence Galida.)

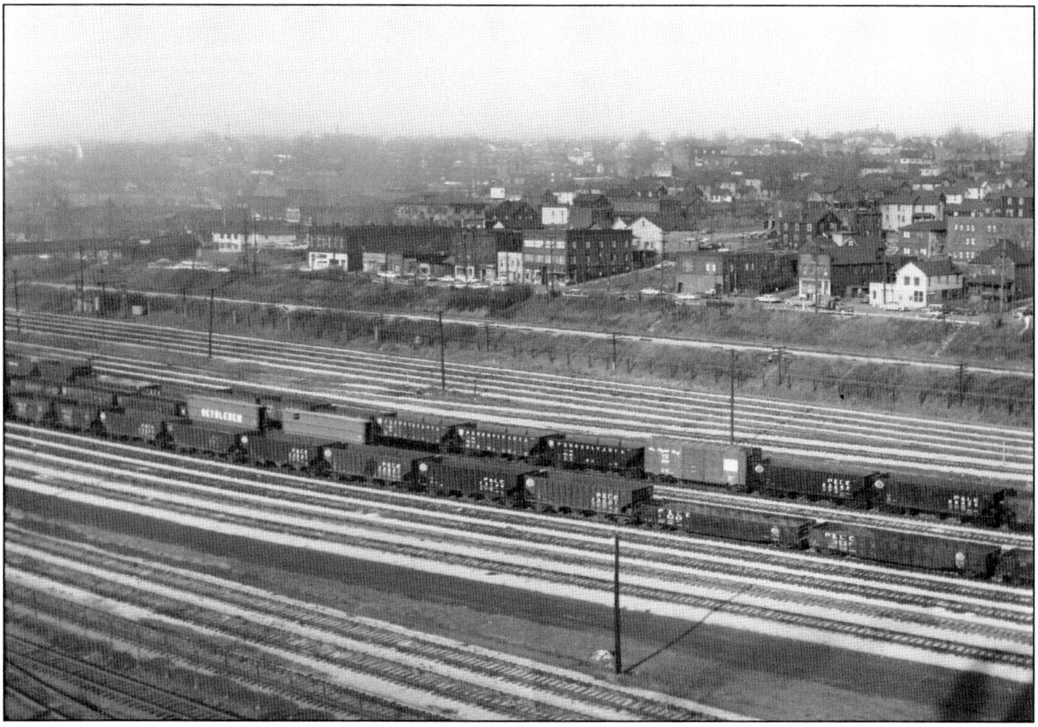

This undated photograph taken from the Youngstown Sheet and Tube Company plant shows how pollution from the mills flowed into the city. Many people who hung their laundry out to dry would often come back outside to find it covered in soot. This posed a problem for many, as clothes were typically washed on the weekend and hung out to dry on Monday. The immigrant families lived a simple life that was reminiscent of their home country and their culture. (Courtesy of Florence Galida.)

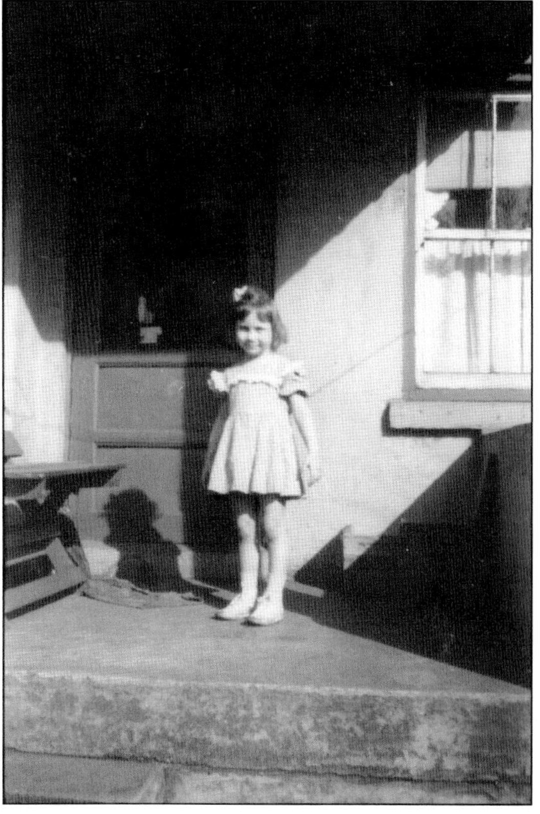

Adele Malys is pictured on the porch of her company home in 1946. The houses were intentionally designed to be small so that the immigrant workers would not be able to shelter an abundance of family members. (Courtesy of Lorraine Sabol.)

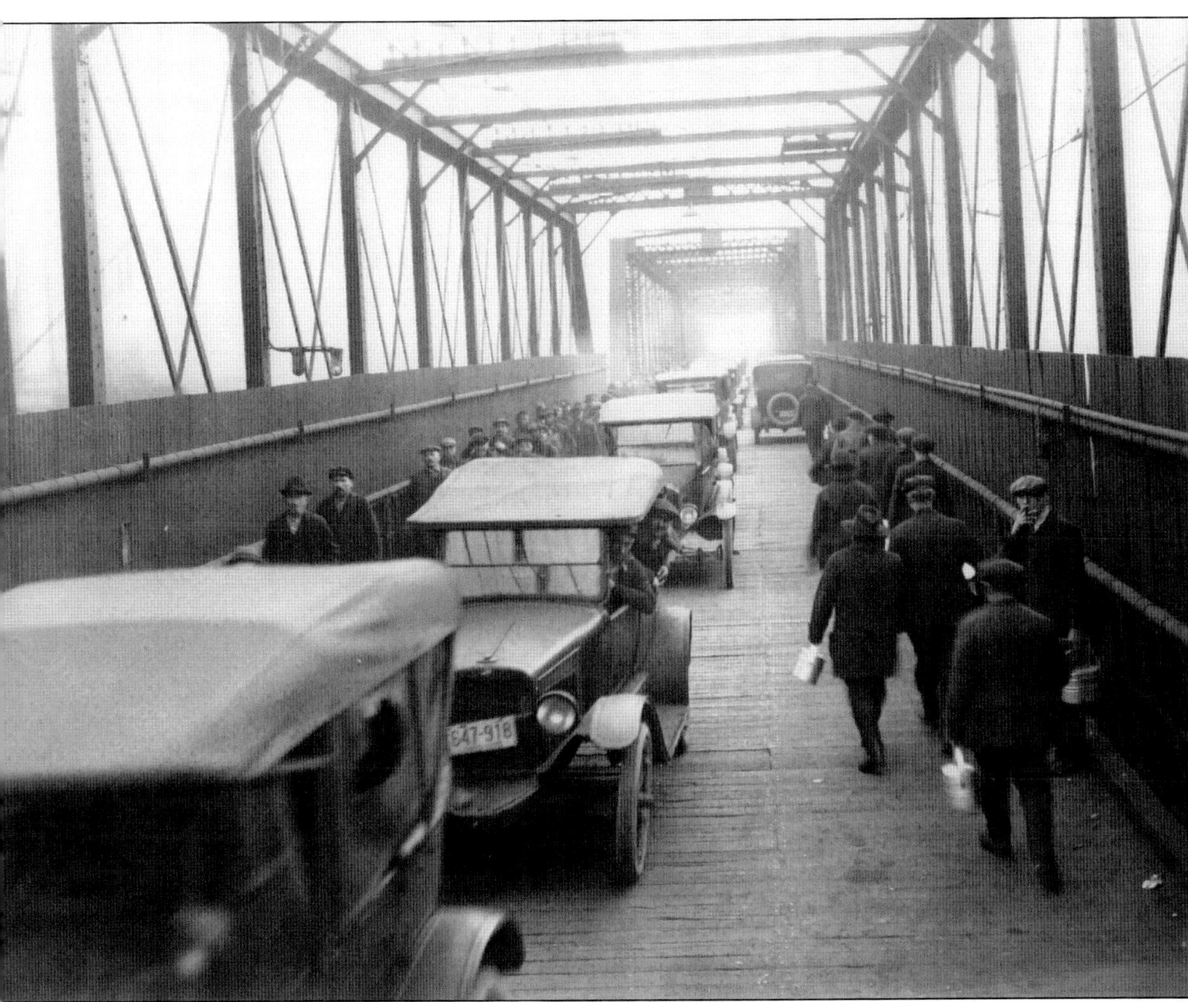

As the Great Depression began to wind down in the 1930s, James Anson Campbell added more renovations to the Campbell Works. Campbell foresaw the national need for various commodities during and after World War II. With his death in 1933, Campbell would not be able to witness the wisdom of his recommendations, as the Youngstown Sheet and Tube Company plants began to drastically expand nationwide. The North Gate Bridge to the Campbell plant is pictured here in 1925. (Courtesy of Florence Galida.)

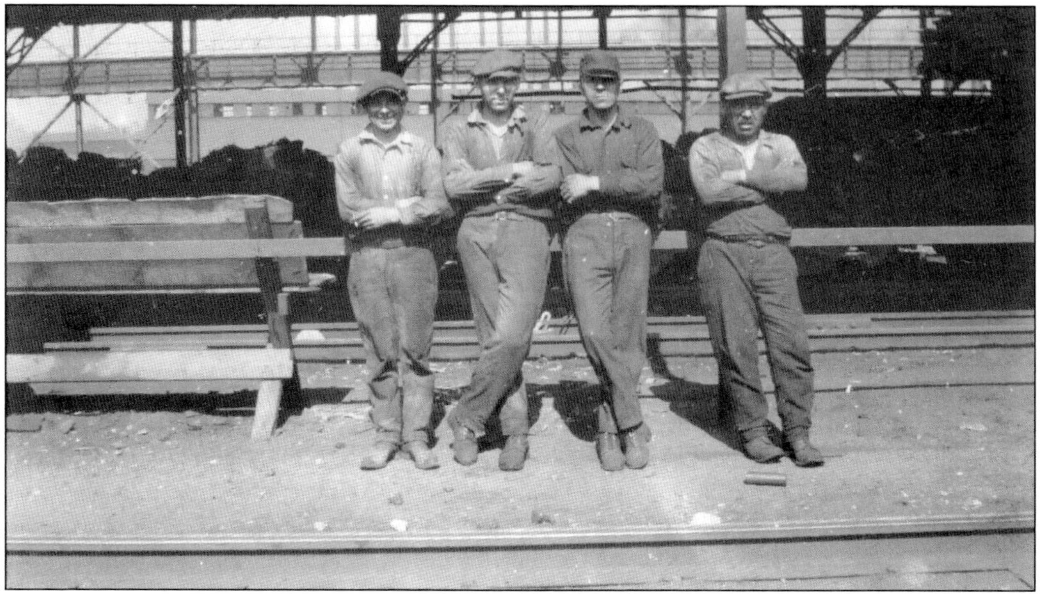

Taking a much-needed break, men from the Youngstown Sheet and Tube Company mill pose for a photograph along a railroad in the 1920s. Second from left is Michael Sosnowchik, who also sang in the Youngstown Sheet and Tube Company choir. The other three men are unidentified. (Courtesy of Florence Galida.)

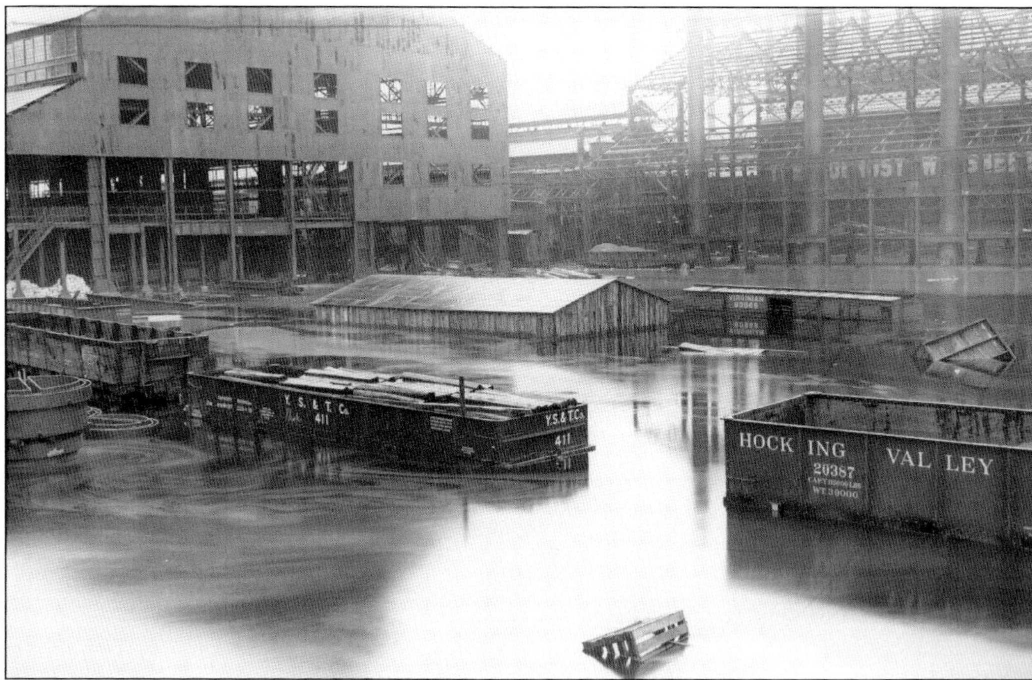

During the flood of 1913, rain began on Easter Sunday in March and continued for four straight days. The Mahoning River rose so far that it had flooded a majority of the Youngstown Sheet and Tube Company buildings before stopping just short of Broad Street (Wilson Avenue). All the railroad tracks were covered, subsequently halting all industry in the Mahoning Valley. (Courtesy of Florence Galida.)

Three

City of Churches

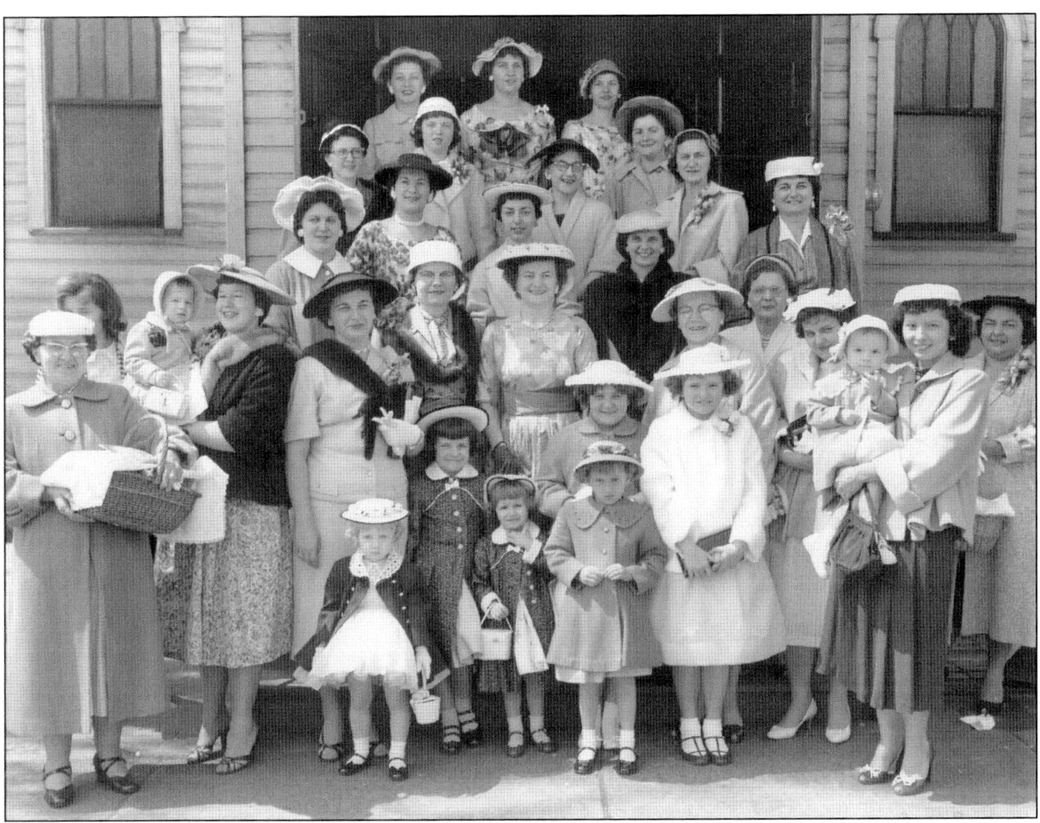

Ladies from St. John the Baptist Russian Orthodox Greek Catholic Church on Fourteenth Street pose for a photograph during an Easter celebration in the early 1950s. With Rev. Nicholas Yuschak serving as the last priest in the old building, Rev. Nicholas Vansuch took over in 1959 at the new church on Struthers-Liberty Road. (Courtesy of Florence Galida.)

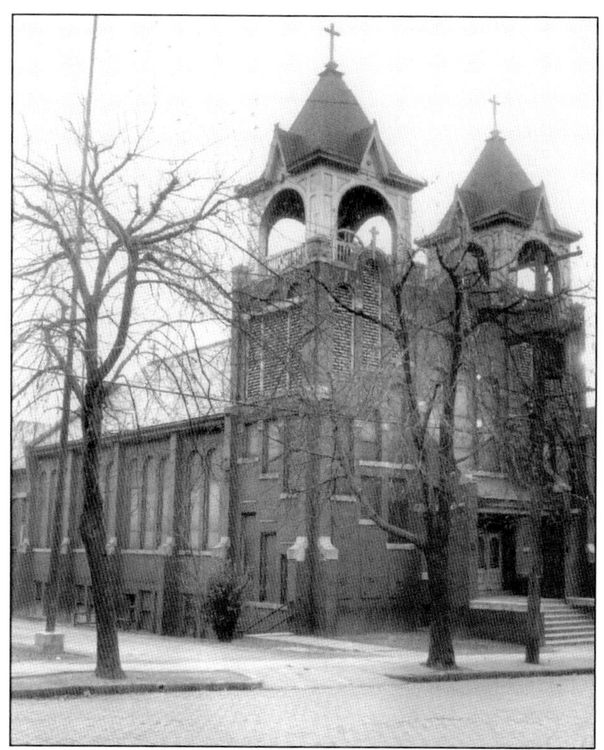

After spending several years traveling to various churches in the area, the Slovak residents of East Youngstown wanted a place to worship that was closer to home. In 1913, a delegation of local Slovaks petitioned the bishop for their own church, which eventually began to form by 1919. The photograph at left of St. John the Baptist Slovak Catholic Church, built in 1952, shows how the structure appeared in the mid-1950s. The photograph below illustrates the beauty of the altar and the interior architecture of the church during the period. (Both, courtesy of Florence Galida.)

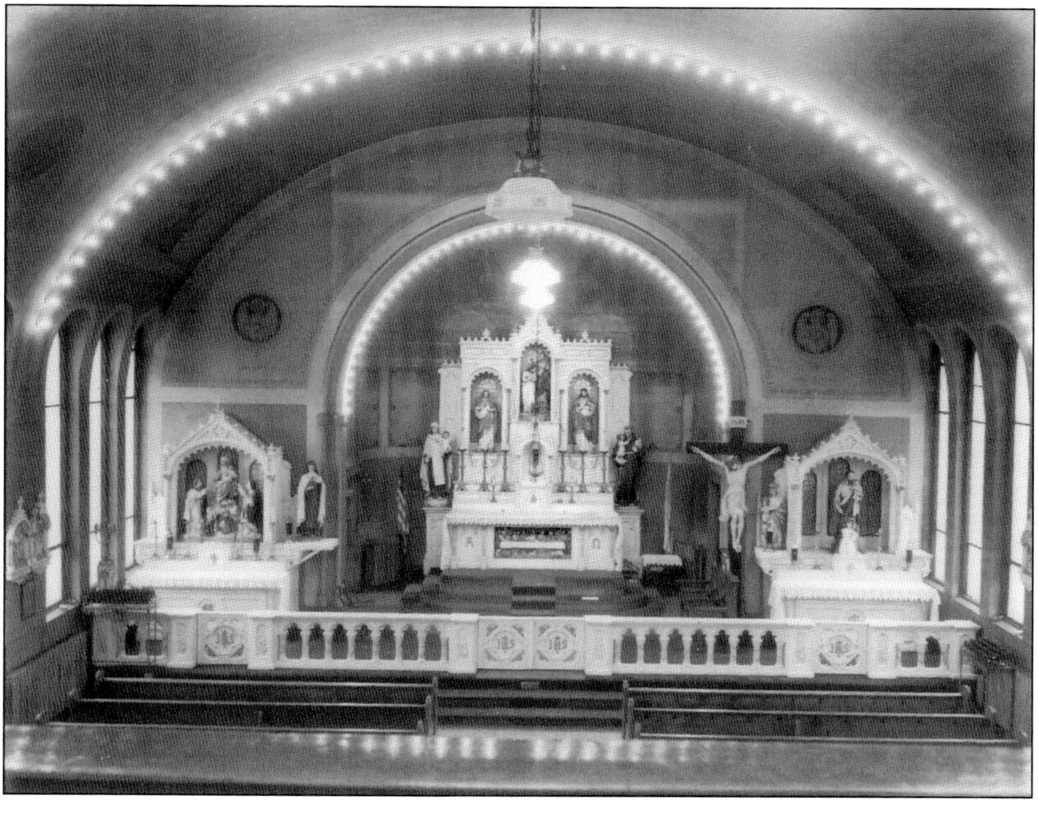

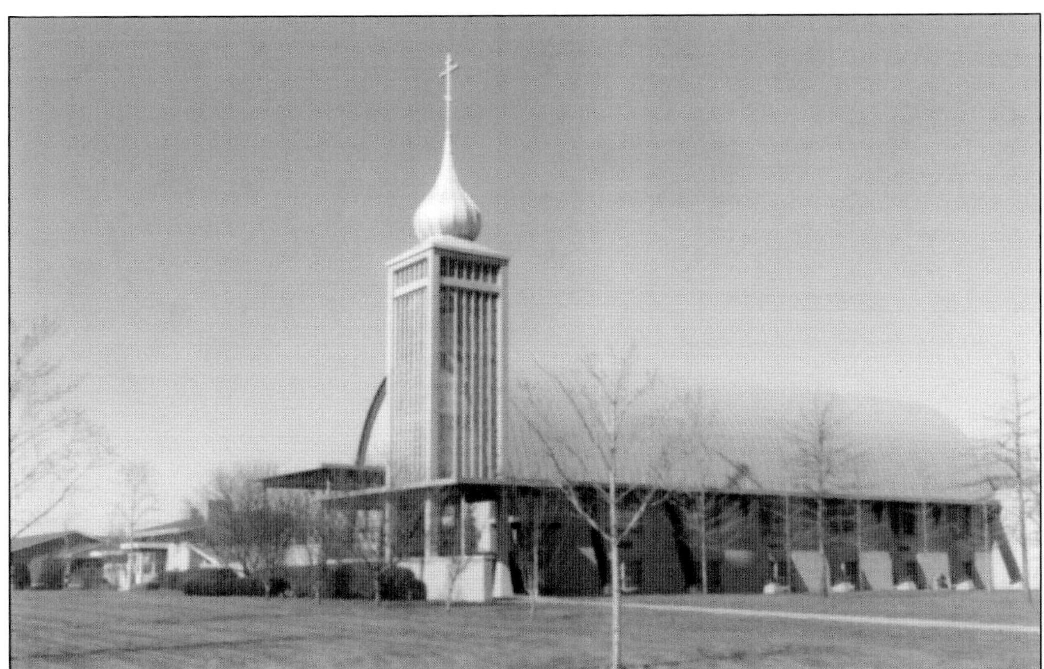

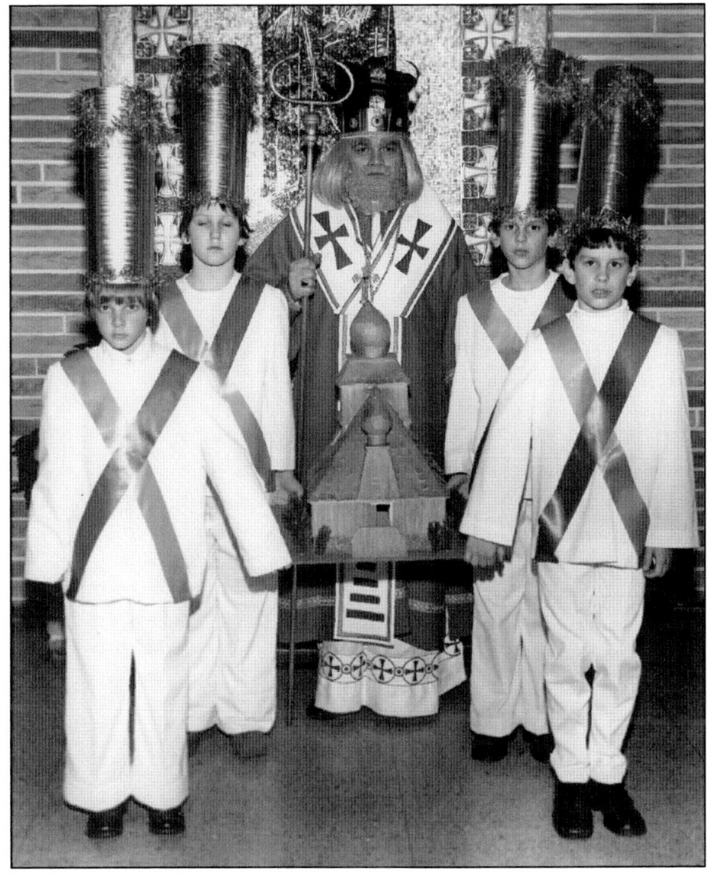

Originally organized in 1917 under the St. George Society, St. John the Baptist Church held its first services on March 3, 1918, in a newly constructed building on Fourteenth Street. Many of the families, from Russian or Ruthenian ancestry, embraced Russian Orthodoxy in 1919, causing a split in the church. Those who followed Catholicism left the church and founded St. Michael's Byzantine Catholic Church, while those who remained joined with the Russian Orthodox Church. To accommodate an increasing congregation, a larger church under the name of St. John the Baptist Eastern Orthodox Church was built on Struthers-Liberty Road at Tenney Avenue on October 23, 1960, as seen above. (Both, courtesy of Florence Galida.)

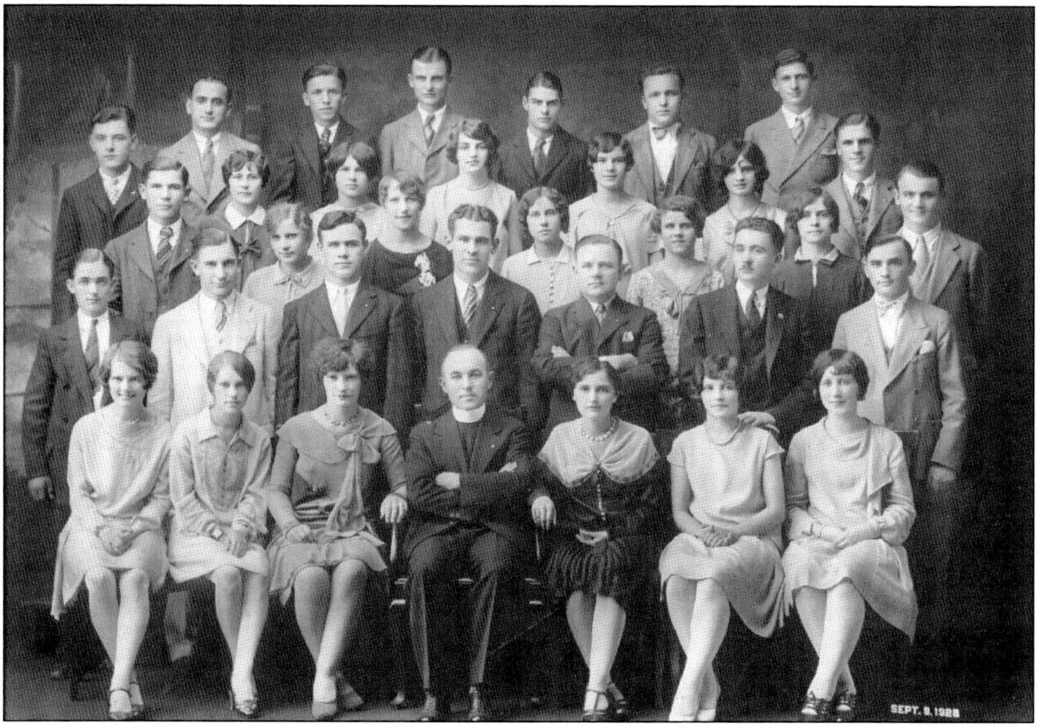

Several members of St. John the Baptist Russian Orthodox Greek Catholic Church participated in the Russian Elite Society. Pictured here on September 9, 1928, are, from left to right, (first row) Sally Gulanich, Helen Gulanich, Betty Tarkanich, Rev. Daniel Krusko, Ann Kovalchick, Mary Kolesar, and Katherine Kolesar; (second row) Andy Pytak, Mike Holliday, Steve Gary, John Sopkovich, Joe Kvasnak, George Paluhanich, and George Kovalchick; (third row) Bill Holliday, Helen Tarkanich, Ann Kirila, Ellen Korchnak, Ann Garaski, Mary Harley, and Joe Gary; (fourth row) Mike Maruschak, Christine Polkabla, Mary Wolfe, Ann Rudy, Ann Wolfe, Ann Harley, and Nick Sopkovich; (fifth row) John Kovalchick, Mike Kovach, Mike Zupko, Mike Katula, Joe Andrasko, and Matt Wansack. (Courtesy of Florence Galida.)

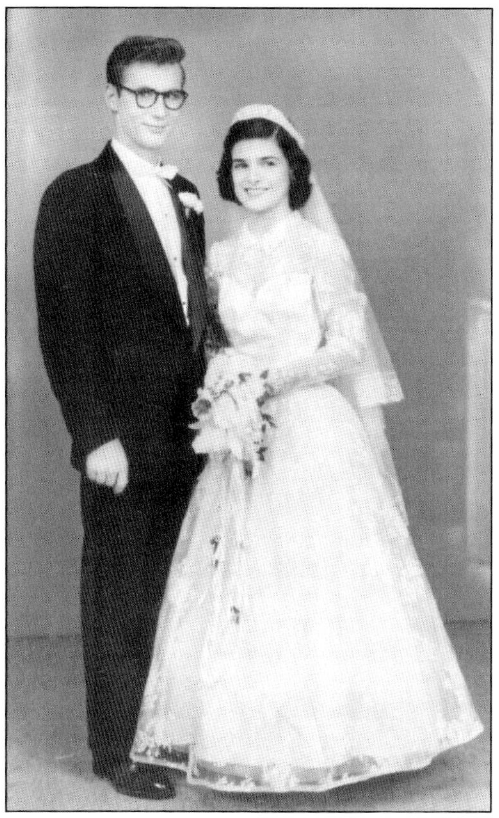

On November 5, 1955, Fr. George Pappas gave the first liturgy at the Archangel Michael Greek Orthodox Church on the corner of Twelfth Street and Porter Avenue. A few weeks later, on November 19, 1955, Richard and Irene Moylan were the first couple to get married in the church. (Courtesy of Irene Moylan.)

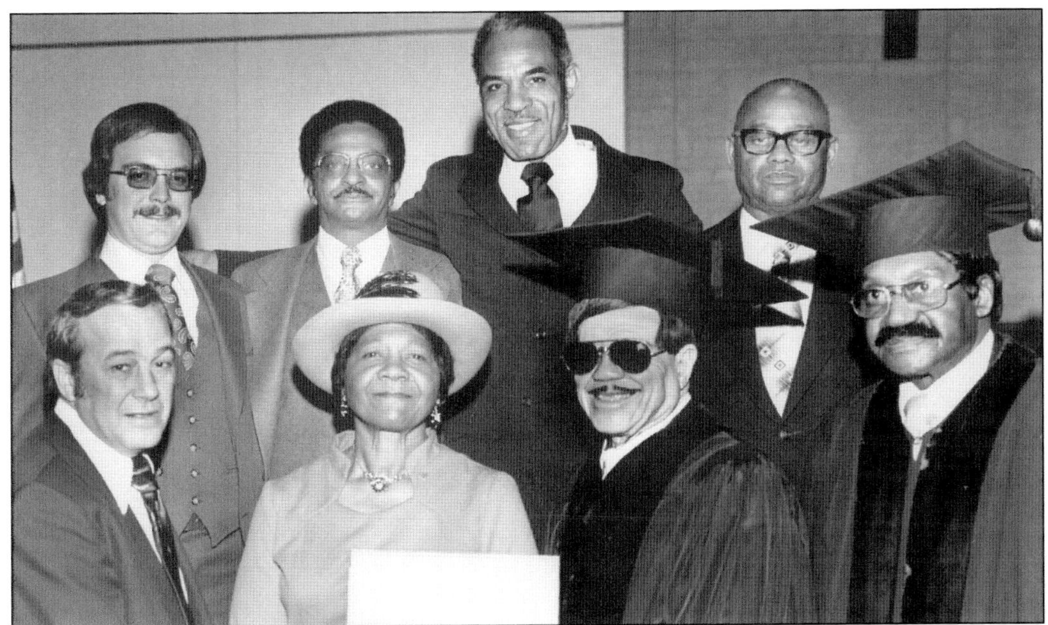

In 1923, several members of the Shiloh Baptist Church left to start their own congregation under the name Gospel Temple Baptist. By 1925, a new building had been established at 36 Ninth Street to house their worshippers. With the congregation steadily growing, Rev. Louis W. Childress and Rev. W.K. Hawkins established a new church at 279 Whipple Avenue on August 27, 1972. From left to right are (first row) George Tablack, Ruby Childress, Rev. Louis Childress, and a Reverend Moore; (second row) James Ciccolelli Jr., Robert Milson, Rev. Wille Gamble, and Rev. Ed Stoneward. (Courtesy of Florence Galida.)

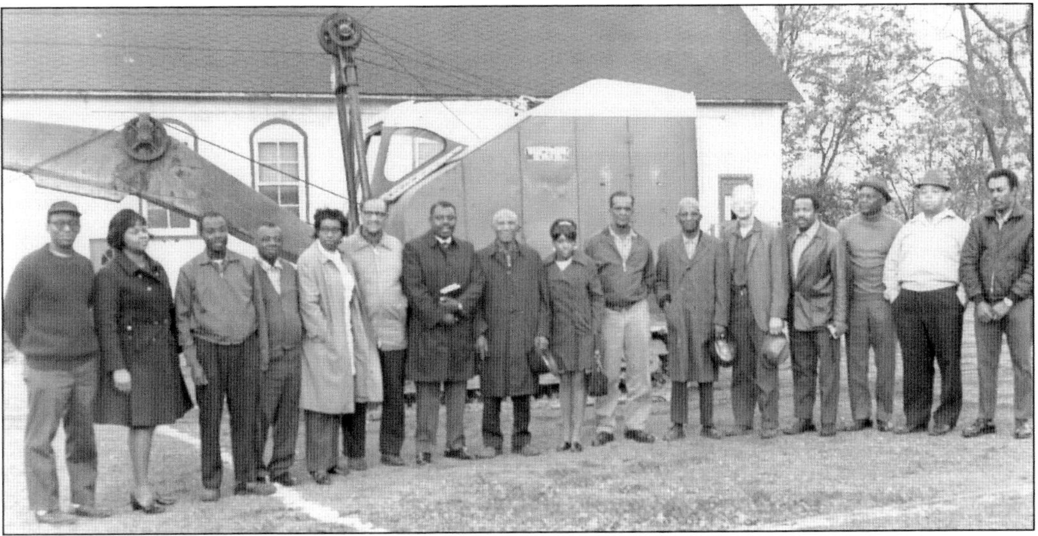

In 1965, the Urban Renewal Program began buying all the property south of Murray Avenue to Wilson Avenue, which subsequently caused Shiloh Baptist Church to find a new building. The congregation eventually moved into the empty Hungarian Baptist Church on the corner of Bright Avenue and Sixteenth Street. In 1970, property was then purchased next to the old church that was large enough to meet the needs of the expanding parish. The Hungarian church was torn down to make room for the parking lot. (Courtesy of Florence Galida.)

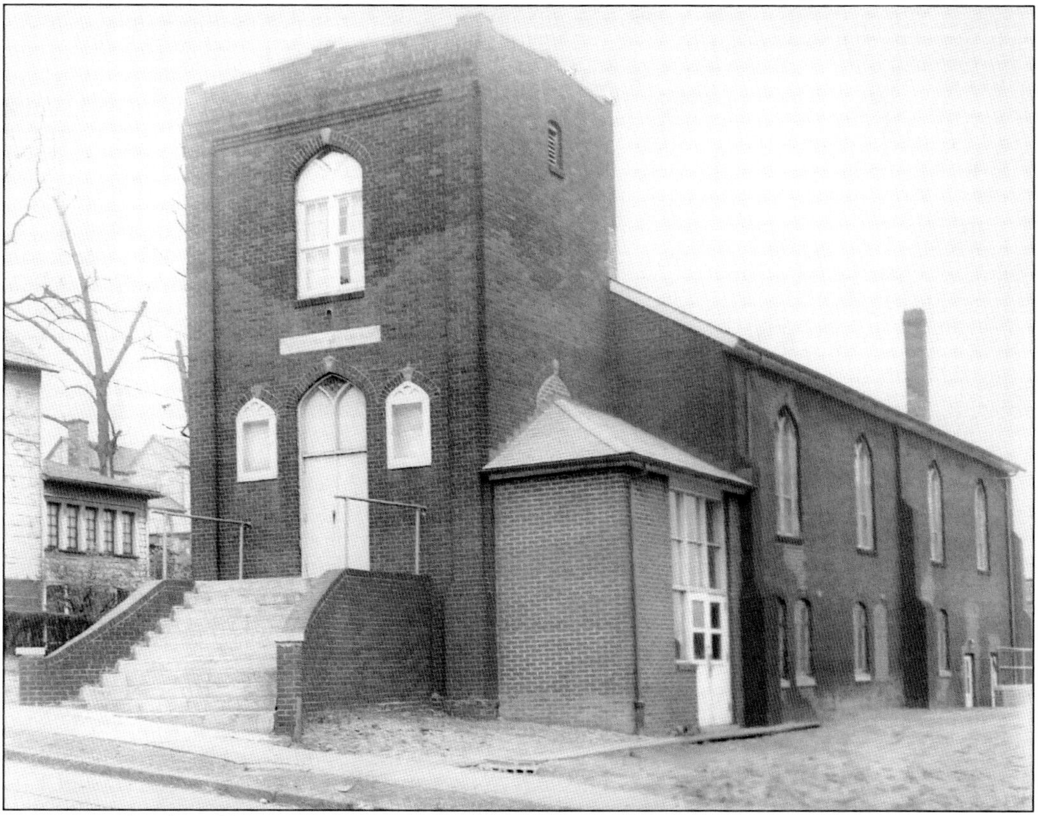

By 1910, only a handful of African American families were living in East Youngstown, and thus, they had to go outside the village for church services. In need of a more local church, these families began holding religious services under the name of Shiloh Baptist at the Higgins' home on August 16, 1917. With the congregation rapidly growing, a new building was constructed at 47 Madison Street in 1924. (Courtesy of Florence Galida.)

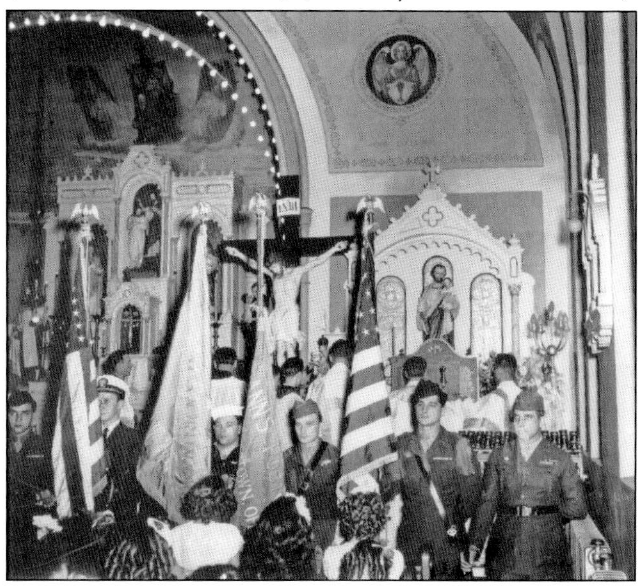

Each year, members from St. John the Baptist Slovak Catholic Church held a special mass in honor of the men and women from the church and the city who served in the military or lost their lives in service of their country. From its early inception, Campbell has had a rich history of honoring its veterans, a display of gratitude that extends to the present day. (Courtesy of Florence Galida.)

Fr. Michael Tondra (sitting) and the eighth grade graduating class from St. John the Baptist Slovak Catholic School are pictured here in June 1948. From left to right are (first row) Joan Verba, Betty Yakubov, Margret Maro, and Norma Mazerik; (second row) Mary Ann Dubos, Edna Smiley, Raymond Brayer, ? Snitzer, Andrew Starinchak, Marjorie Rusnak, and Helen Texter; (third row) Mary Duboy, Martha Hudak, Eleanor Hamrock, Ann Vargo, Marion Phillips, and Betty Pavliga. (Courtesy of Florence Galida.)

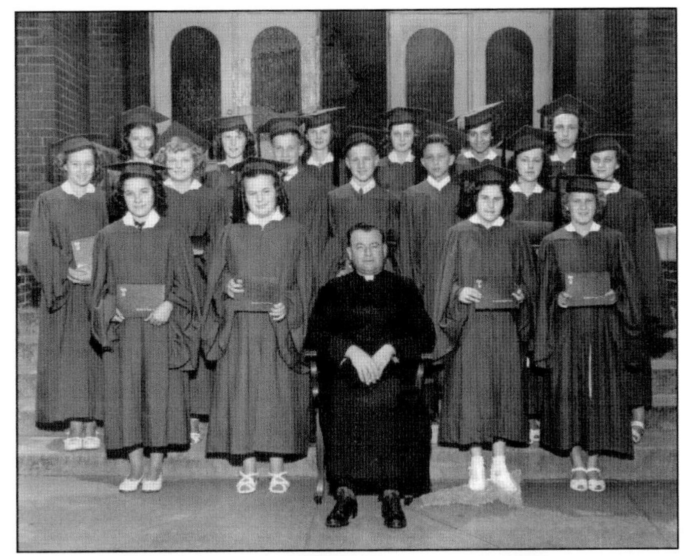

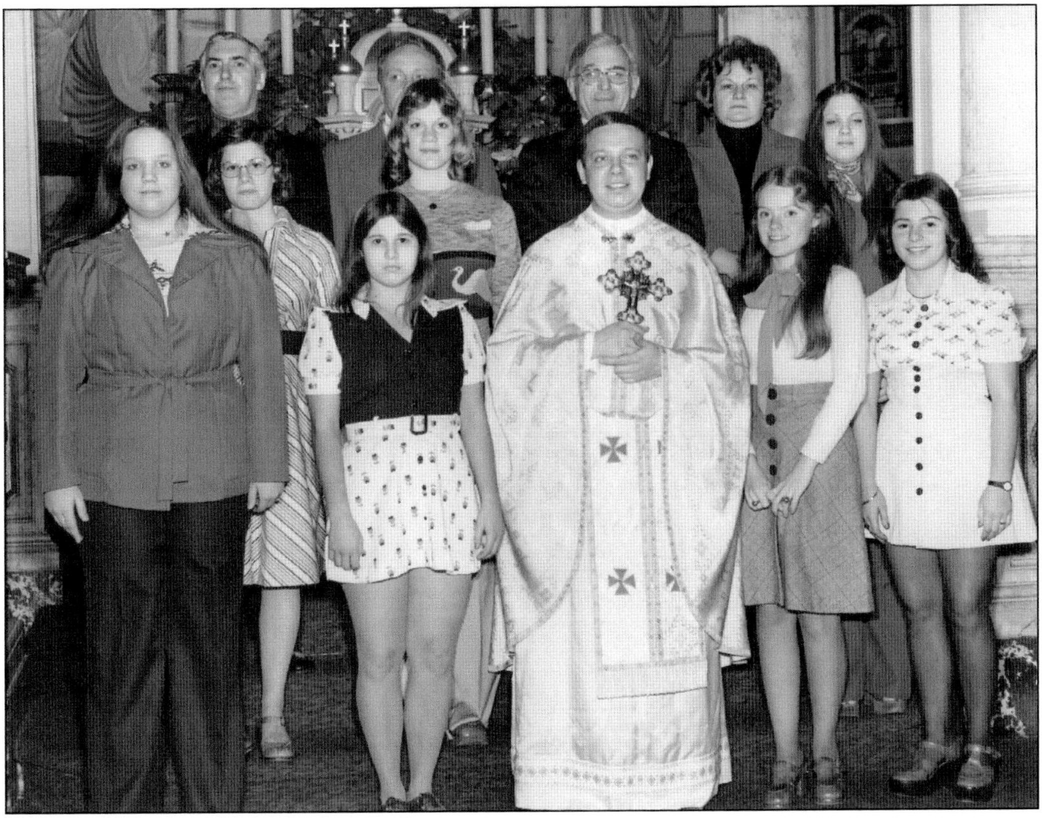

As Slovak immigrants moved into the Youngstown area during the early 1900s, they looked to establish their own parish near their new settlement. Many years of hardships would plague the church and its parishioners until a permanent building could be established. After several appeals to the bishop in Cleveland, the St. Elizabeth Parish was created at the Sacred Heart Church on April 16, 1922. When Fr. Joseph L. Kostik took over as priest, a new rectory was established at 92 Haseltine Avenue. (Courtesy of Florence Galida.)

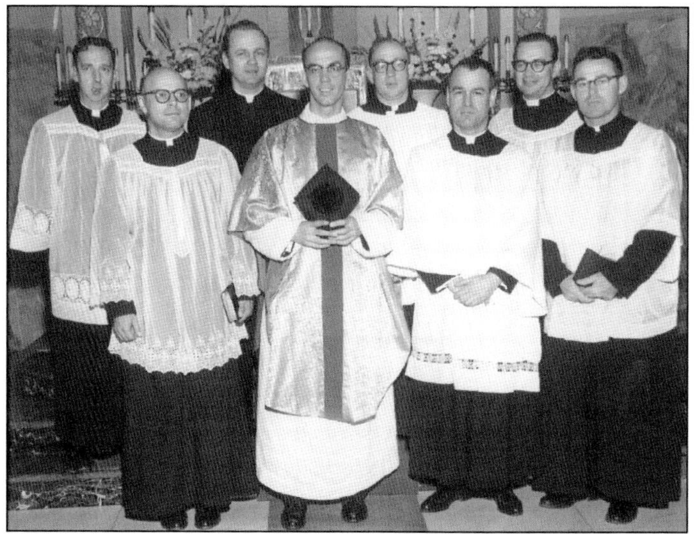

After decades of struggling, the motivated members of St. Elizabeth Church put forth such a great effort through festivals and other activities that enough money was raised for a new church. On August 22, 1954, ground breaking began on the corner of Gladstone and Keystone Streets. The church was then dedicated on September 29, 1956, with a replica of the Lady of Lourdes Shrine in France dedicated on May 21, 1961. (Courtesy of Florence Galida.)

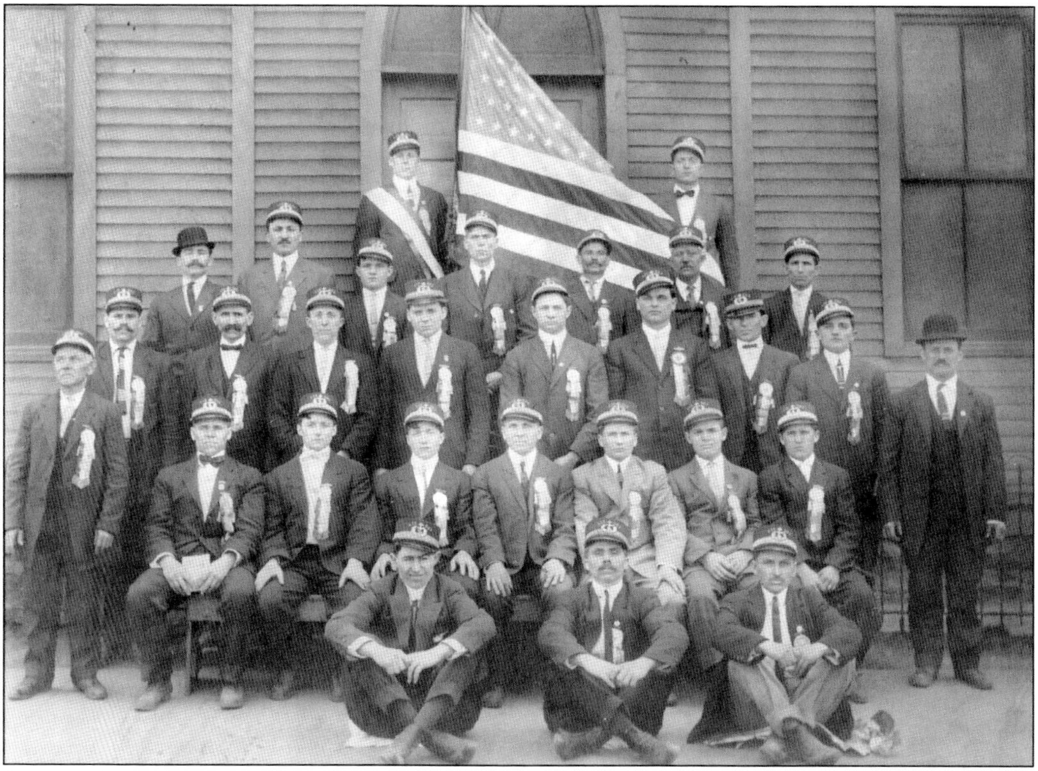

During the early years of East Youngstown, many of the immigrants came together in various social lodges. The Greek Catholic Union No. 576 is shown in front of their lodge on Wilson Avenue around 1913. From left to right are (first row) John Kornyak and two unidentified; (second row, seated) M. Cebula, S. Vrabel, G. Vrabel, J. Cebula, A. Polkabla, unidentified, and J. Dubos; (third row, standing) John Furin Sr., ? Sharshan, ? Kovalchick, J. Vansuch, P. Macala, J. Vansuch, J. Kolesar, M. Andrasko, D. Shirilla, and John Furin Jr.; (fourth row) ? Polkabla, J. Lisko, M. Rosko, M. Lisko, ? Kuzma, S. Lisko, and M. Dudik; (fifth row) G. Lisko and M. Lisko. (Courtesy of Florence Galida.)

Four

School Days

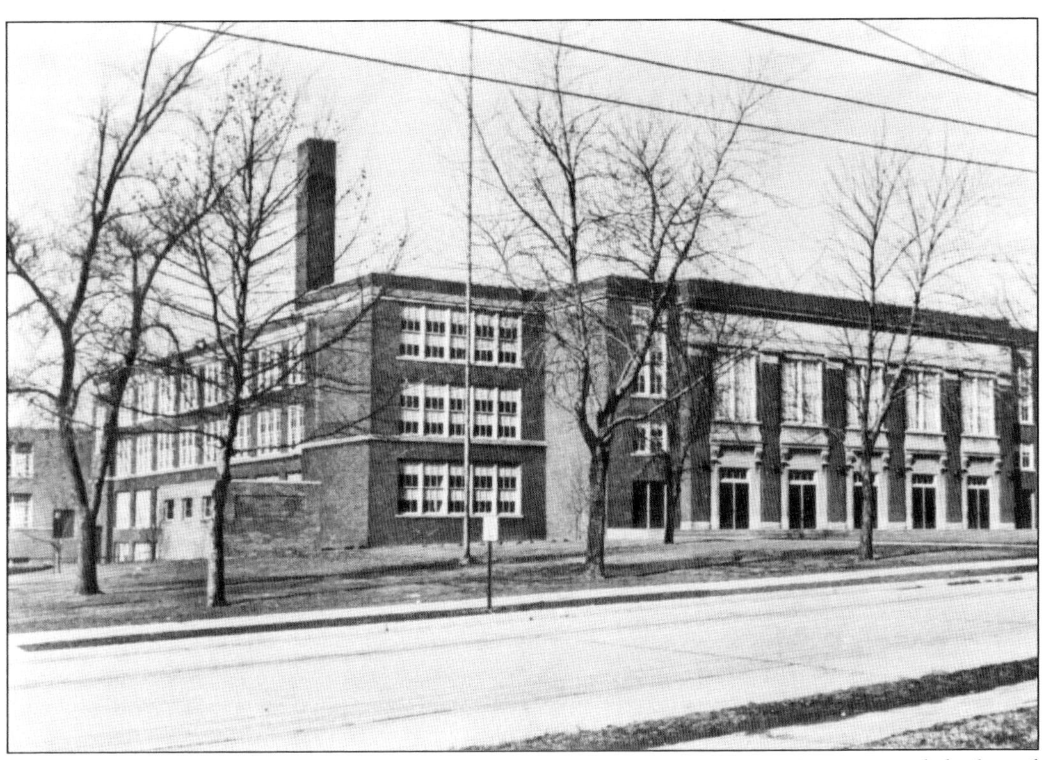

With a school population exceeding 3,000 students in 1922, Supt. W.M. Coursen and the board of education began preparation for a new high school. After buying farmland from the Creed and Reed families, respectively, work on the new building began in May 1924. Named Memorial High by James McCartney on June 24, 1924, the school opened its doors on September 8, 1925, and the first class graduated on June 10, 1926. (Courtesy of Florence Galida.)

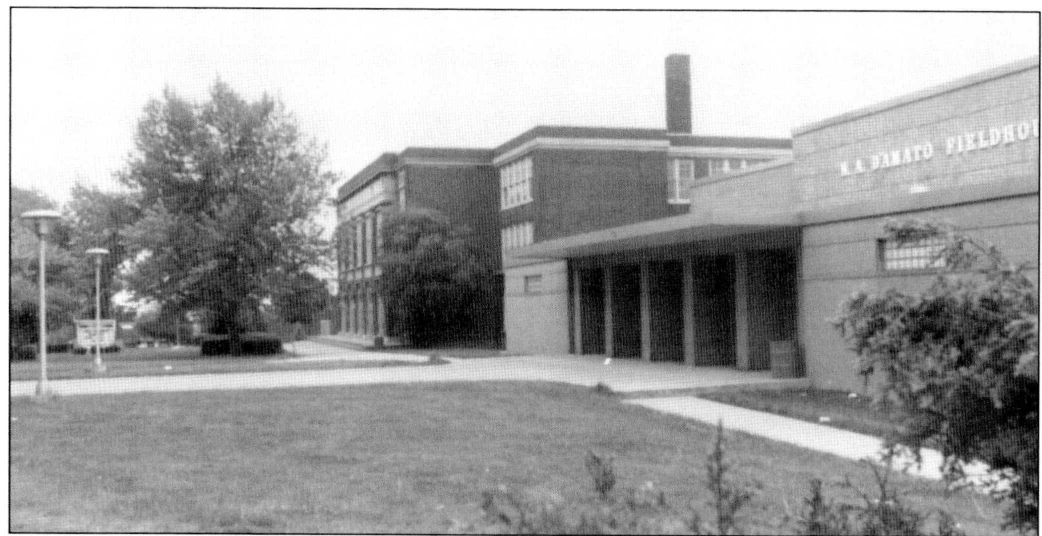

The remaining farmland behind the school was converted to the football stadium during the summer of 1929. Supt. Nicholas D'Amato added a field house to the north end of the school in 1965 and, later, an athletic building to the north side of the stadium in 1967. An interesting fact is the front of the school contained stone caskets that were removed in 1935 after an outcry from parents. (Courtesy of Florence Galida.)

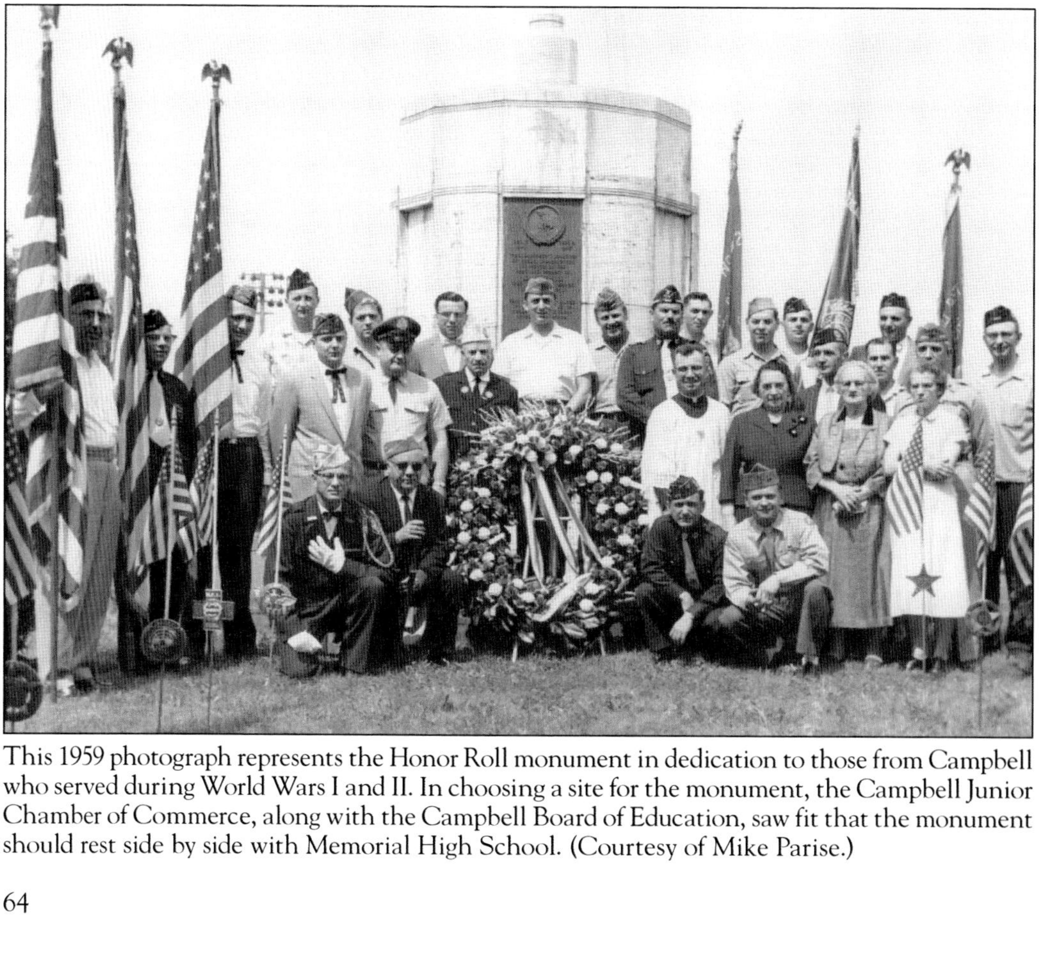

This 1959 photograph represents the Honor Roll monument in dedication to those from Campbell who served during World Wars I and II. In choosing a site for the monument, the Campbell Junior Chamber of Commerce, along with the Campbell Board of Education, saw fit that the monument should rest side by side with Memorial High School. (Courtesy of Mike Parise.)

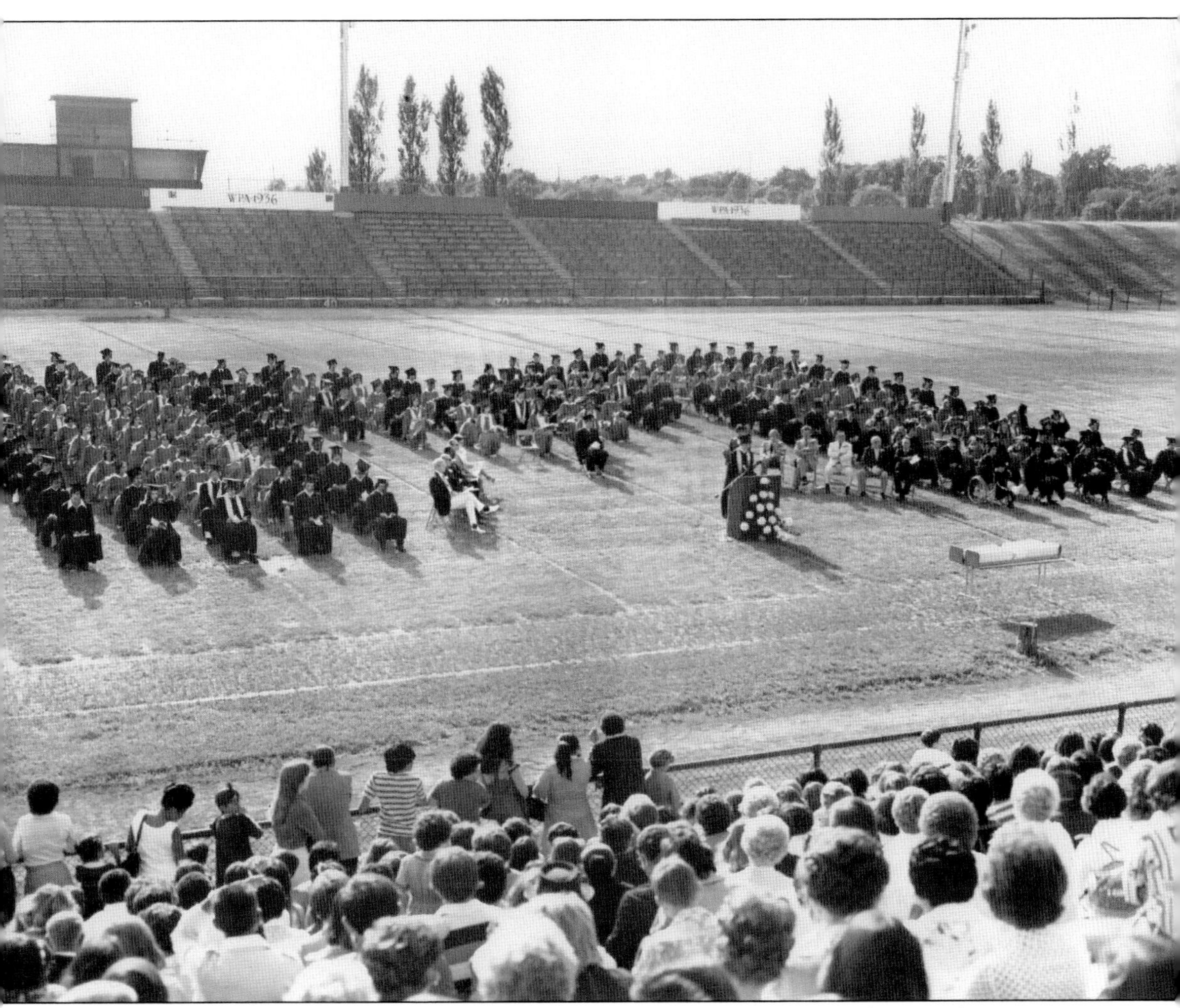

Since 1939, commencement has been held on the football field with the graduating class sitting in the formation of an "M." During inclement weather, commencement is held in the D'Amato Fieldhouse. In 1972, 1973, 1974, and 1975, the Campbell school system endured a teacher's strike due to strict guidelines put in place by the board of education and the superintendent. The strikes took a serious turn in 1974 when a former student bombed the high school principal's office, which subsequently destroyed over 50 years of high school records. Pictured here are the 1977 graduates of Memorial High School. (Courtesy of Florence Galida.)

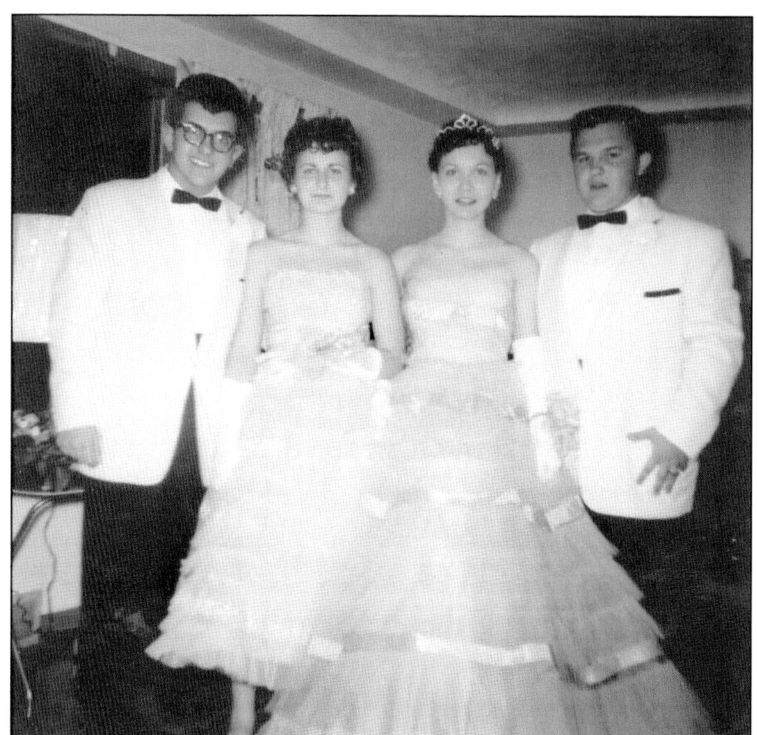

This photograph of two Campbell couples was taken at a residence on Neoka Drive prior to the 1959 prom. That year, the high school prom was held at St. John's Roman Catholic Church Hall. From left to right are John Leombruno, Monica Tikson, Adele Malys, and Mel Sabol. (Courtesy of Lorraine Sabol.)

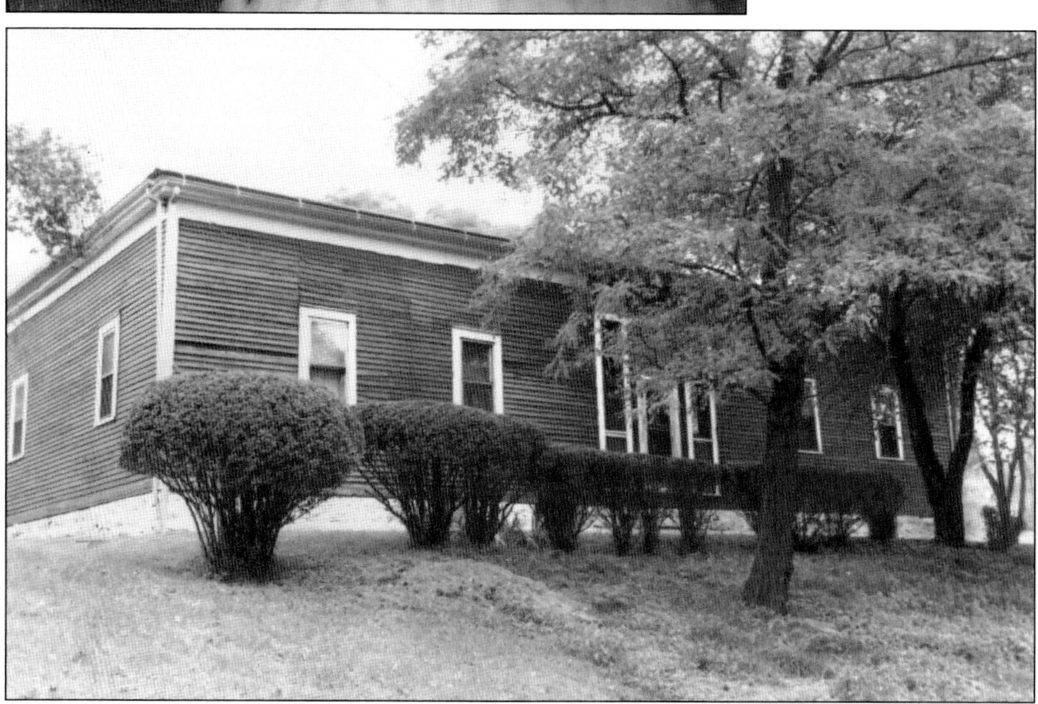

Built between 1903 and 1905, the Seventh Street School, more commonly known as the Stop 7 School, was established to serve children in the area along Warhurst Road and Broad Street (Wilson Avenue). After 1916, the school closed down and was transferred to a private owner. The building no longer stands due to a recent fire. (Courtesy of Florence Galida.)

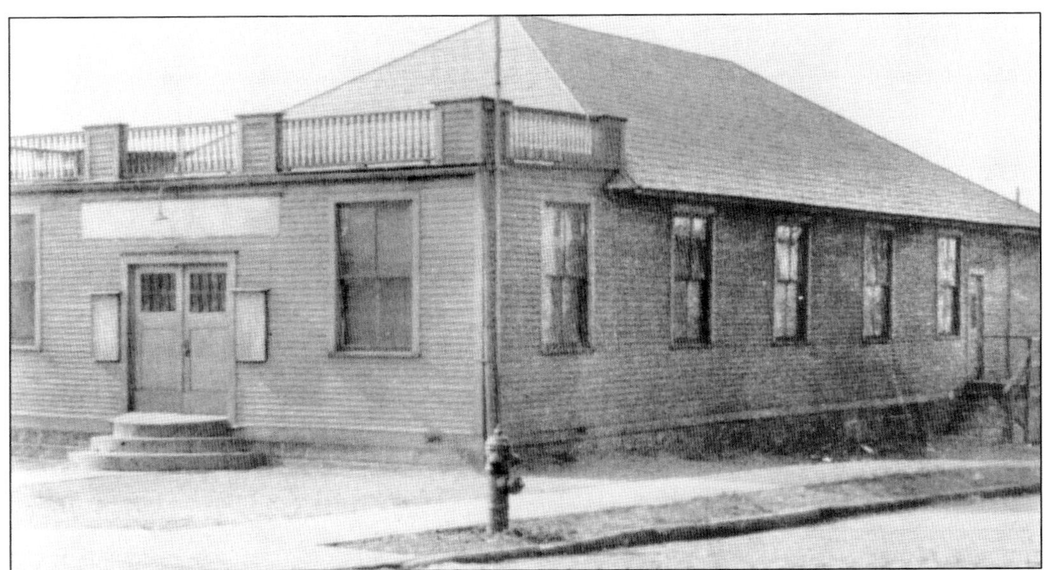

Built on the corner of Twelfth Street and Gordon Avenue in 1905, this two-room school was known as the 12th Street School and sometimes referred to as the Gordon School. After spending years as an overflow to the newer Gordon School and a storage facility for the Pittsburgh and Lake Erie YMCA, the building was purchased by the Italian Catholic Society in 1933. Following renovations, it took on the name of St. Lucy's Church until 1952. In 1975, the building began to operate as a Grecian lounge, but it is no longer standing today. (Courtesy of Florence Galida.)

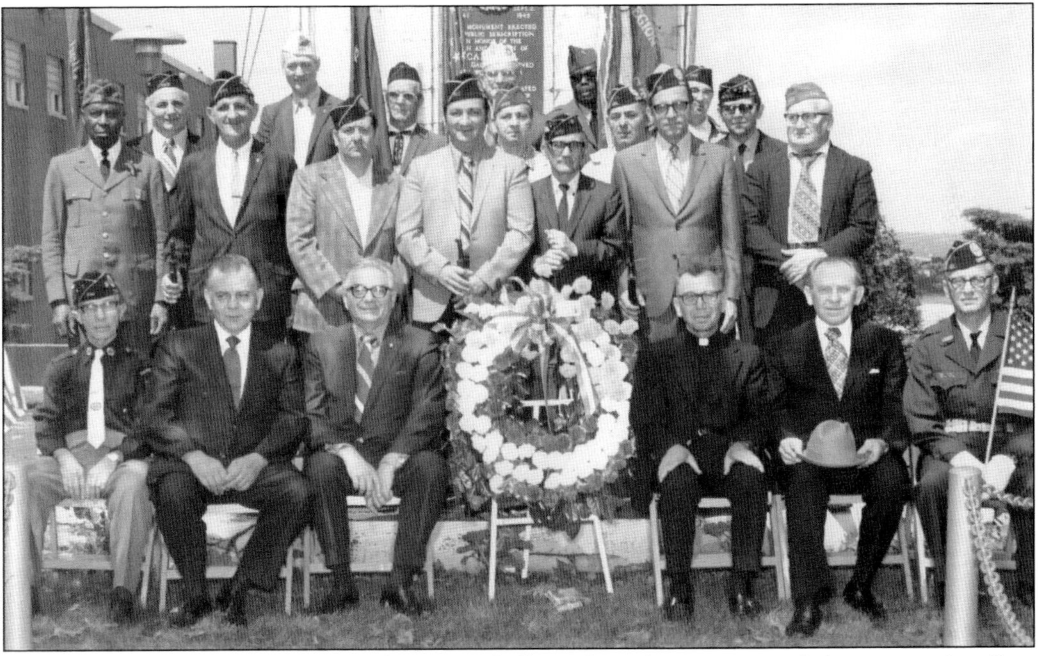

From World War I to the present day, Campbell residents have answered their nation's call to service. Some have returned home, while others were prisoners of war, but too many have made the ultimate sacrifice. Veterans, city officials, and residents gather each year at the Soldiers Monument at Memorial High School to pay their respects and acknowledge these brave men and women. (Courtesy of Florence Galida.)

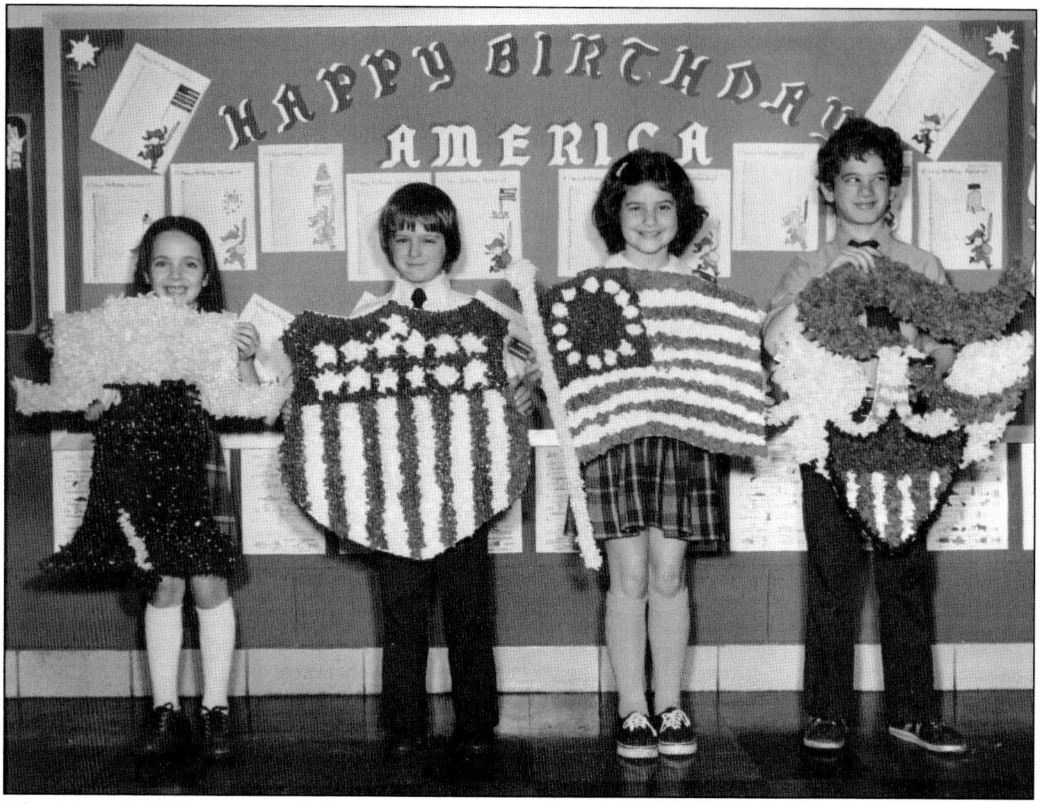

The Campbell Bicentennial Committee organized several events in 1976 to bring the history of America and Campbell to life. Along with city churches and businesses, schoolchildren were encouraged to participate in the celebration by creating historical flags, decorations, clothing, and dances. This was a busy year for the city as everyone from youngsters to politicians participated in making this an exciting event. (Courtesy of Florence Galida.)

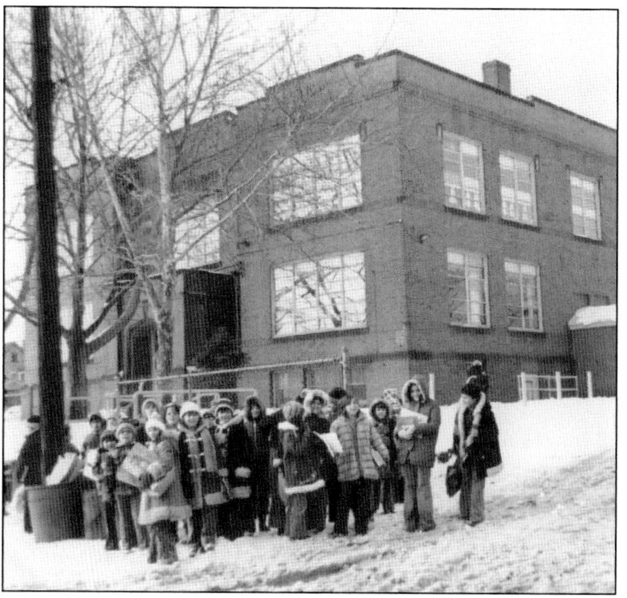

The Gordon School was built in 1913 on farmland purchased from the Gordon family on Twelfth Street, between Gordon and Tremble Avenues. Additions to the school were made in 1915 and 1919 as more land was purchased from private owners. In 1949, a gymnasium was built in a citywide effort to improve local schools. Over the years, the Gordon School served as a hospital during the flu epidemic of 1918, a draft board during World War II, and a recreational center for adults. The Sycamore Place apartment complex currently occupies the site. (Courtesy of Florence Galida.)

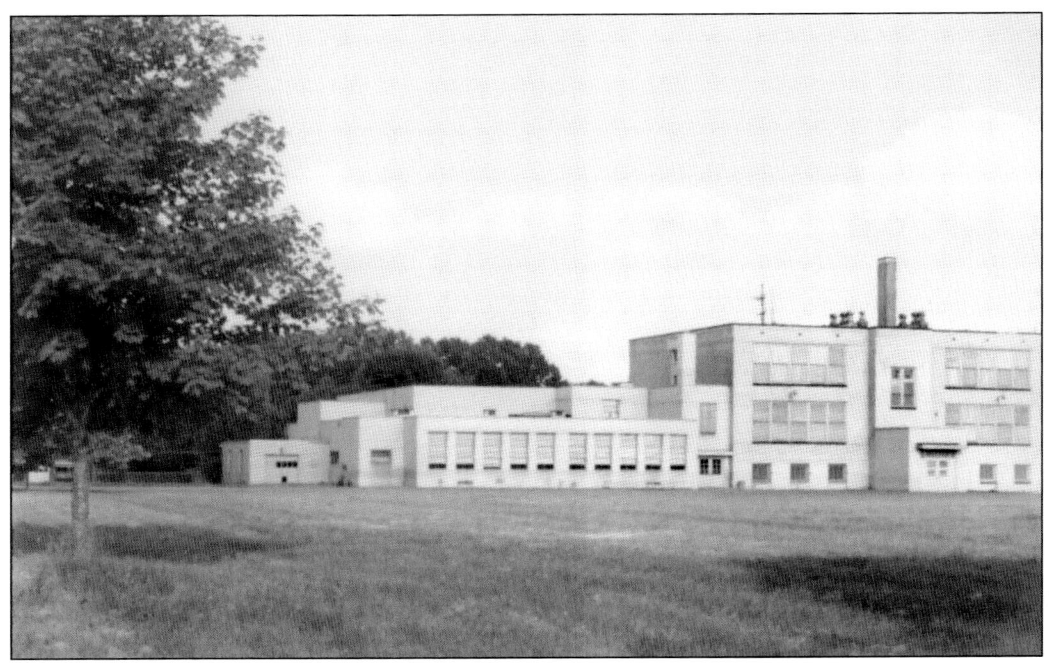

Located on the old McCartney farmlands that date back to the 1830s, the McCartney School was constructed starting in 1918, with classes beginning in 1919, and the school grounds were finally completed in 1922. In 1974, the elementary school was closed due to its small size and projected expenses on repairs. The school grounds occupied the area of Monette Street and Woodland Avenue, the current location of the Vertner W. Tandy Apartments. Below is a c. 1945 photograph of an elementary class. (Both, courtesy of Florence Galida.)

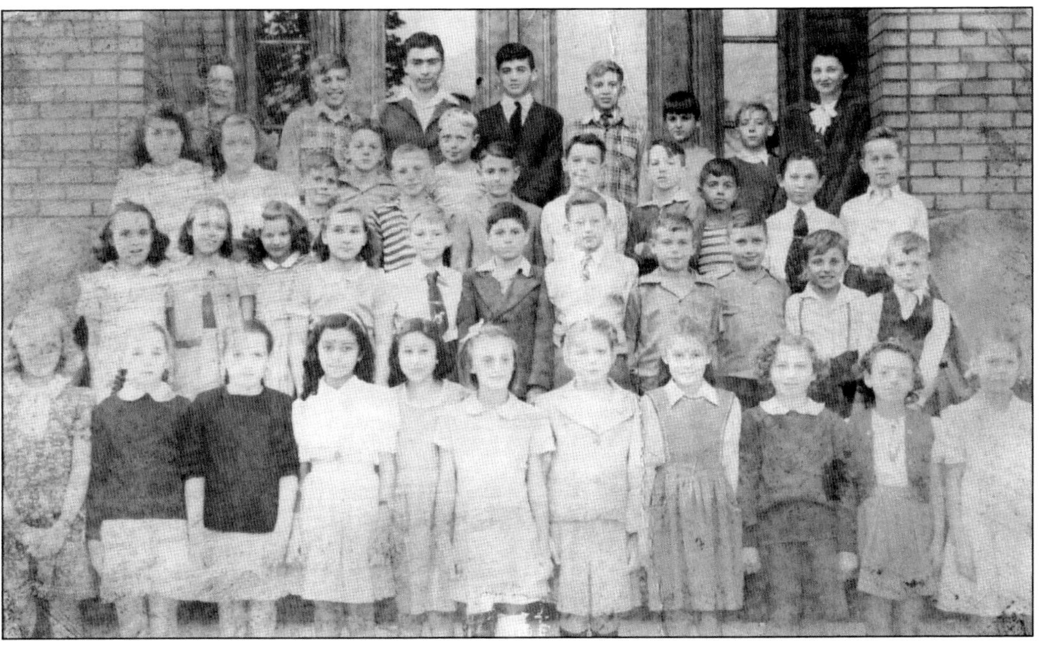

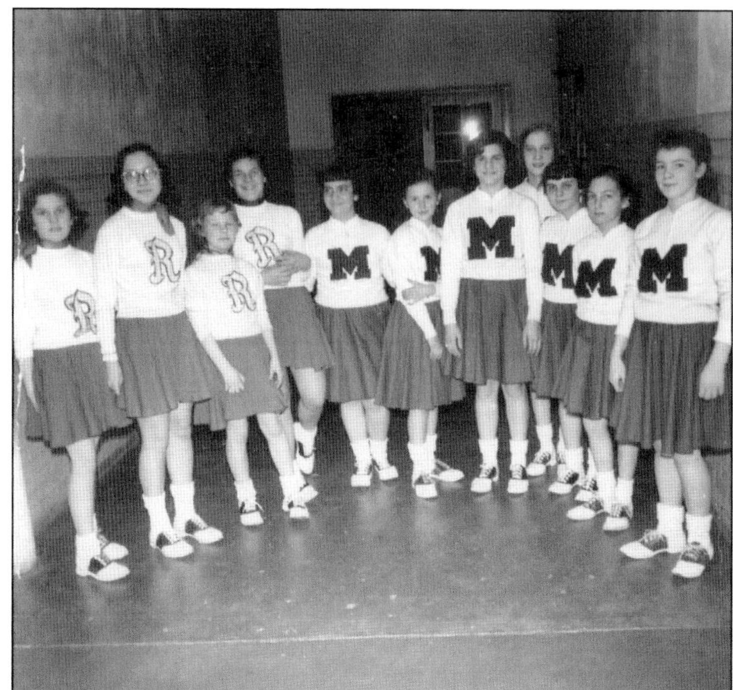

During a March 1955 basketball game between Reed Middle School and McCartney Middle School, the cheerleaders from each team paused for a quick photograph before the action began. From left to right are Ginger O'Dea, Adele Malys, Claudia Graben, Marie Kennedy, Sandra Esso, Laverne Putko, Beth Ann Conti, Mary Ann Mingo, Patty Chito, unidentified, and Martha Colbert. (Courtesy of Lorraine Sabol.)

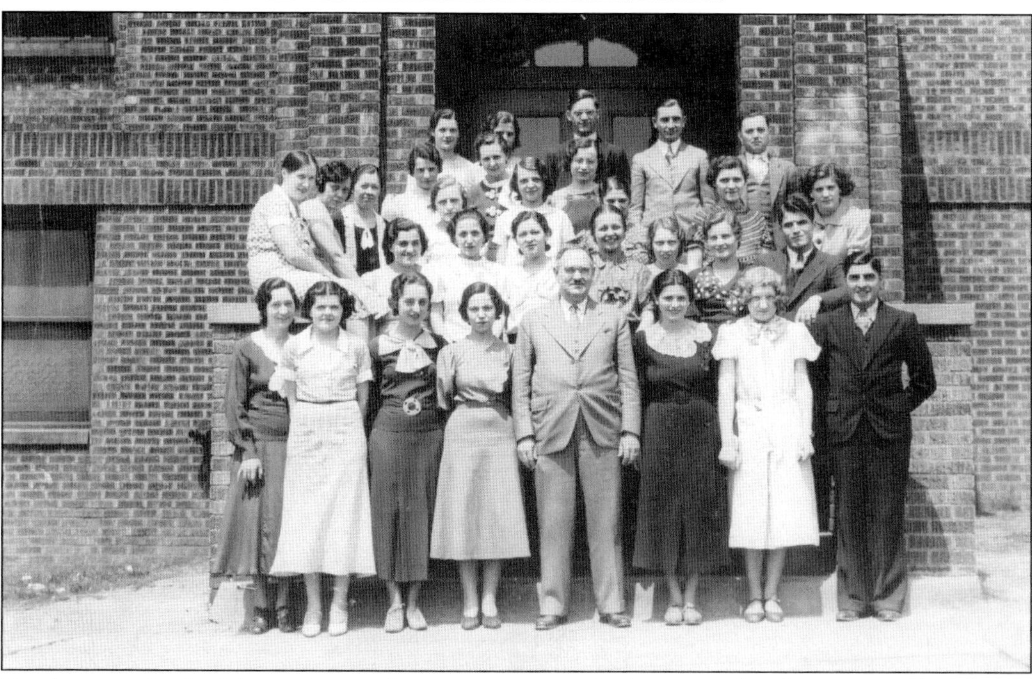

Teachers are the backbone of any education system and often provide a home away from home for many students. During the early years of Campbell's school system, teachers had to deal with many issues, such as cultural disconnect, lack of training, language barriers, and more. Those with specialized training were sent where they would be most productive, while others followed a more arts and crafts curriculum. The Reed School teachers are pictured in front of their building in the 1930s. (Courtesy of Florence Galida.)

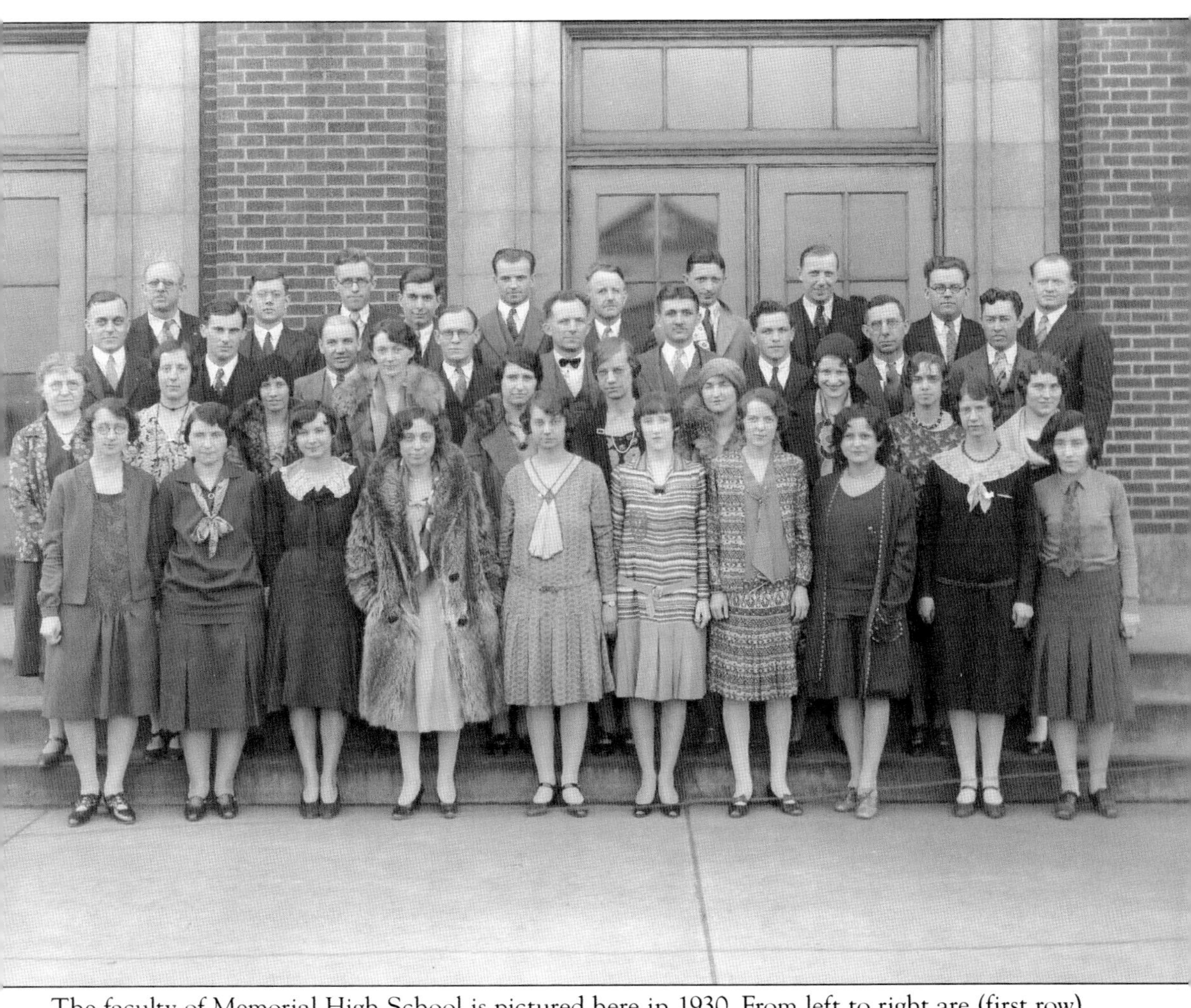

The faculty of Memorial High School is pictured here in 1930. From left to right are (first row) Mary Fulton, a Mrs. Klinger, Dorothy Thorton, a Miss Scardina, Florence Cook, Ann Murray, Susan Watt, Albina Resetar, Evelyn Runkle, and Irma Marinelli; (second row) Jennie Swogger, Margaret Morr, Miss Moinet, Mary French, a Miss Wysner, Martha Cook, Hildgarde O'Brien, a Miss Holcomb, Phyllis Kendall, and a Miss Canterbury; (third row) a Mr. Stewart, Walter Caldwell, Dick Barrett, Arnold Butler, Harry Dewey, Andrew Klinko, C.R. McNeal, D.W. Weisel, and David Parks; (fourth row) W.H. Goodwin, Kenneth Kay, Horatio Bugby, Ernest Gustinella, John Fedor, Harrison Sexton, Matthew Stephens, William Reed, N.T. Knight, and George Patton. (Courtesy of Florence Galida.)

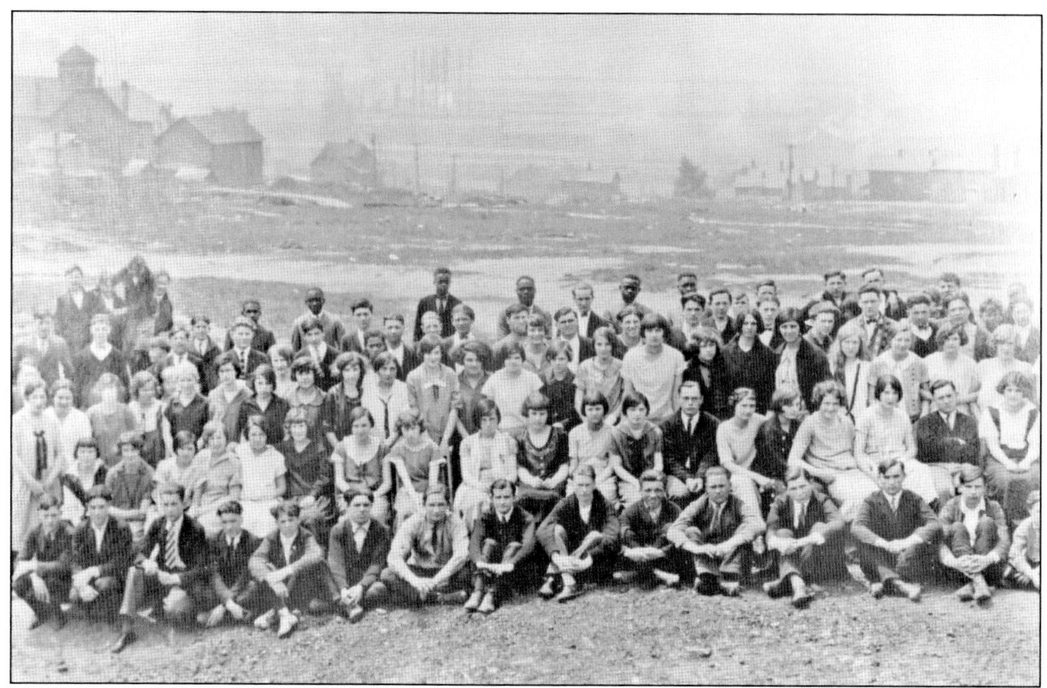

Students of the 1925 Penhale High School are shown before they moved to the new Memorial High School. In the background is the Youngstown Sheet and Tube Company, with St. John the Baptist Polish Church to the left. (Courtesy of Florence Galida.)

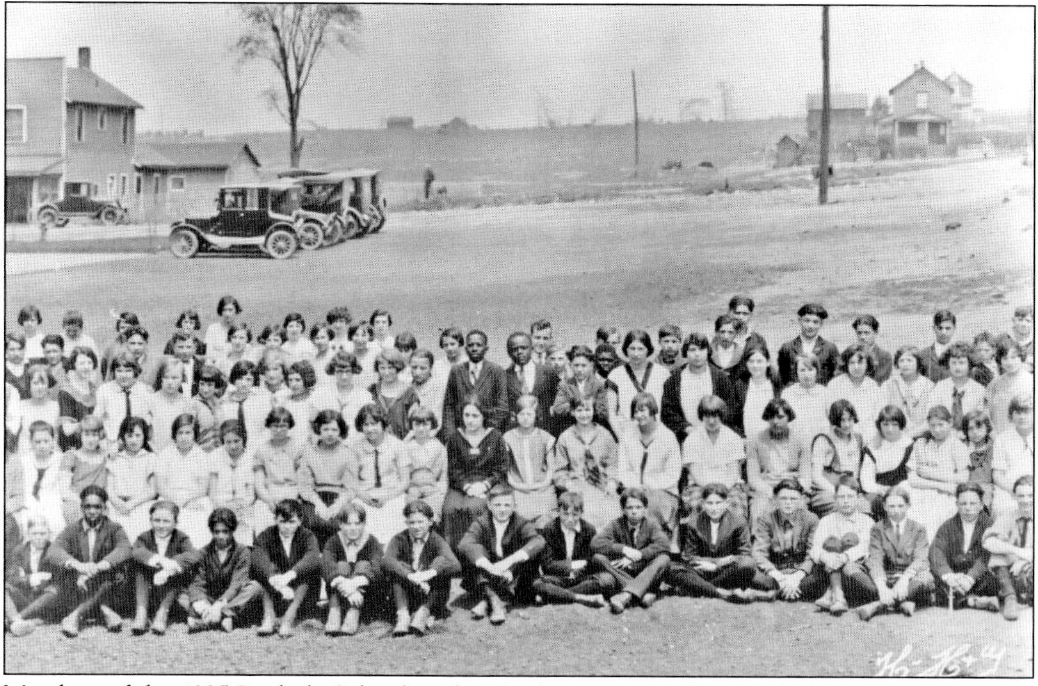

Members of the 1925 Penhale School student body are pictured on Penhale Avenue with their teachers' automobiles in the background. At this time, most of the land in East Youngstown (Campbell) consisted of farmlands and swamps. (Courtesy of Florence Galida.)

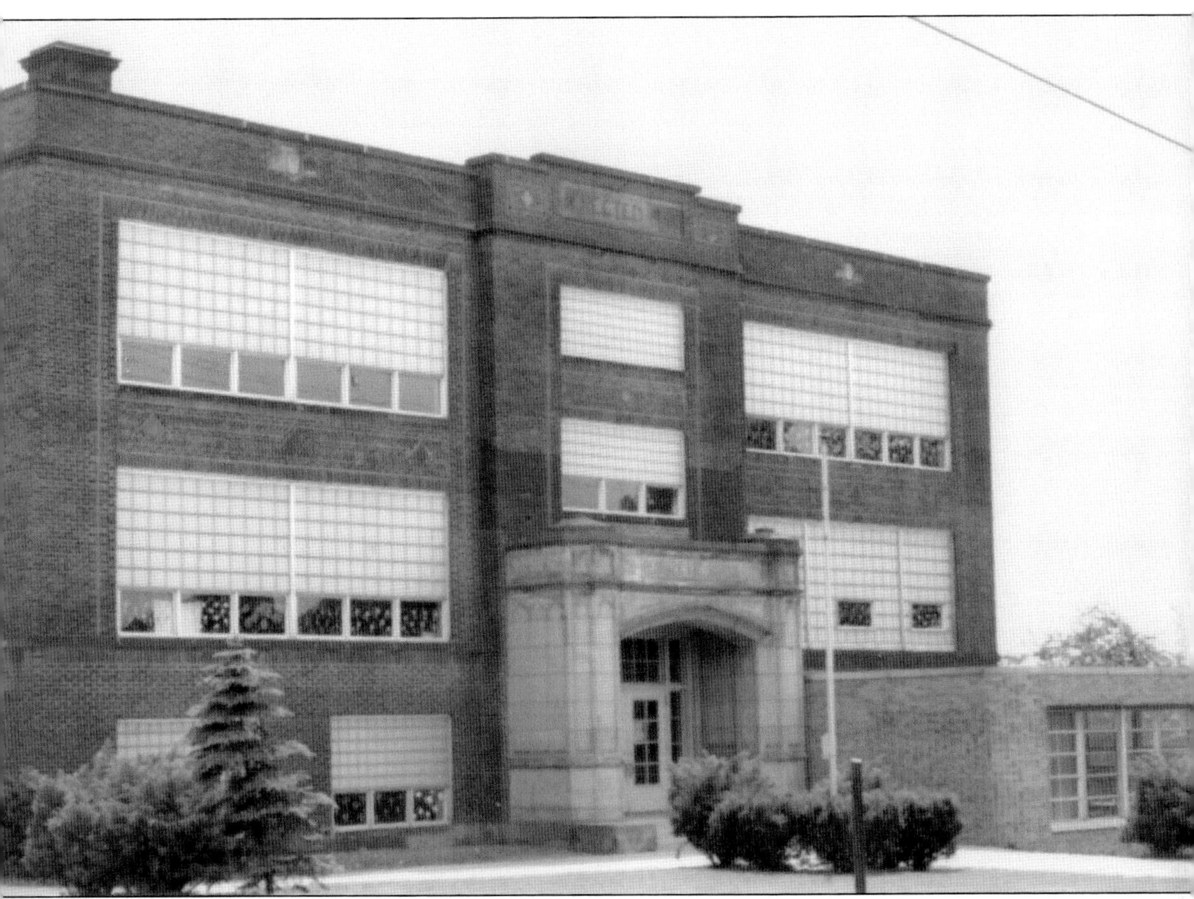

The Penhale Avenue School was built for $175,000 in 1919 and held its first class in 1920. In 1921, the school became the first junior high in Mahoning County. By 1922, the school had become a junior-senior high and subsequently graduated the first senior class in the city of East Youngstown. The building remained relatively unchanged until the addition of a gymnasium in 1949. (Courtesy of Florence Galida.)

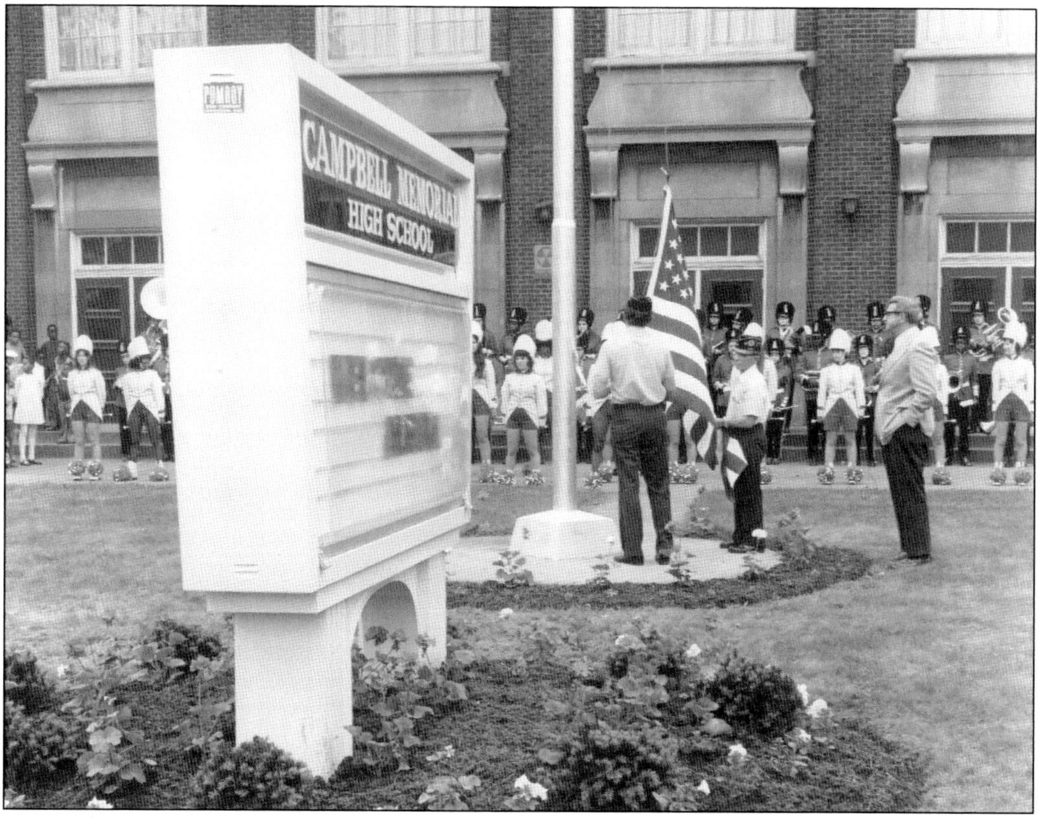

In October 1972, the Campbell Memorial Parent-Teacher Association came together to begin the organization of an alumni celebration. The goal of the group was to honor the graduates of Campbell from the 1922 class at Penhale High School (where one girl and one boy graduated) to the current class of 1973. On Sunday, May 27, 1973, a parade and banquet were held to honor all the past, present, and future Campbell alums. (Courtesy of Florence Galida.)

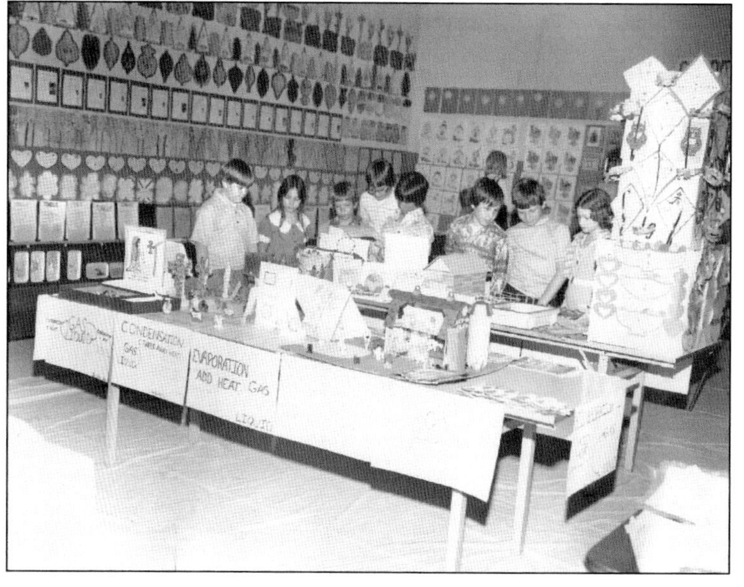

In 1967, St. John the Baptist Roman Catholic School was closed when a more modern school building was erected in its place behind the St. Joseph the Provider Church. The new school, which contained more classroom space and a gymnasium, was renamed St. Joseph the Provider Parochial School. Schoolchildren are shown participating in the Learning Fair on April 24, 1977. (Courtesy of Florence Galida.)

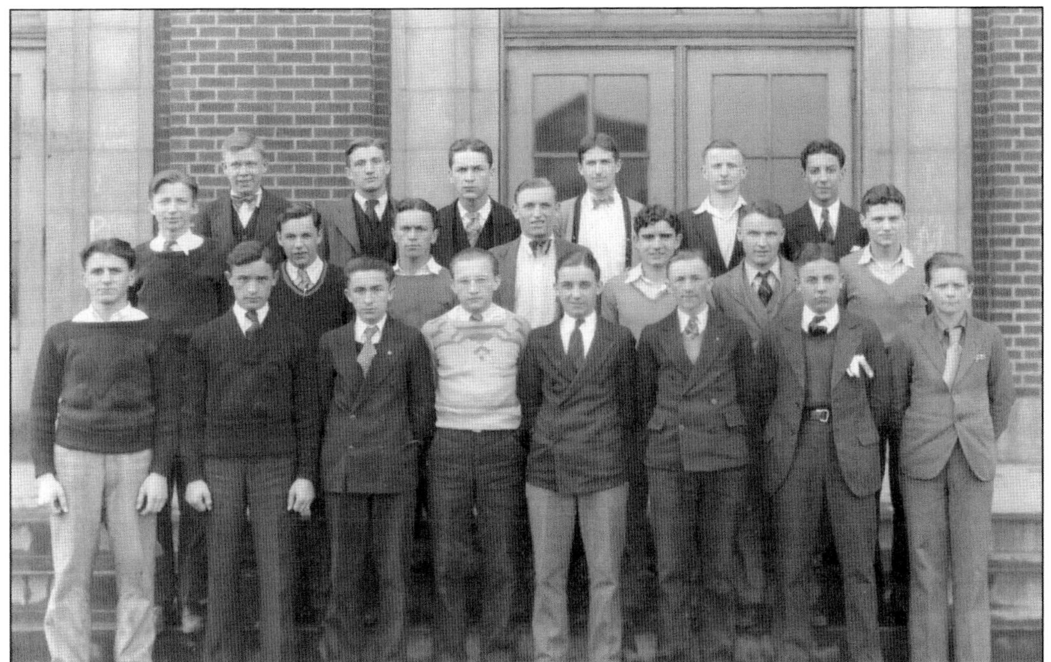

Shown is the Campbell Memorial Four Square Club of 1930. From left to right are (first row) Ledo Ross, Jimmie Dambrogio, John Tkaczychyn, Joe Vansuch, Andrew Pytak, John Grysinsky, Patsy Nolfi, and Peter Spitt; (second row) Thomas Kranynak, John Miksec, John Siembieda, Paul Zbell, George Dann, Bill Dulkiwicz, and Stanley Danilov; (third row) Albert Shipka, John Schwatz, Alex Lucicosky, Matt Wansack, Ally Hamrock, and Alex Philips. (Courtesy of Florence Galida.)

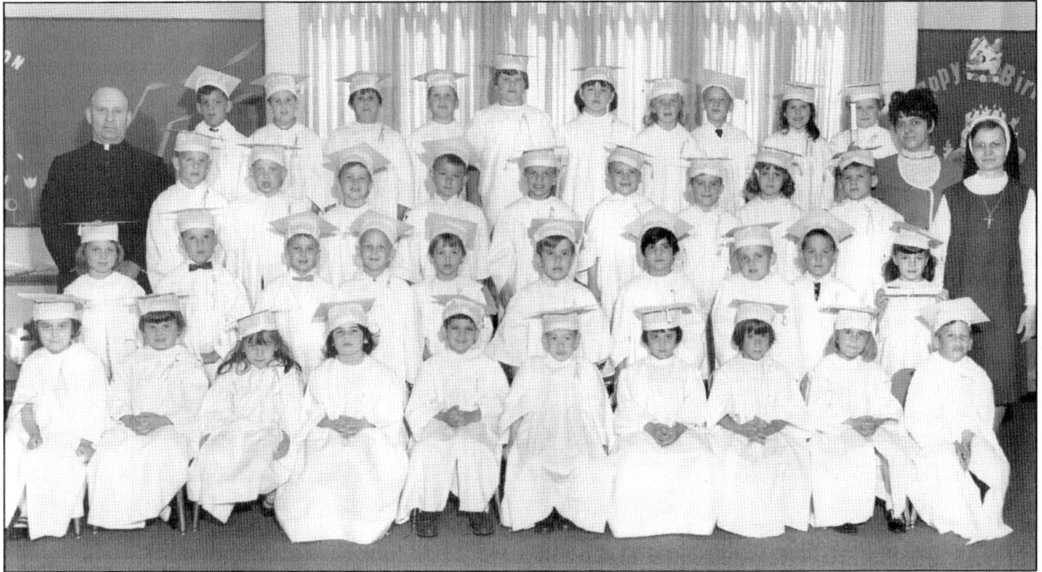

In 1967, a newer and larger building was added behind St. Joseph the Provider Church to house the students from St. John the Baptist Roman Catholic School. The building on Ninth Street closed that same year when the children moved to their new classrooms at St. Joseph the Provider Parochial School. The 1968 kindergarten class is pictured during their graduation. (Courtesy of Florence Galida.)

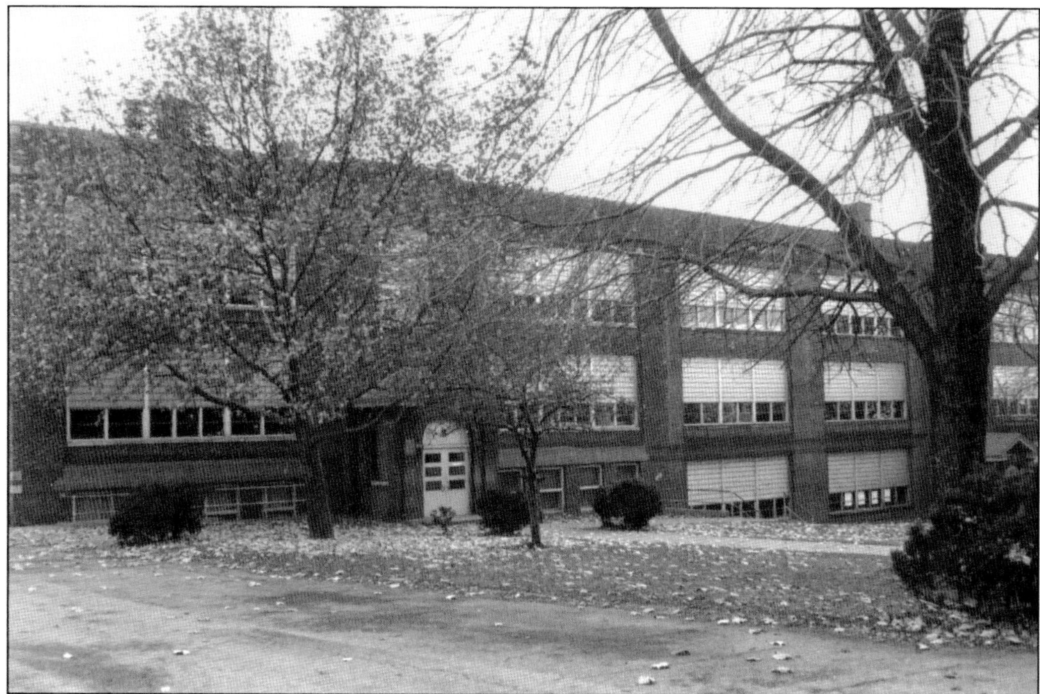

Opened in 1917, the Reed School occupied land bought from Elmer and Audley Robinson. In 1921, an addition allowed for more classrooms at the school and thereby the ability to take on students in kindergarten through eighth grade. By 1974, Reed has been changed to a middle school, enrolling only sixth through eighth graders. The school was located on Sixteenth Street, between Reed and Gordon Avenues. (Courtesy of Florence Galida.)

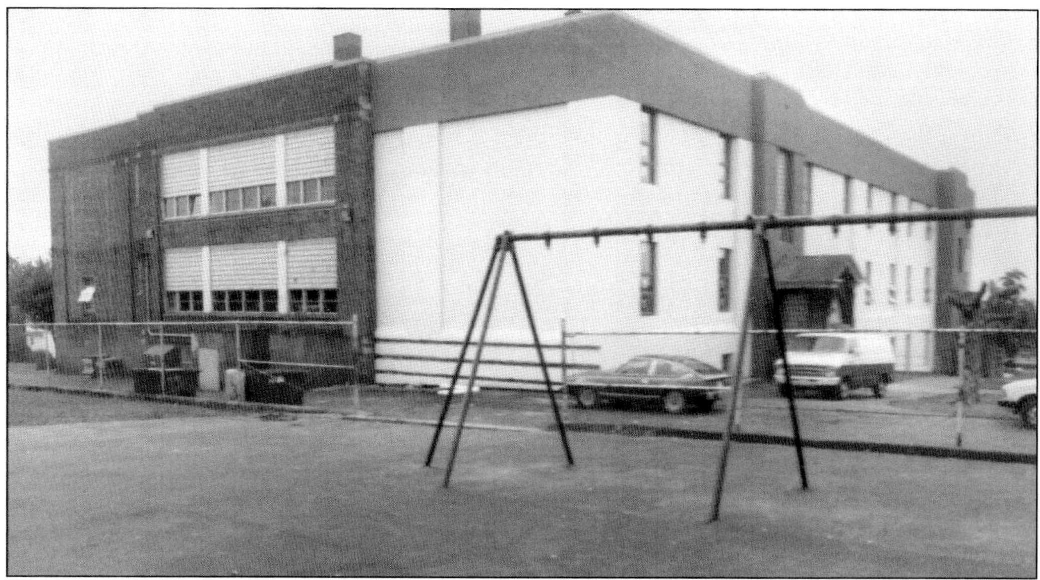

Depending on when students attended Reed Middle School will determine which building they remember most fondly. The Campbell School District began renovating the Reed School during the late 1970s and early 1980s to repair and cover the weathered bricks and give the building a newer look. (Courtesy of Eugene Skelley.)

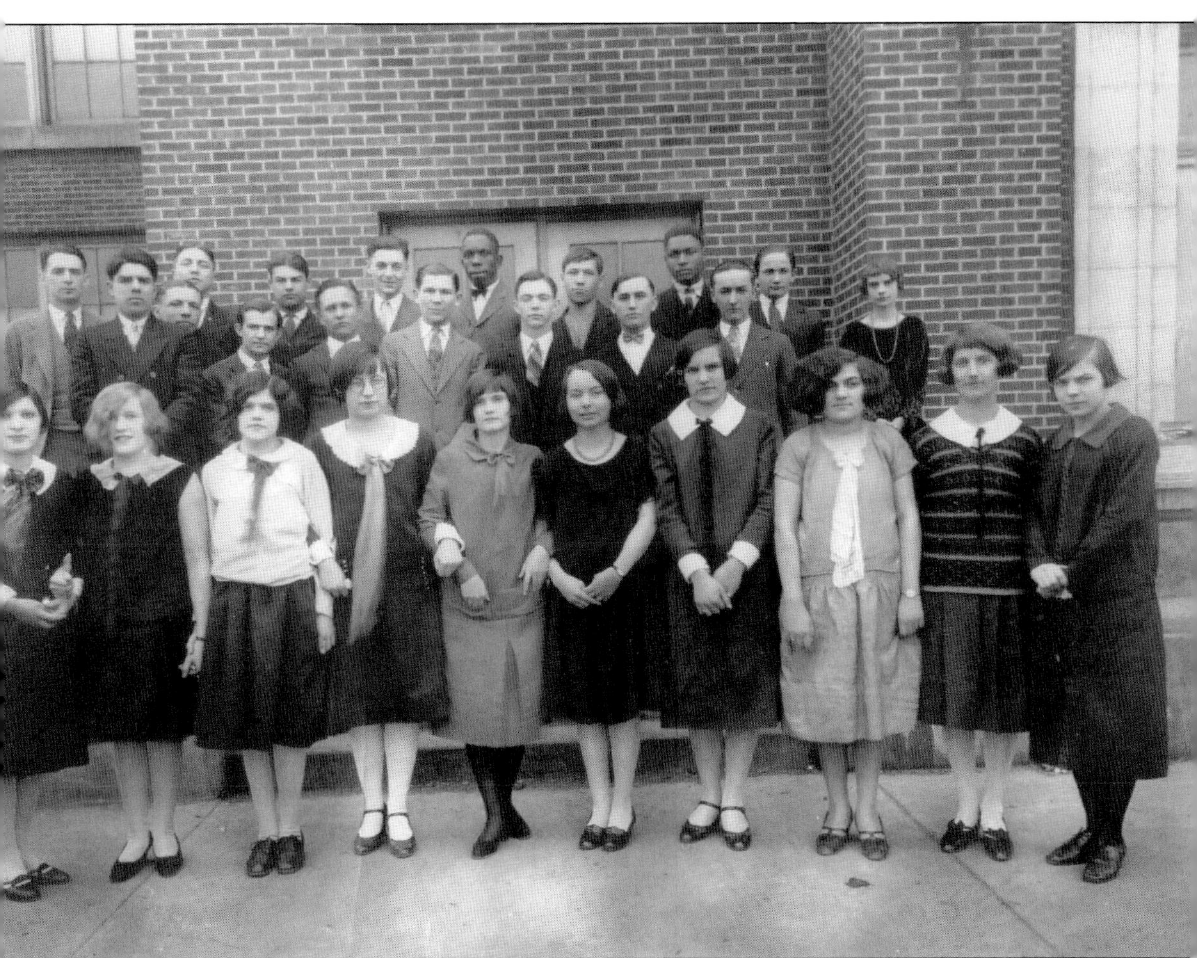

In 1926, the first class graduated from Memorial High School. From left to right are (first row) Stella Julius, Dorothy Moore, Cornelia Honda, Margaret Hamrock, Louise Jones, Loretta Donovan, Mary Witkiewiecz, Angeline Marsola, Rose Brakovic, and Blanche Lysowska; (second row) Anthony Dann, George Gulovich, Paul Fedor, Mike Grecko, William Holliday, Elmo Holleran, George Kovalchick, and John Richards; (third row) Edward Reese, Joe Vrabel, Michael Katula, Charles Vojnovich, Lymas Riddle, George Forgach, Nathaniel Patton, Steve Stavich, and Weltha Keck. (Courtesy of Florence Galida.)

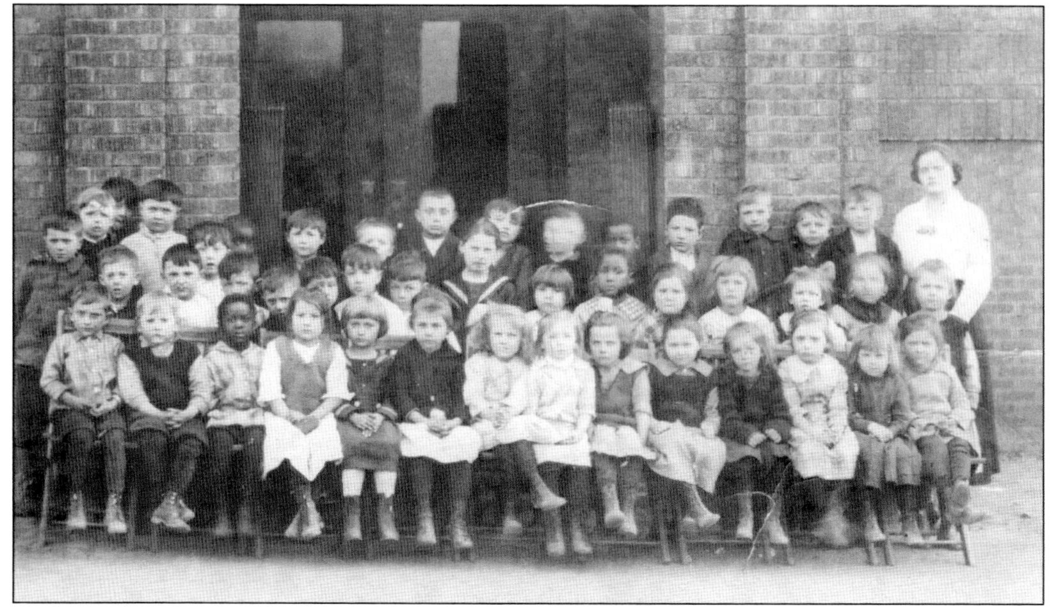

During the first 28 years of its inception, the Reed School, which contained grades one through eight, had the highest enrollment of any elementary school in the city. The Grade 1-B class is shown posing in front of the building on January 1, 1921. (Courtesy of Florence Galida.)

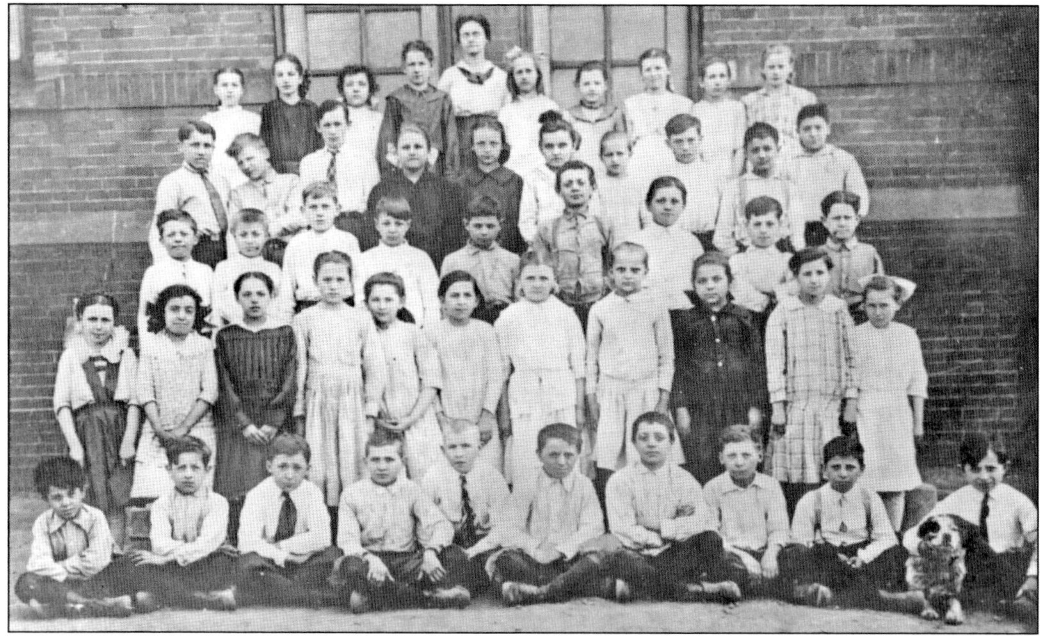

During the early days of Coitsville Township, only three schools were operating for the settlers: Fairview, 12th Street, and 7th Street Schools. As the area's population soared above 13,000, the East Youngstown School District quickly grew to more than 12 schools. One of the major problems that troubled teachers during this school expansion was learning how to educate the immigrant children of various cultural backgrounds. However, these motivated educators met the challenges head-on and produced some of the finest young men and women of the area, most of whom would help shape the city of Campbell. (Courtesy of Florence Galida.)

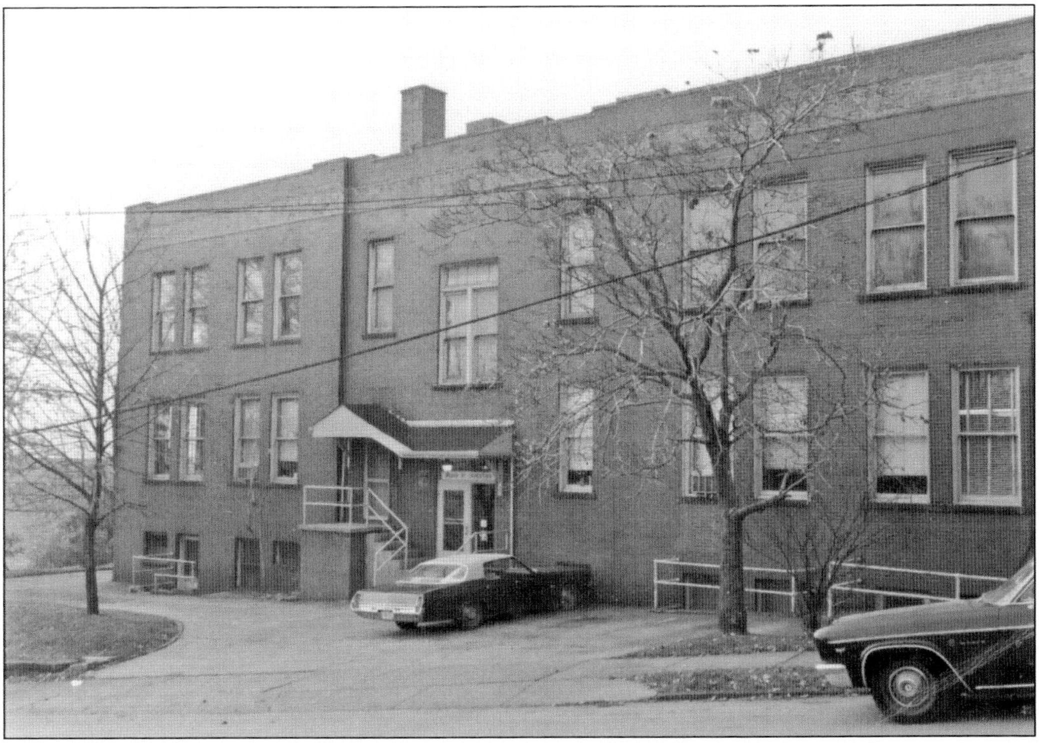

During the old Coitsville Township days of the mid-1800s, Samuel Fitch owned 137 acres near the present-day area of First and Main Streets. A schoolhouse, nicknamed the "Wildcat School," sat on the land in the mid-1870s. In 1903, a new school known as the Main Street School or Riverside School was built on the corner of First and Main Streets. With enrollment on the rise, the board of education had a larger school built on the corner of Wilson Avenue and First Street in 1910, with classes starting in 1911. In 1956, the school closed its doors to students and became the new home of the board of education. (Courtesy of Florence Galida.)

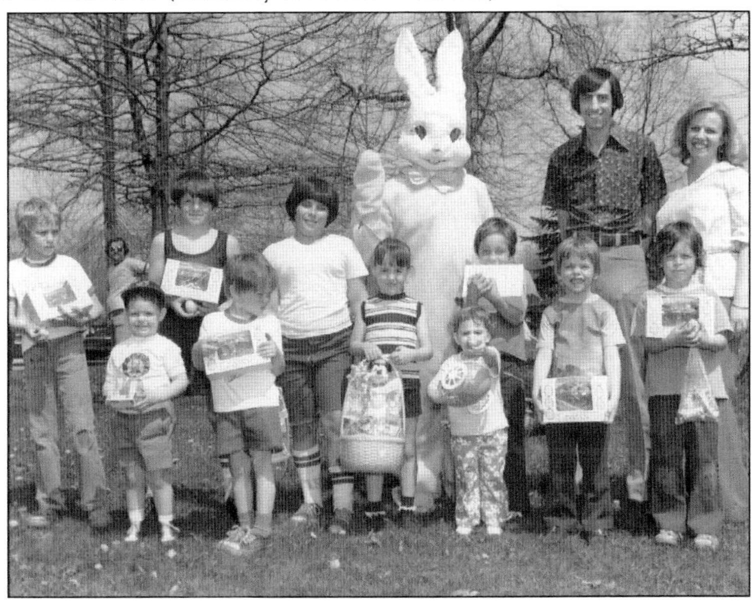

Mayor Michael J. Katula Jr. (right of the Easter Bunny) celebrates the Easter holiday with schoolchildren in the mid-1970s. During its time as a city, Campbell has always had both a public and parochial school system. The parochial elementary schools containing grades one through eight were operated under the Youngstown Catholic Diocese. (Courtesy of Florence Galida.)

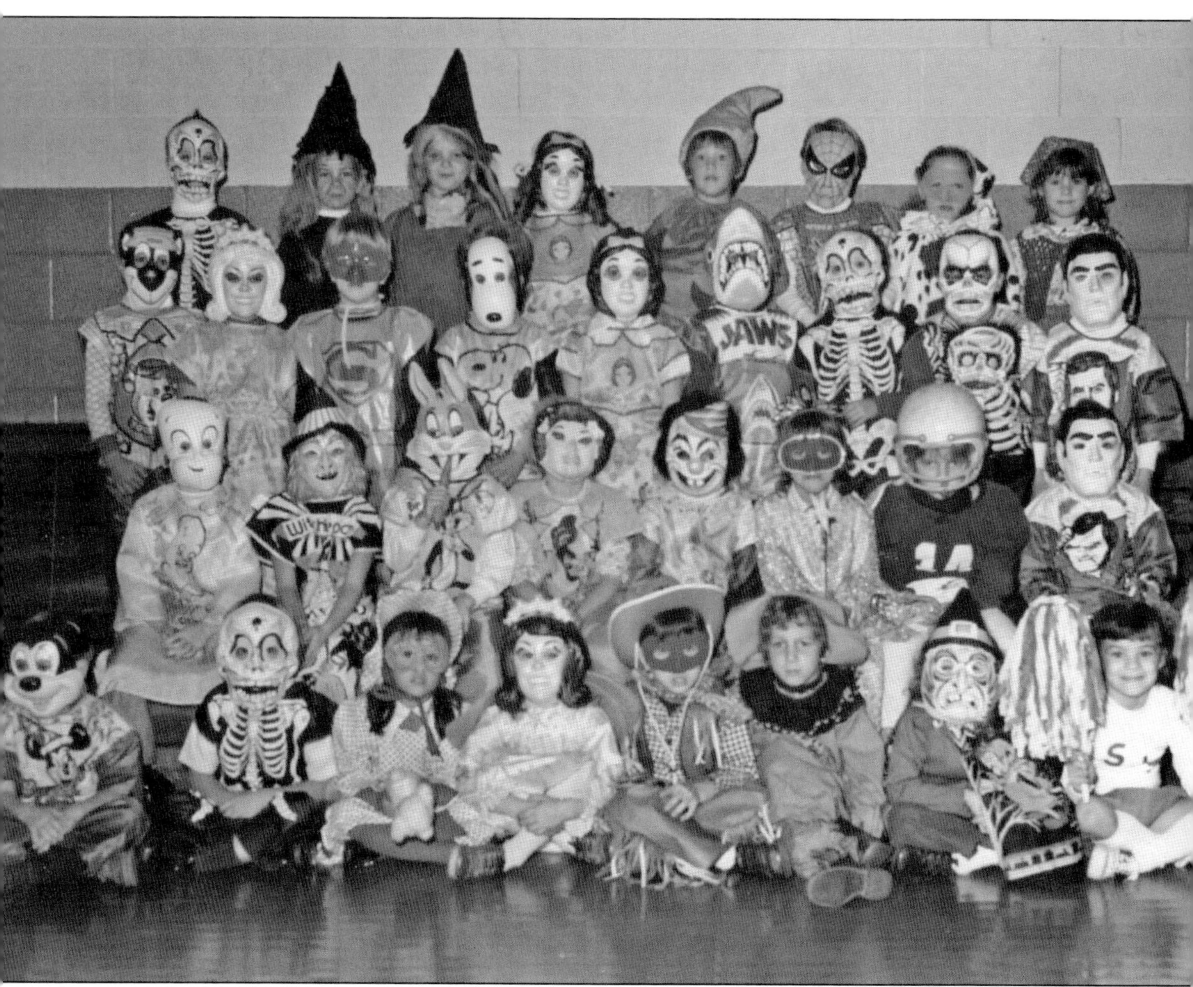

St. Joseph the Provider Parochial School was started in 1947 under the name of St. John the Baptist (Polish) Roman Catholic School and was located on Ninth Street. Students are shown posing in their favorite costumes during an undated Halloween party at St. Joseph the Provider Parochial School. (Courtesy of Florence Galida.)

During the late 1940s, several members of the Memorial High School student body started their own band called The Downbeats. From left to right are musicians (first row) Gene Trimacco, Frank Dravecki, and Lennie Costantino; (second row) Mickey Tirpak, Jerry Toti, and George Chugden. (Courtesy of Florence Galida.)

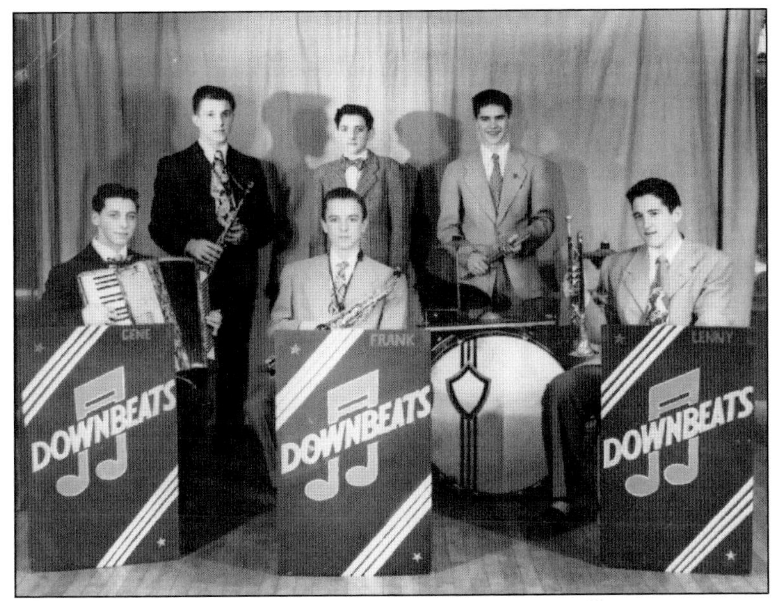

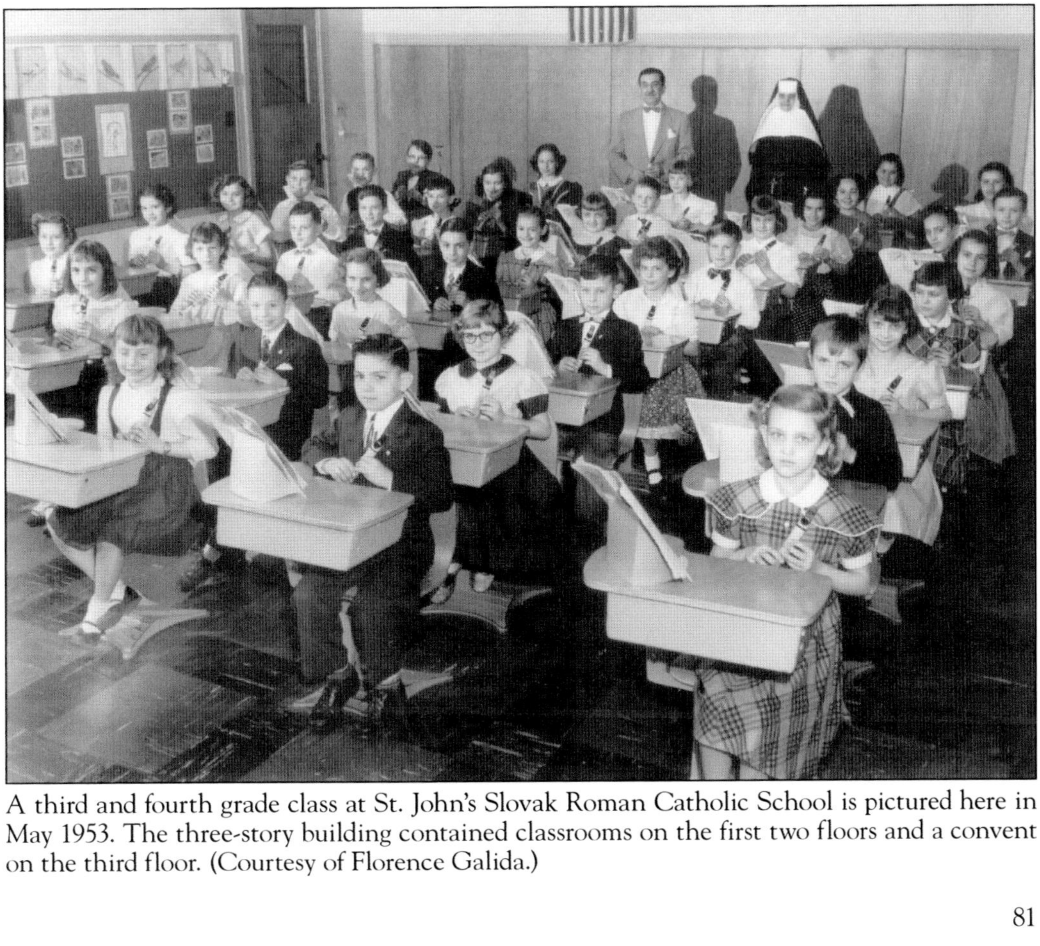

A third and fourth grade class at St. John's Slovak Roman Catholic School is pictured here in May 1953. The three-story building contained classrooms on the first two floors and a convent on the third floor. (Courtesy of Florence Galida.)

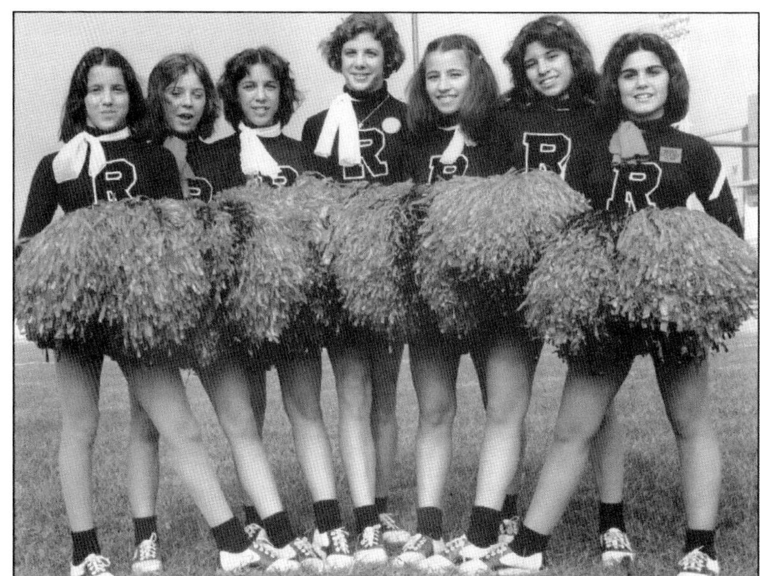

Reed School cheerleaders are shown in this c. 1979 photograph. From left to right are Wanda Marino, Wanda McDonald, Georgienne Antonas, Linda Valerio, Mary Ann Lopez, Lori Vavles, and Chrissy Mammo. (Courtesy of Florence Galida.)

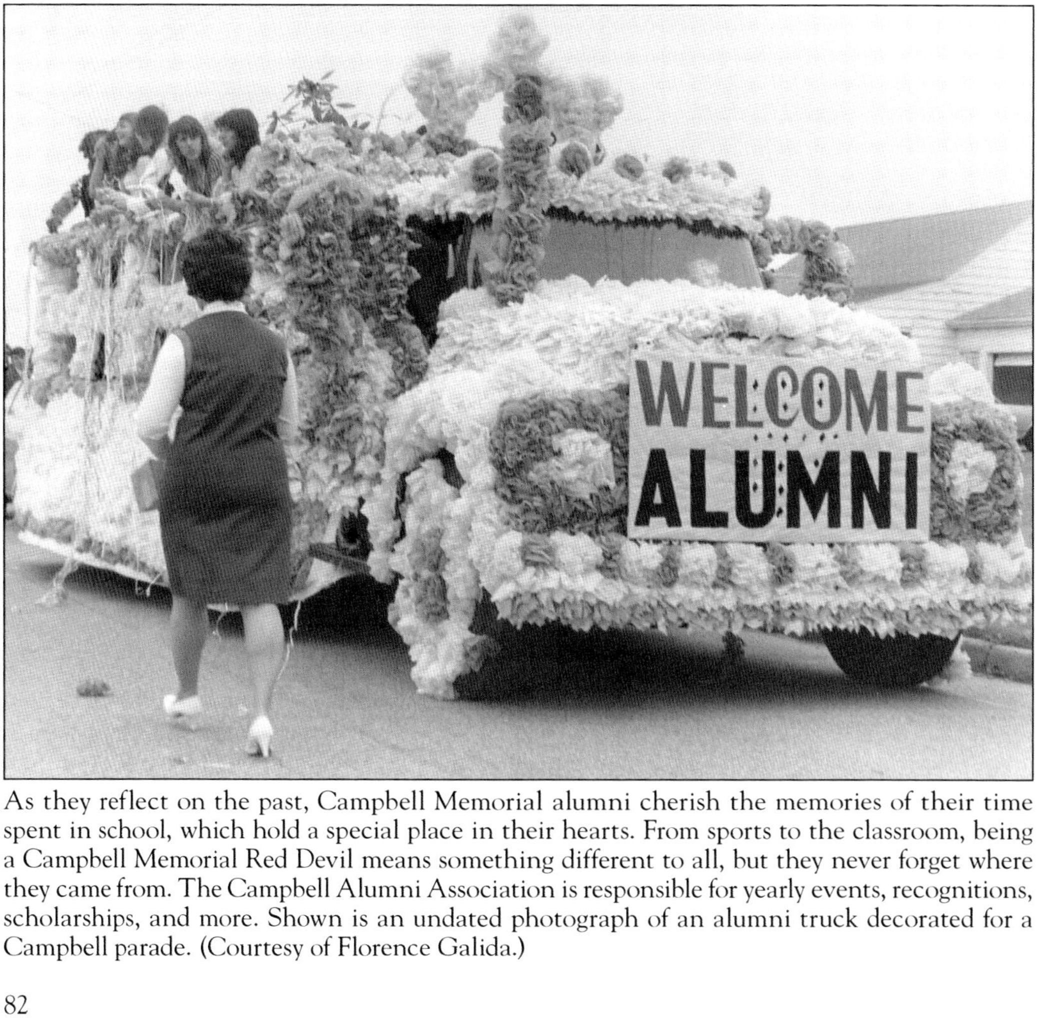

As they reflect on the past, Campbell Memorial alumni cherish the memories of their time spent in school, which hold a special place in their hearts. From sports to the classroom, being a Campbell Memorial Red Devil means something different to all, but they never forget where they came from. The Campbell Alumni Association is responsible for yearly events, recognitions, scholarships, and more. Shown is an undated photograph of an alumni truck decorated for a Campbell parade. (Courtesy of Florence Galida.)

Five

HOME OF THE RED DEVILS

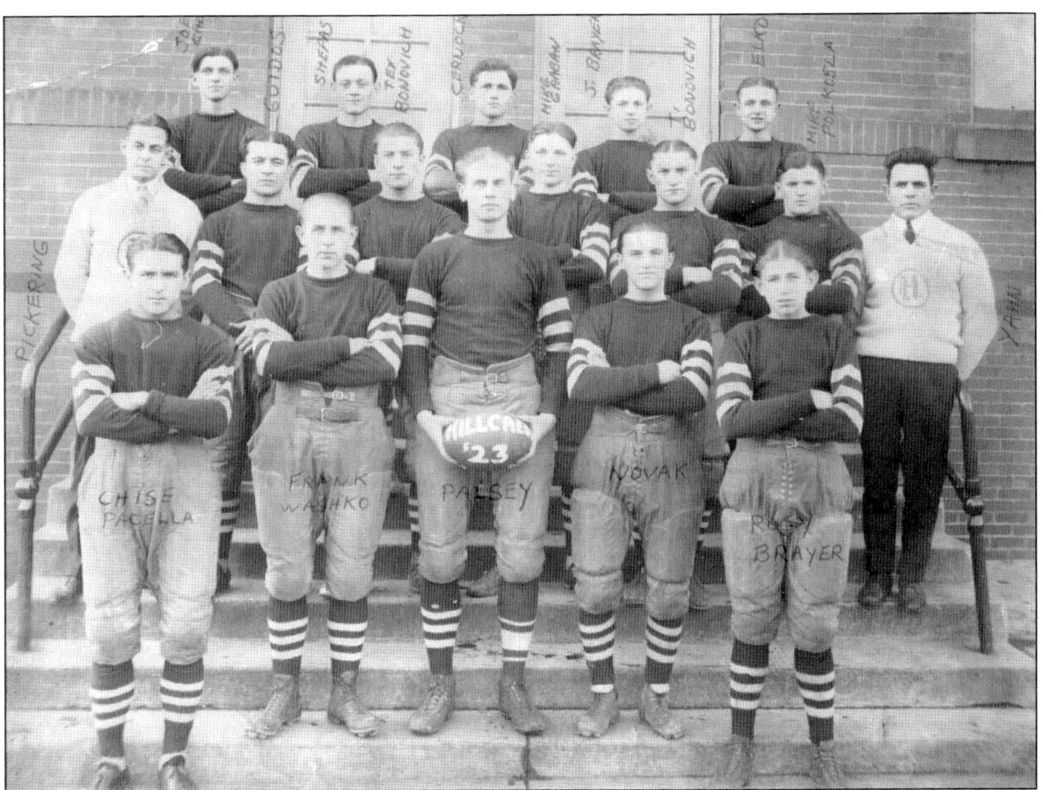

In 1922, the Hillcrest Club of Campbell was formed to give young boys in the area a chance to play organized baseball, basketball, and football. The members of the 1923 East Youngstown Hillcrest football team are, from left to right, (first row) Chise Pacella, Frank Washko, ? Palsey, ? Novak, and Rosy Brayer; (second row) head coach Ken Pickering, ? Guidos, Tex Bonovich, Mike Graban, T. Bonovich, Mike Polkobla, and Coach Yahn; (third row) Joe Check, ? Shepas, ? Cernock, J. Brayer, and ? Elko. (Courtesy of Florence Galida.)

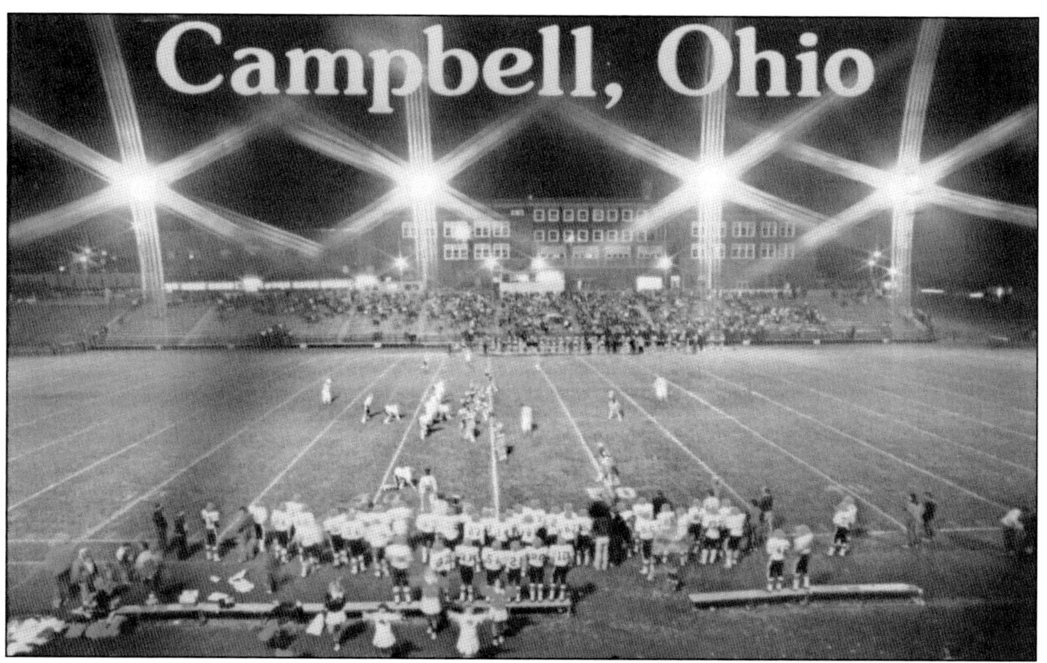

This is a postcard image of the Memorial High School football stadium, as seen from the visitors' side. The 1975 photograph depicts two football teams from out of the city. During football playoffs, many teams would play at John Knapick Field due to the size of the bleachers and the overall beauty of the stadium. (Courtesy of Mike Parise.)

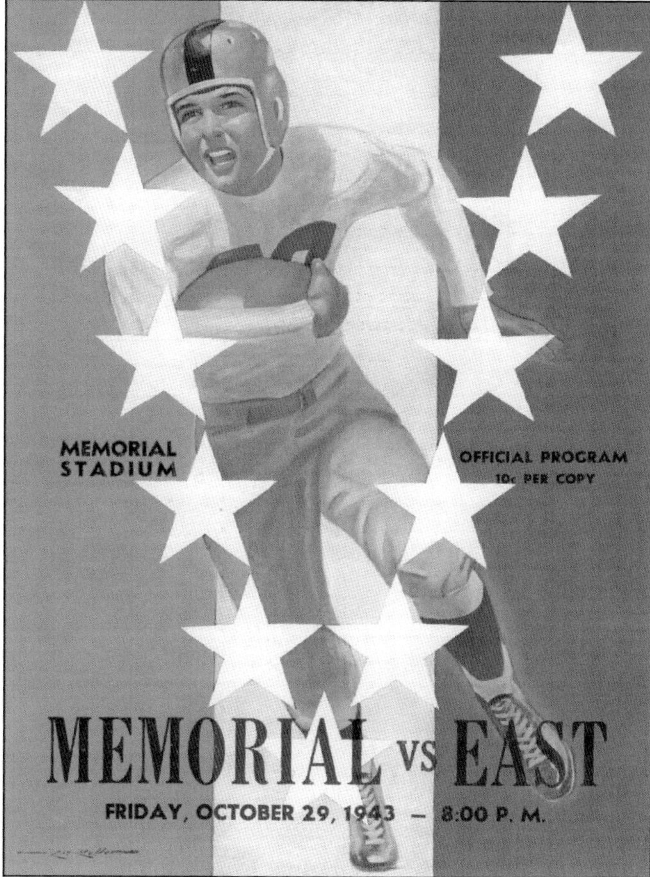

Memorial High School football began in 1924 when the East Youngstown Penhale team took the field and finished with a 5-1 season under coach Ken Pickering. In 1927, Dick Barrett took the helm as head coach after the departure of Pickering. Barrett would lead several successful seasons until Johnny Knapick moved from assistant coach to head coach in 1935—the same year Campbell received their nickname "Red Devils." (Courtesy of Mike Parise.)

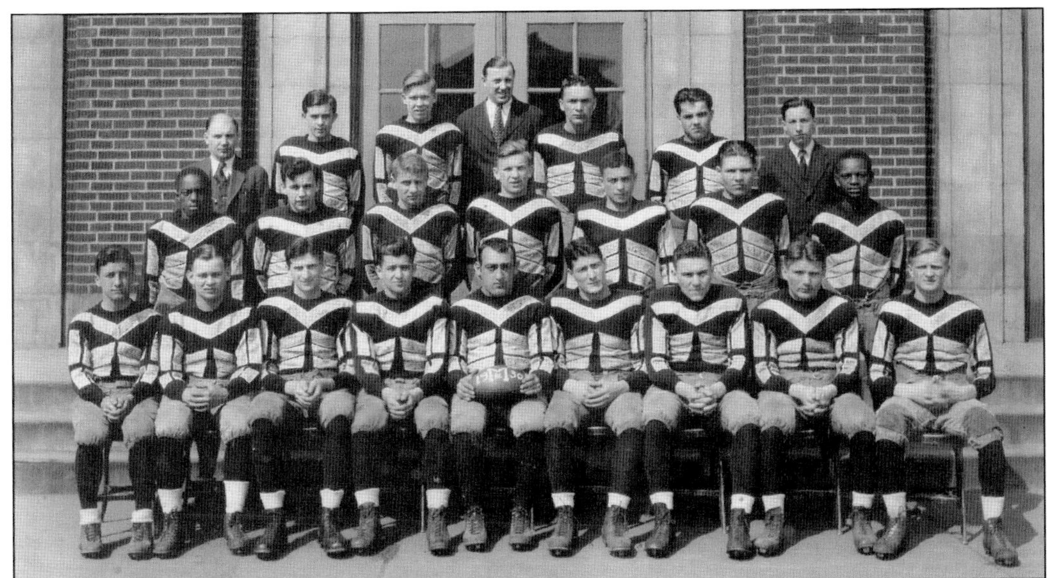

Members of the 1930 Campbell Memorial football team are, from left to right, (first row) Ben Tucci, John Putko, Matt Wansach, Nick Masters, Sam Barillaire, Tony DePiero, Andy Sabol, John Komarc, and John Jakubek; (second row) Bob Foster, Sam Vail, Mike Miller, Andy Shipka, Carmen Julius, John Kulick, and Al Stonework; (third row) coach Dick Barret, Paul Matvey, Al Shipka, Bill Reed, Alex Lucicosky, Dick Nechiporchik, and Lewis Cegledy. (Courtesy of Florence Galida.)

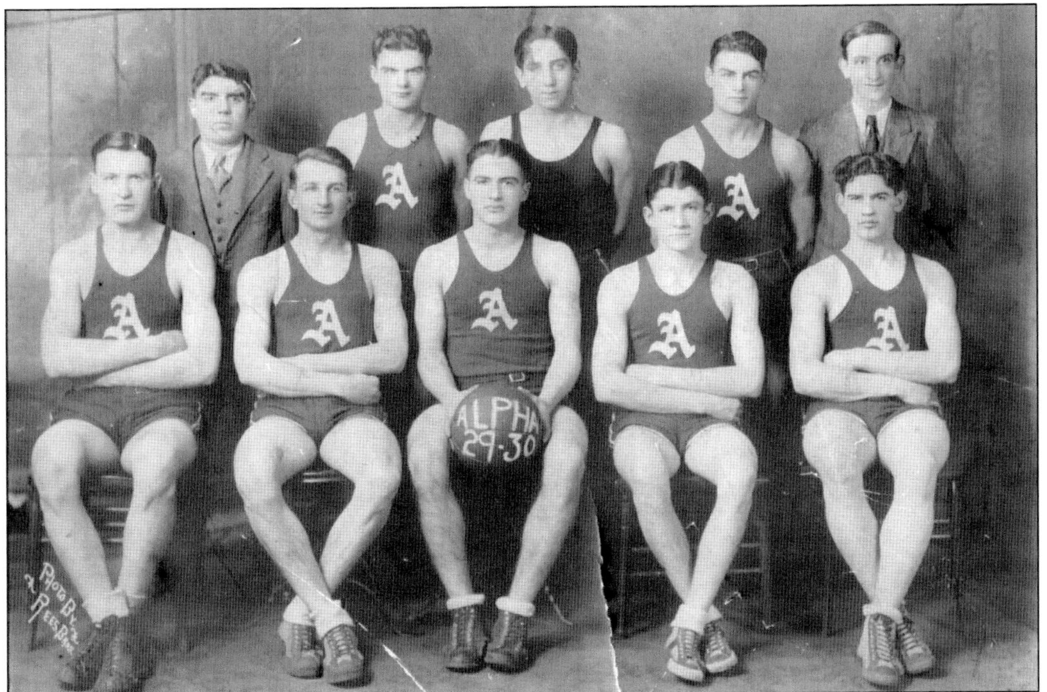

Members of the 1929–1930 Alpha Club basketball team are, from left to right, (first row) George Muretic, Willy Kondart, Matt Yurak, Joe Davis, and Joe Kopp; (second row) coach Tony Dann, Ted Katula, Rocco Armaline, Mike Katula, and coach Charles Testa. (Courtesy of Florence Galida.)

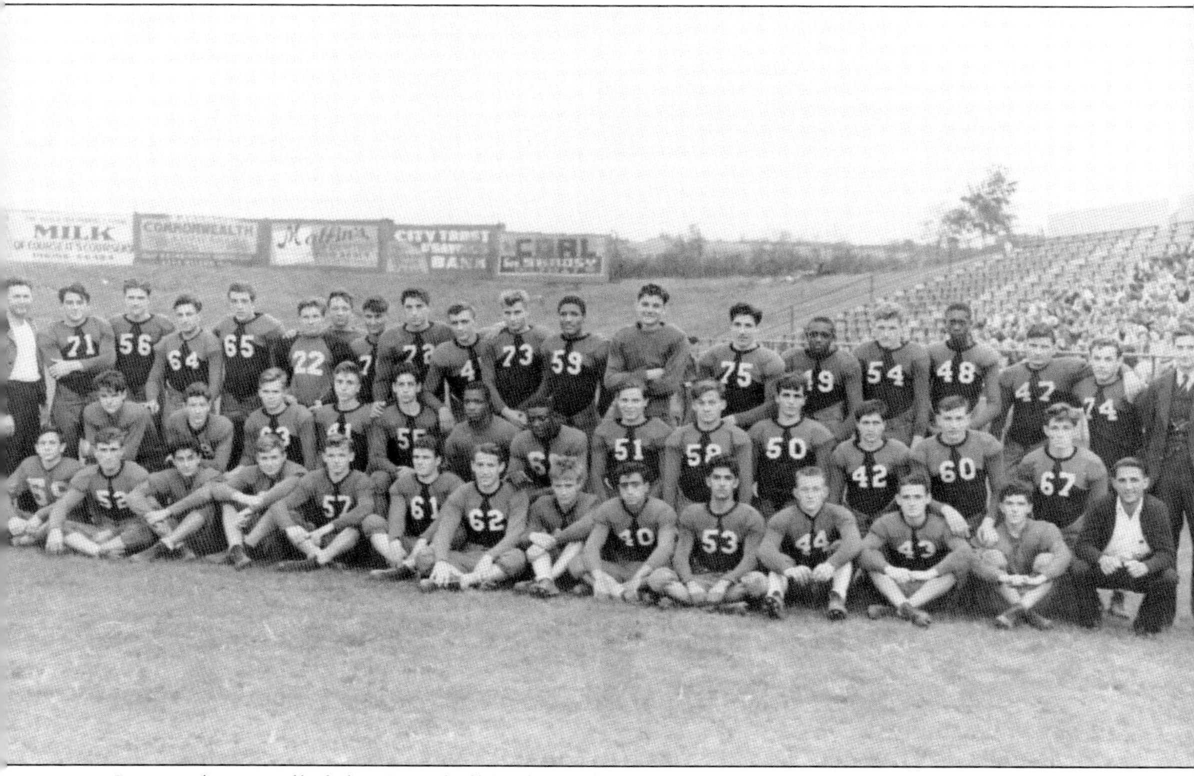

Prior to being called the Campbell Red Devils, Memorial High School sports teams went by the Red Rams and, later, the Red Raiders. In 1935, a newspaper reporter from Elyria, Ohio, stated that the Campbell Memorial football players were playing like devils on the field. From this, the name "Red Devils" stuck, and it is still used as the mascot to this day. Although the uniforms have changed over the decades, the black, red, and white colors have remained a staple of all Campbell sports uniforms. The 1937 Campbell Memorial Red Devils football squad is shown posing for a photograph in the high school football stadium. The banners in the background are from city businesses. (Courtesy of Florence Galida.)

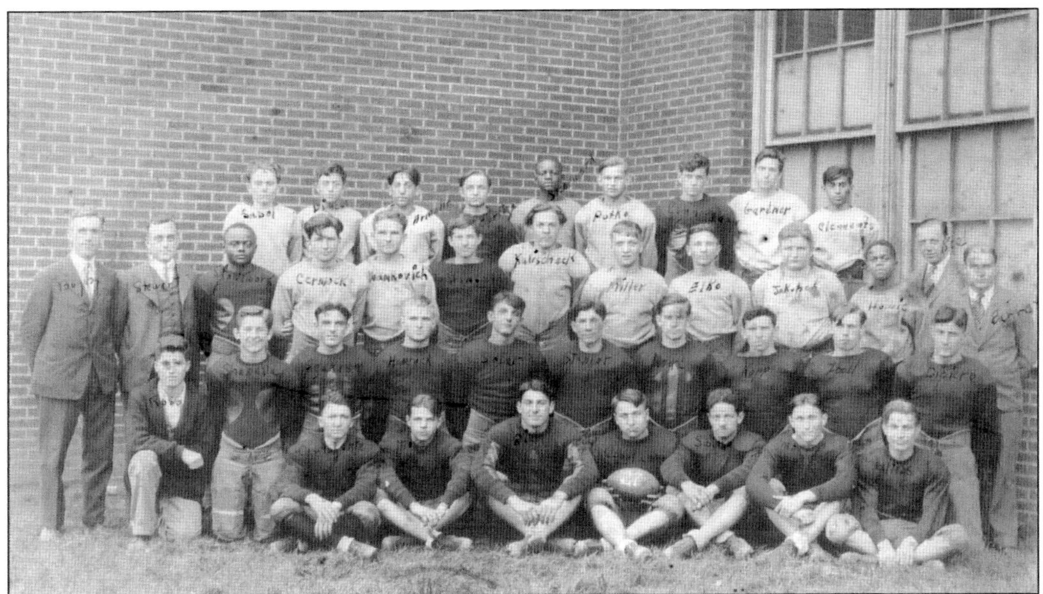

Members of the 1927 Campbell Memorial football team are, from left to right, (first row) Centafonte, Mose, Rich, Cebula, Switka, Morro, and Walters; (second row) unidentified, Shapella, Sakacs, Hamrock, Solar, Stanoar, Moore, Kopp, Zbell, and Dipiero; (third row) Bugby, Stewart, Stonework, Cernock, Wankovich, Wansack, Kalischack, Miller, Elko, Jakobek, Howie, Beed, and head coach Dick Barrett; (fourth row) Sabol, Dimeco, Armalie, Opretega, Stonework, Putko, Cunningham, Gardner, and Clements. (Courtesy of Florence Galida.)

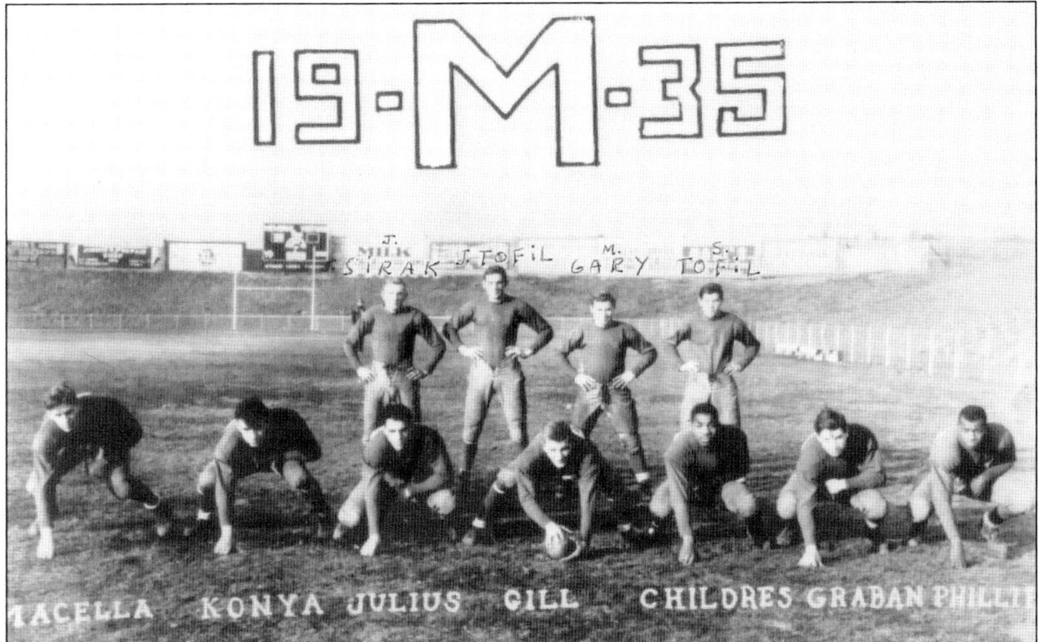

John Knapick, a great football player in his own right, became the head coach of the Campbell Memorial football team in 1935. Members of the team from that year are, from left to right, (first row) Andy Macela, Lou Konya, Joe Julius, Sloko Gill, Bill Childress, John Graban, and Monroe Phillips; (second row) Joe Sirak, Joe Tofil, Mike Gary, and Stan Tofil. (Courtesy of Florence Galida.)

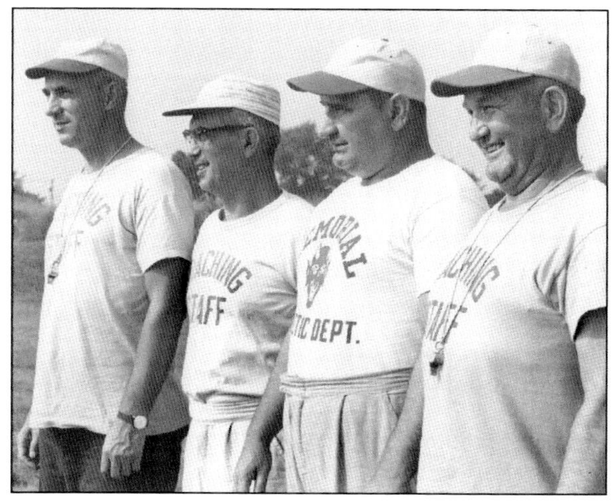

In this undated photograph, the Campbell Memorial football coaches are, from left to right, Lou Konya, Carmen Julius, Walter Malys, and head coach John Knapick. Spanning a head-coaching career at Memorial from 1935 to 1964, Knapick is solidified in Campbell football history with an impressive 172 wins, 86 losses, and 30 ties. In honor of his dedication, commitment, and contributions to Campbell athletics and education, the gridiron became known as John Knapick Field at Campbell Memorial Stadium on September 17, 1982. (Courtesy of Florence Galida.)

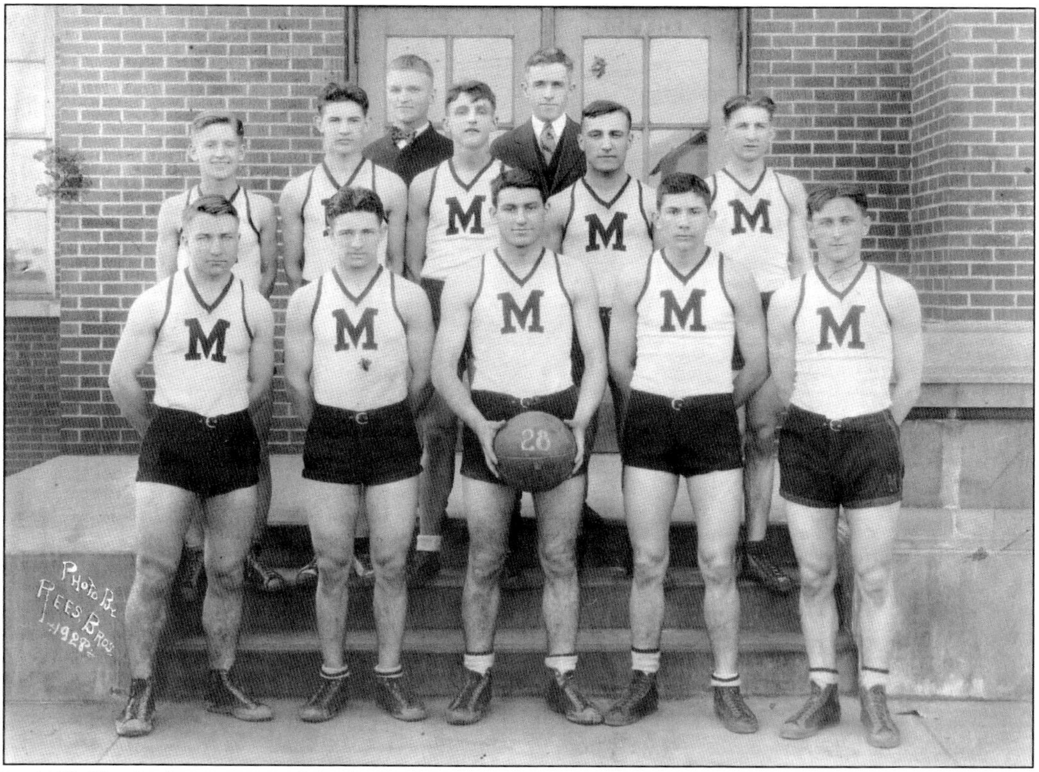

In 1927, Ken Pickering turned the basketball coaching position over to Horatio Bugby, who remained there until Arnold Butler took over in 1929. Members of the 1928 Campbell Memorial men's basketball team are, from left to right, (first row) George Cebula, Joe Switka, Jim Rich, Frank Stanfor, and Mike Maro; (second row) Joe Shabella, John Kopp, Pete Sollar, Bugsy Barillaire, and Willie Kondart; (third row) Al Hamrock and head coach Horatio Bugby. (Courtesy of Florence Galida.)

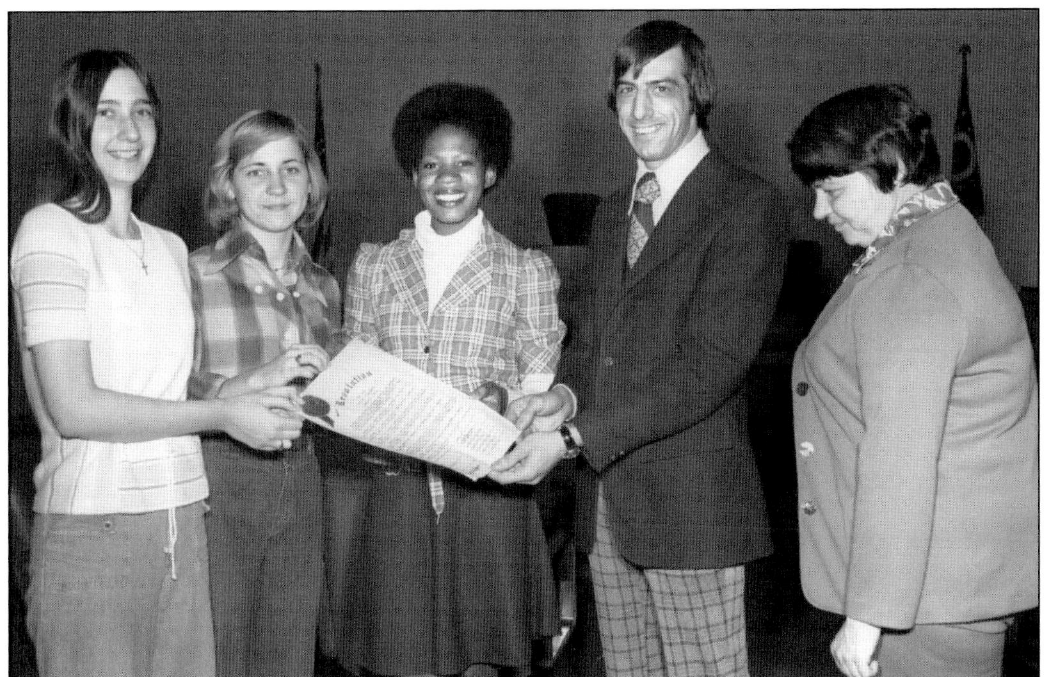

From left to right, Michelle Dintino, Donna Mingo, and Peggy Johnson of the Campbell Memorial women's basketball team receive a proclamation from Mayor Michael J. Katula Jr. for being the 1975–1976 District Champions. Coach Priscilla Sirilla (far right) looks on in admiration at the accomplishments her team has made throughout the season. (Courtesy of Florence Galida.)

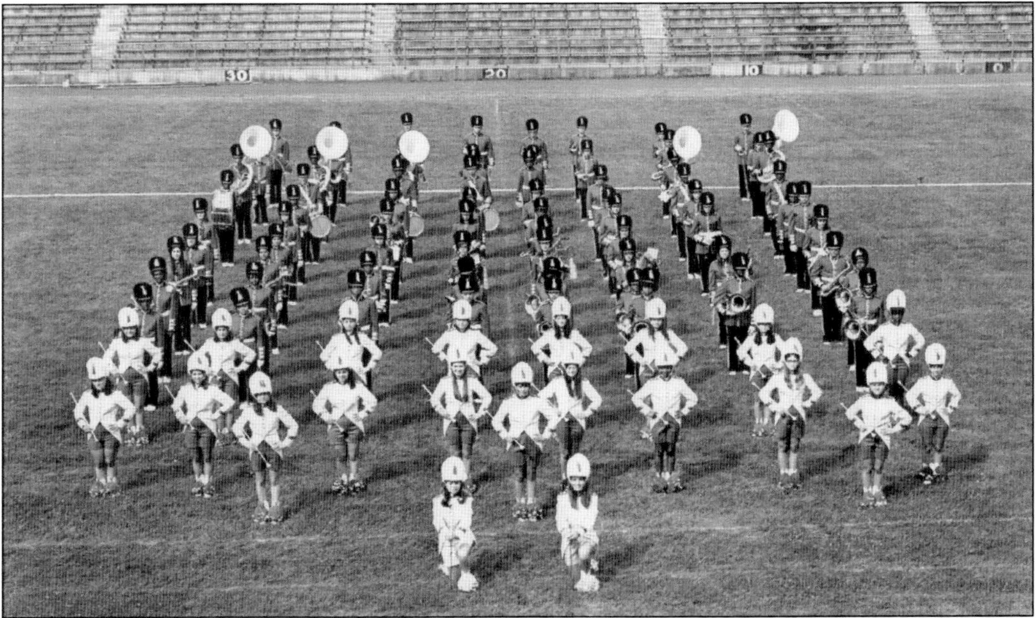

The Campbell Memorial band started in 1930 to provide musical support and entertainment at the football and basketball games. During its inception, the band would pair with the high school orchestra to perform an annual concert to raise money for new uniforms and musical instruments. (Courtesy of Florence Galida.)

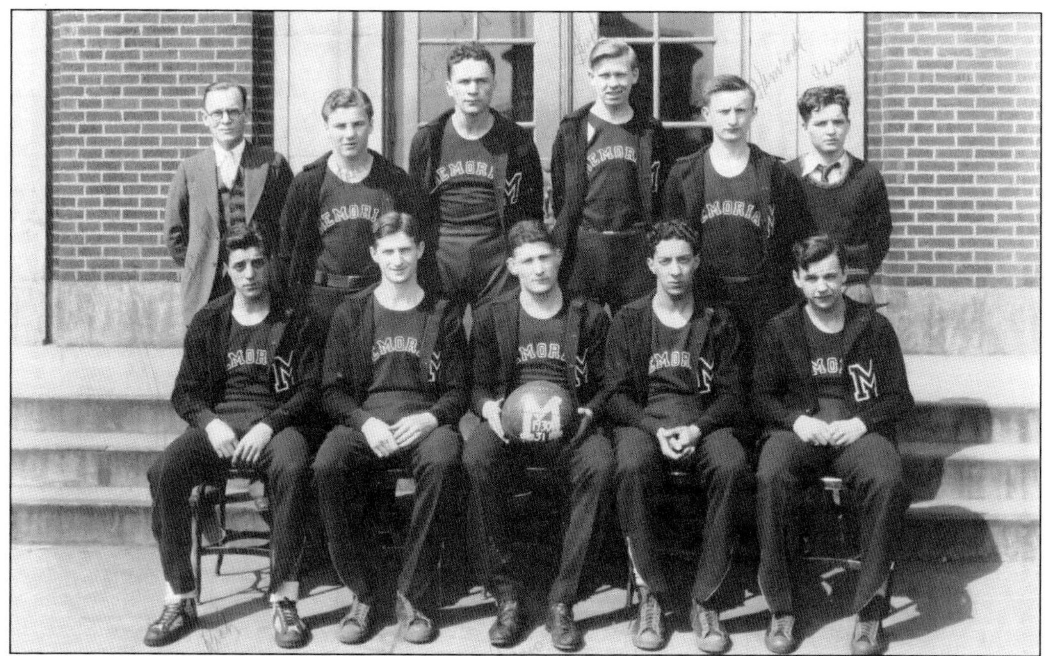

Members of the 1930–1931 Campbell Memorial men's basketball team are, from left to right, (first row) Louis Rich, Matt Wansach, Tony DePiero, Alex Phillipides, and John Vale; (second row) coach Arnold Butler, Steve Sabol, Alex Lucicoski, Al Shipka, Alvin Hamrock, and Charles Carney. Coach Arnold Butler remained with the basketball team from 1929 to 1931. The 1932 season opened under the guidance of coach Ernest Gustinella, who stayed with the Red Devils until 1942 and never had a losing season. (Courtesy of Florence Galida.)

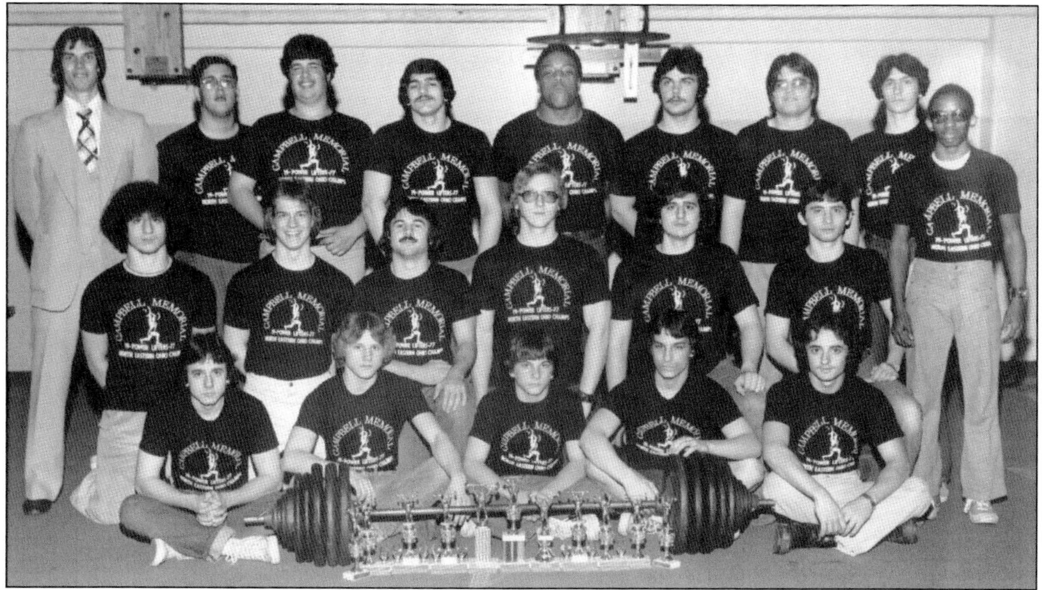

Competitive weight lifting was introduced to Campbell Memorial during the 1968–1969 school year. During the first year of competition, the weight-lifting squad took second place and proved that they could contend with the strongest in the area. Members of the 1977 Campbell Memorial Power Lifters, Northeast Ohio champions, are pictured here. (Courtesy of Florence Galida.)

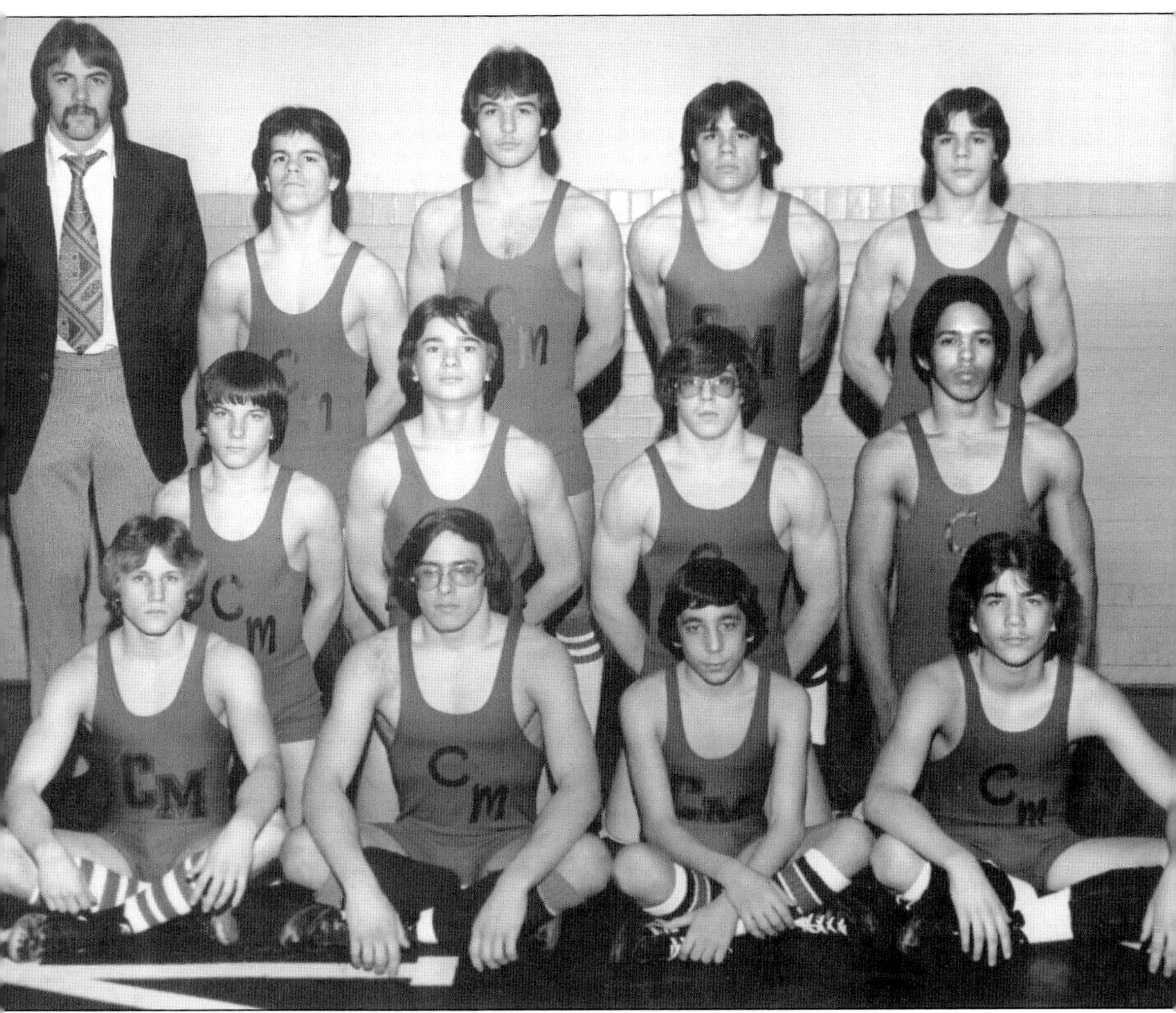

Wrestling began in 1974 under the guidance of Steve Mistovich, but it was a short-lived sport for students of Memorial High School. Coach Ed Rozum is pictured with his 1978 team. Other sports offered to Campbell Memorial students during the 1960s and 1970s were tennis, cross-country racing, track and field, golf, bowling, and weight lifting. Since that time, many sports have come and gone, partly due to declining enrollment, city population, and overall interest. However, when a student dons a Red Devil uniform, opposing teams know they are in for one heck of a fight. (Courtesy of Florence Galida.)

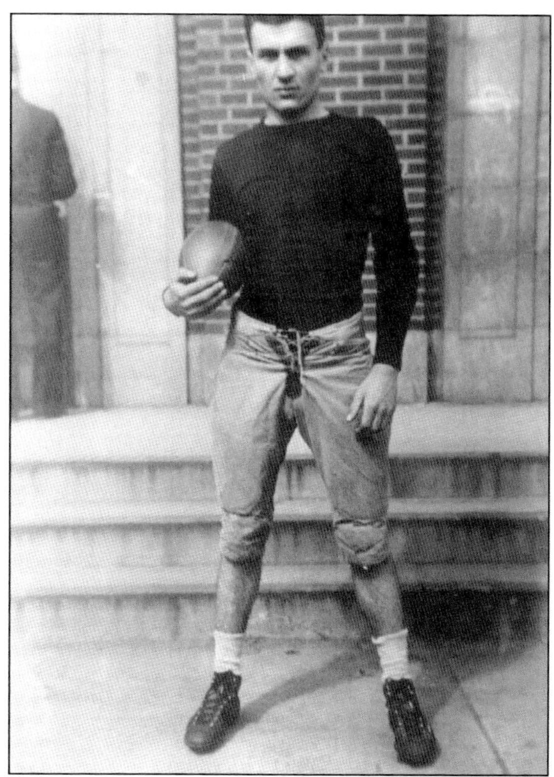

Campbell has a long and proud tradition of sports, especially football, in which students played for entertainment, personal growth, or preparation for life after school. Many athletes used the roughness of football to ready themselves for the long and arduous hours in the mills or to physically and mentally train for military service. Adolph Malys is pictured in his football uniform around 1932. (Courtesy of Lorraine Sabol.)

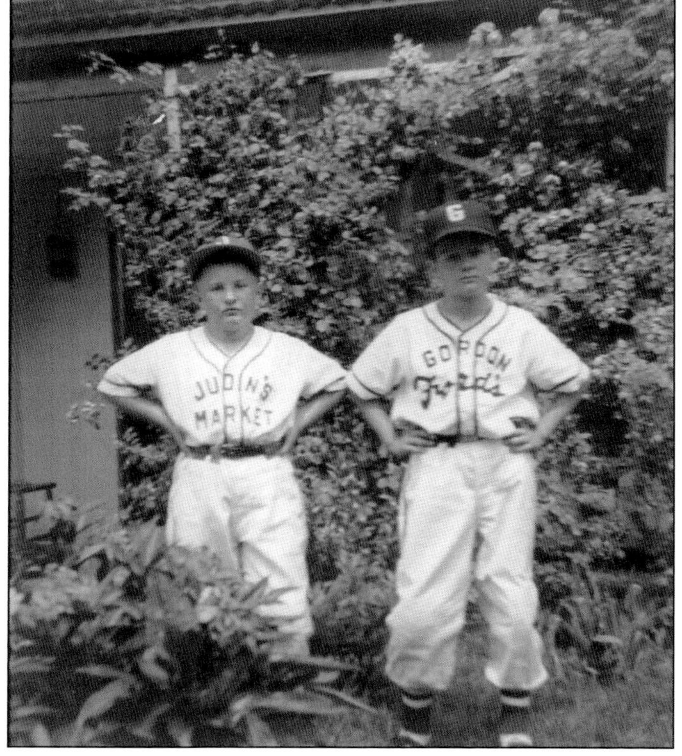

Dressed in their baseball uniforms, Melvin Sabol (left) and Rudy Arlow (right) pose for a photograph in front of the Youngstown Sheet and Tube Company homes during the summer of 1952. In 1951, the Campbell Boosters Association began developing their Little League program. The first four team sponsors consisted of Reed Builders Supply, Judin's Food Market, T. Roy Gordon Foods Inc., and the Campbell Sash Works. On June 15, 1952, the first pitch was thrown in front of a crowd of 2,500 parents, friends, and sports enthusiasts. (Courtesy of Lorraine Sabol.)

Since its early days as a booming city, Campbell's youngsters have always been sports oriented and taken great pride in representing their hometown. Stella Sabol and Melvin Sabol are pictured in the company homes around 1952. Judin Food Mart, owned by Steve Judin, was an original sponsor of the Little League during its formation in 1952. (Courtesy of Lorraine Sabol.)

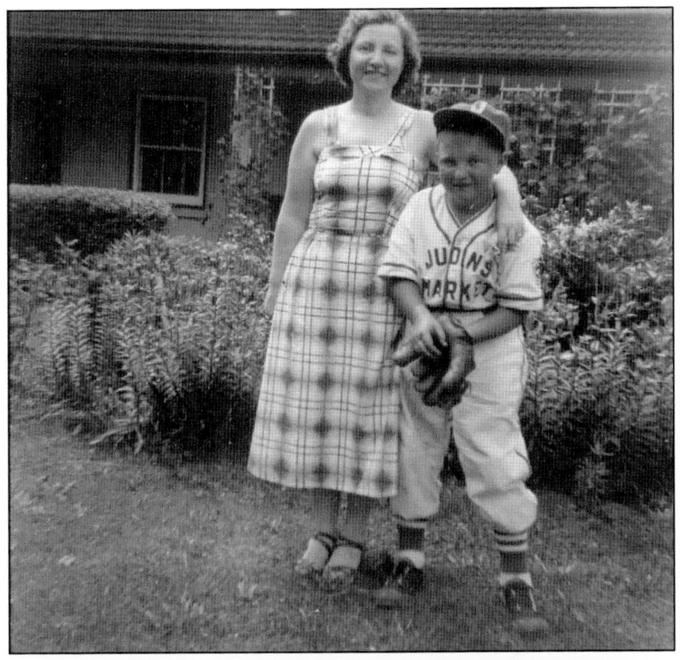

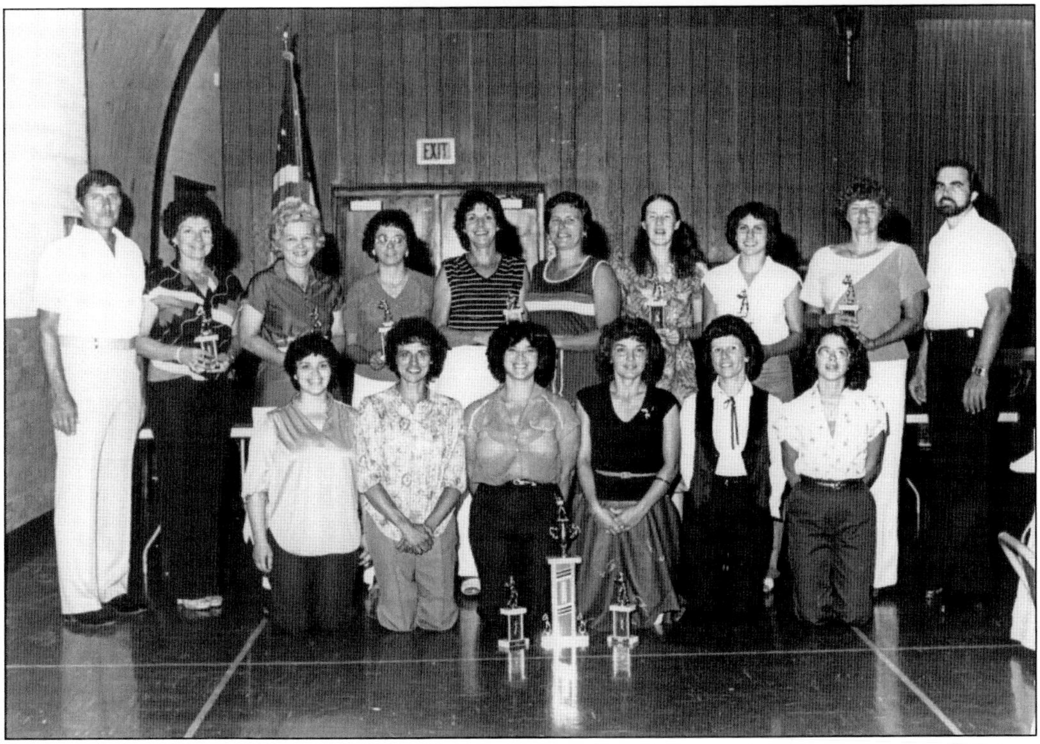

The 1980 Teresa's Villa ladies softball champions are, from left to right, (first row) Lisa Marino, Florence Galida, Rose Gonzalez, Joan Hamrock, Vernie Navarre, and Lourie Navarre; (second row) coach John Marenkovic, Dorothy Korchnak, Aggie Del Signore, Norene Kotasek, Gloria Katula, Dee Schrieber, Dana Bozick, Gale Galida, Jane Marenkovic, and coach Bill Navarre. (Courtesy of Florence Galida.)

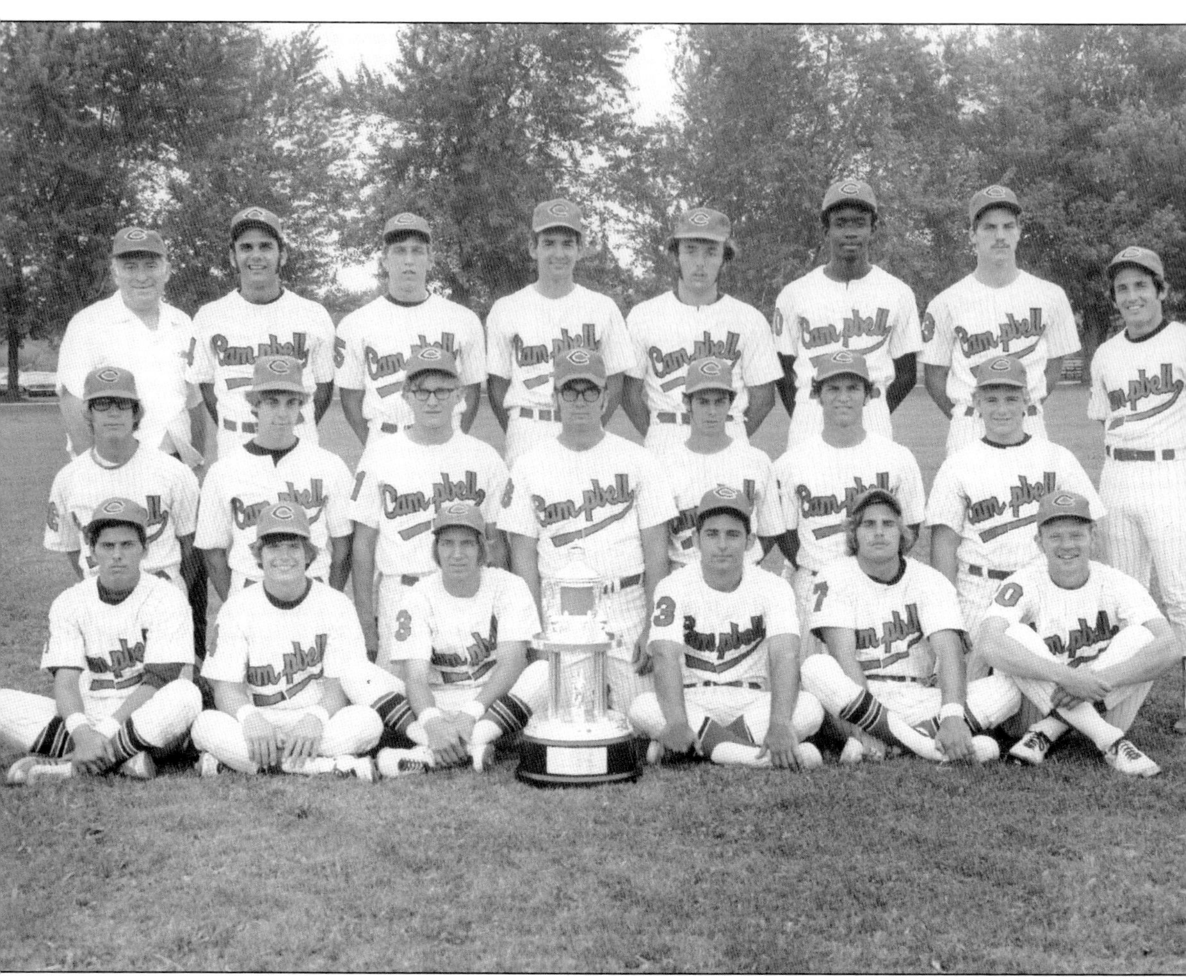

In 1971, the Campbell Athletic Club brought home the National Amateur Baseball Federation Junior Tournament championship. From left to right are (first row, seated) Mike Szenborn, Joe Malys, John Linden, Chris White, Gary Tondy, and Alan Rogers; (second row, kneeling) Ken Linden, Jan Terlecky, Rick Beck, Chip Hanuschak, Ralph DePizzo, George Cappuzello, and Jeff Marconi; (third row, standing) business manager Vlad Tikson, coach Al Frasco, Mike Zaluski, Dave Mootz, Charles Carnahan, Louis Packer, Mike Morris, and manager Steve Krivonak. (Courtesy of Florence Galida.)

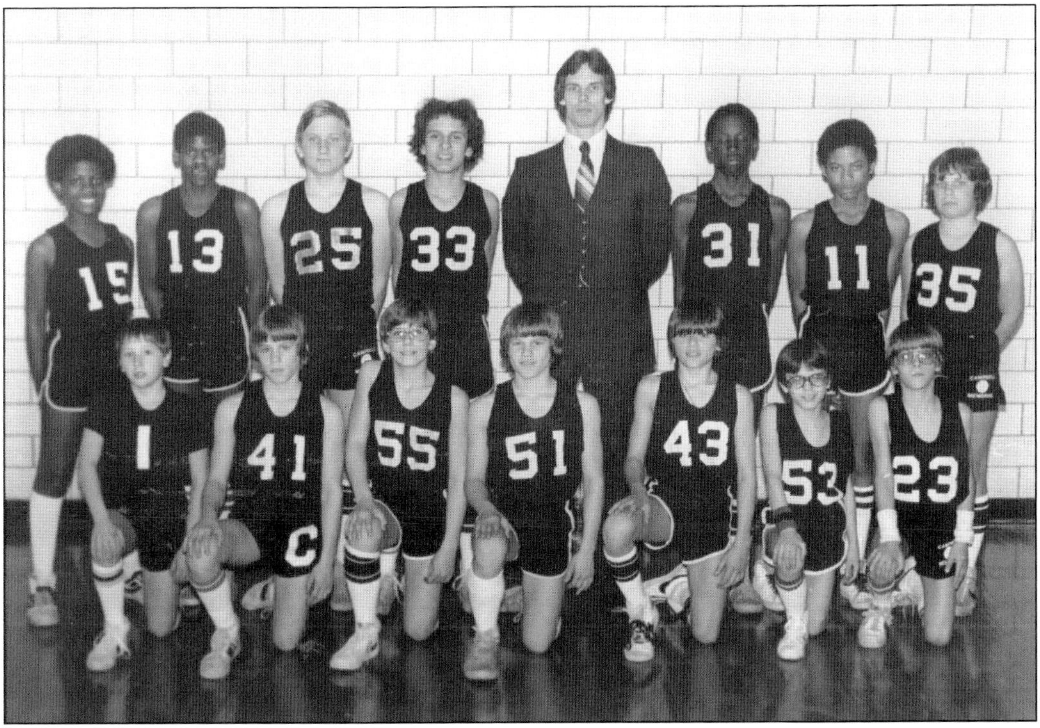

The 1980–1981 Campbell Reed Middle School seventh grade basketball team was the undefeated champion of the Mahoning Valley Conference. From left to right are (first row) Ed Bozic, Carmen Costantino, Pete Patelis, John Costantino, Mike Marantes, George Mastrovesalis, and George Lavendis; (second row) Luther Stubbs, Maurice Love, Andy Duraney, Brian Foster, coach Tom Carney, Terry Berry, Jim Corbett, and Paul Kish. Lessons learned in sports, coupled with academics, have permitted Campbell students to excel during their life. Many of these students have gone on to become Campbell community leaders, public servants, and successes in their own right. (Courtesy of Florence Galida.)

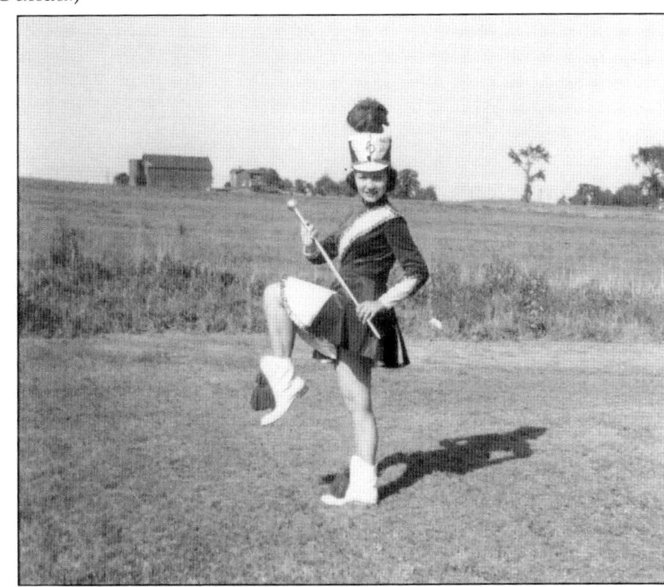

This photograph of Adele Malys in her majorette uniform was taken in September 1958 near the area of Creed Circle and Edward Lane. The Breetz barn and farmhouse can be seen in the background. (Courtesy of Lorraine Sabol.)

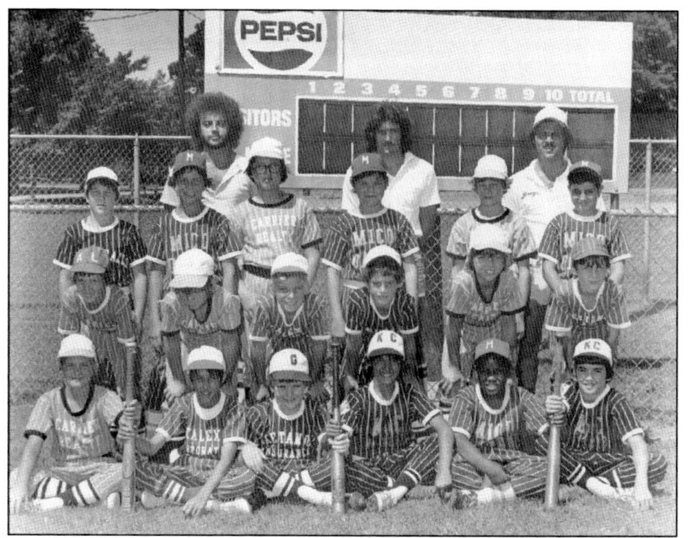

In 1957, and again in 1959, the Campbell Little League All-Stars took the Ohio state championship but were ultimately defeated in the US regional competition each time. Here are the 1977 Campbell Little League All-Stars, consisting of members from Carrier Realty, Knights of Columbus, Mico Dairy, Calex Corporation, Hellenic Athletic Club, St. Michael's Civic Club, and Bill's Mini-Mart. (Courtesy of Florence Galida.)

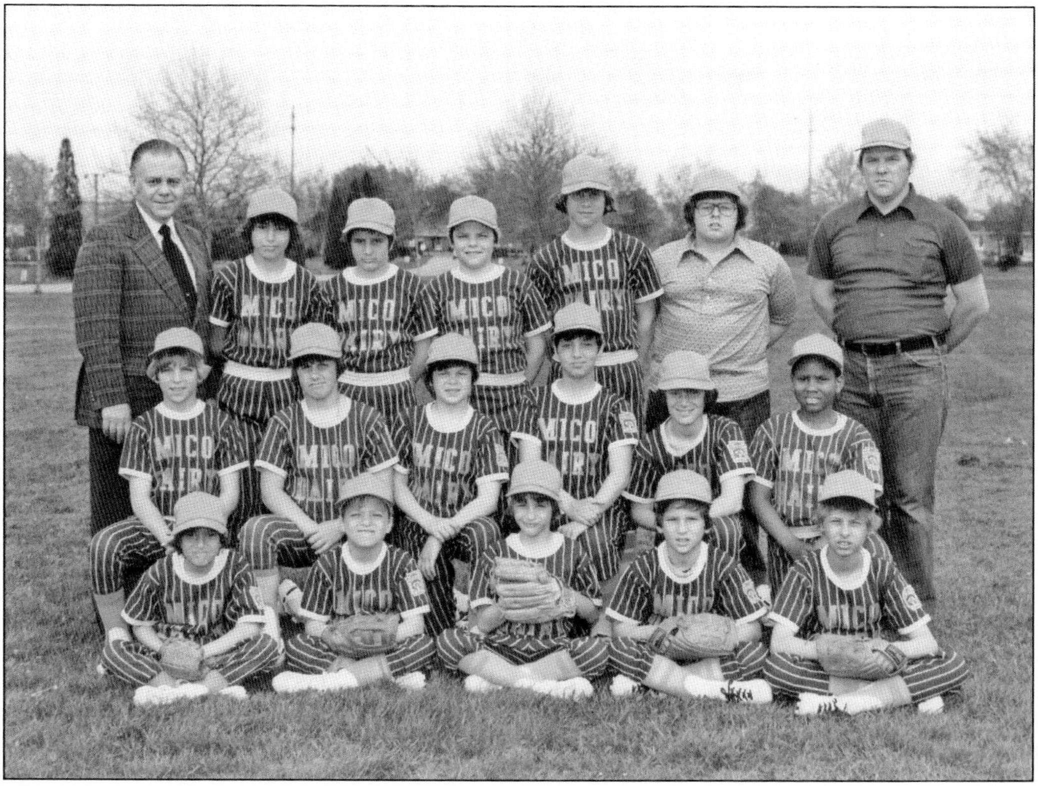

The Mico Dairy team of the Campbell Little League is shown in this undated photograph. From left to right are (first row) Joe Tiratto, Russ Osman, Mike Krotky, Brian Gaitanis, and Jeff Gull; (second row) Frank Carron, Dave Cramer, John Spencer, Tony Cena, Bob Schellito, and Chris Ingram; (third row) Mayor Rocco Mico, Pete Maillis, Kevin Kish, Joe Haus, Bob Beeson, manager Joe Snitzer, and coach Joe Haus. (Courtesy of Florence Galida.)

Six

The City's Finest

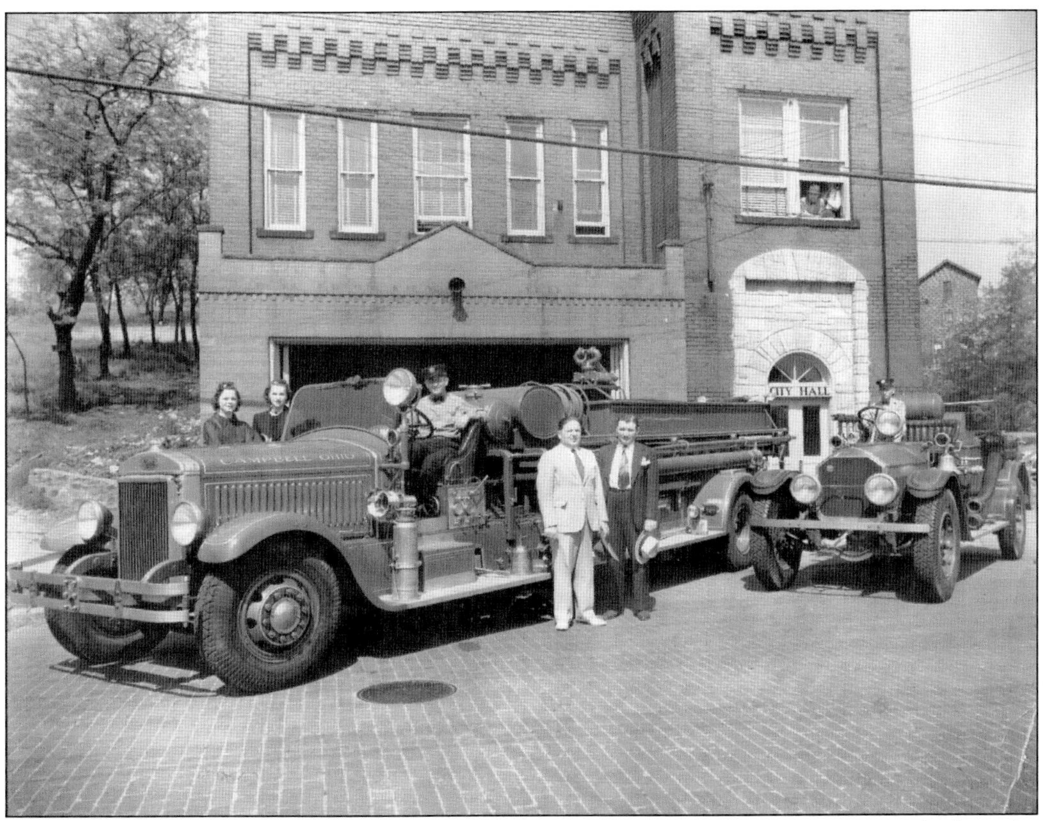

City officials and employees pose with a newly purchased fire truck in front of city hall in the 1930s. From left to right are Sofie Tofil, Helen Vansuch, Julius Torok, Mayor John B. Borak, safety service director John Petruska, and ? Ducat. Pete Butchko is pictured in the second-floor window. (Courtesy of Florence Galida.)

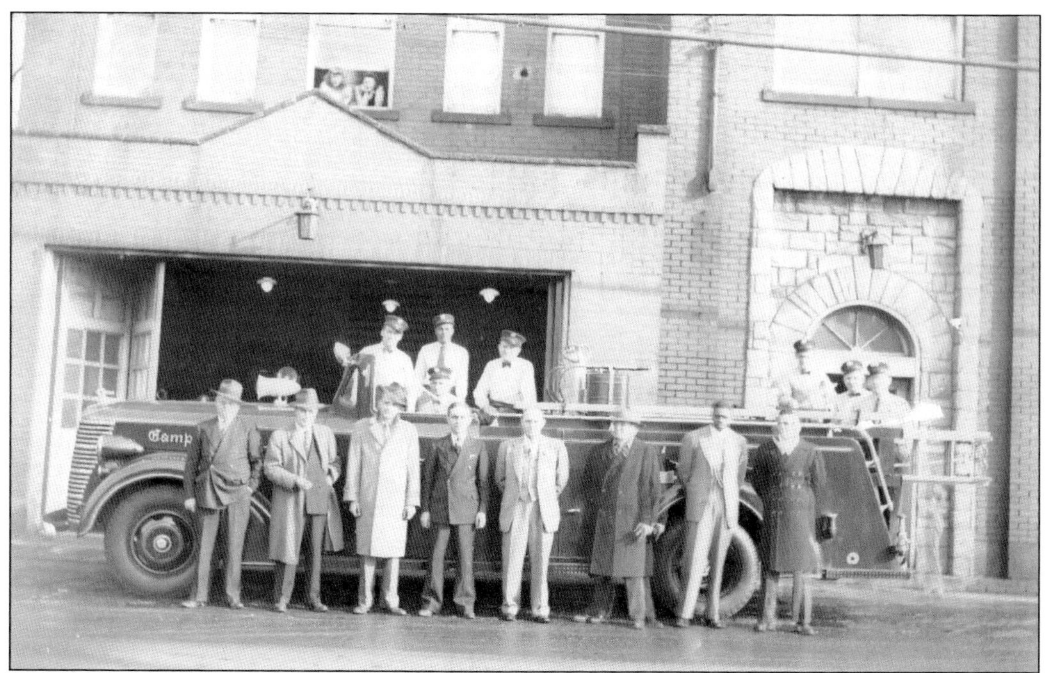

A newly purchased fire truck is being showcased in front of city hall on Wilson Avenue, near Eighth Street, during the late 1940s. Various city officials and firefighters are pictured with Mayor Andrew J. Hamrock (first row, fourth from right). The site has changed hands many times over the years and is now privately owned. The city hall building is no longer standing. (Courtesy of Florence Galida.)

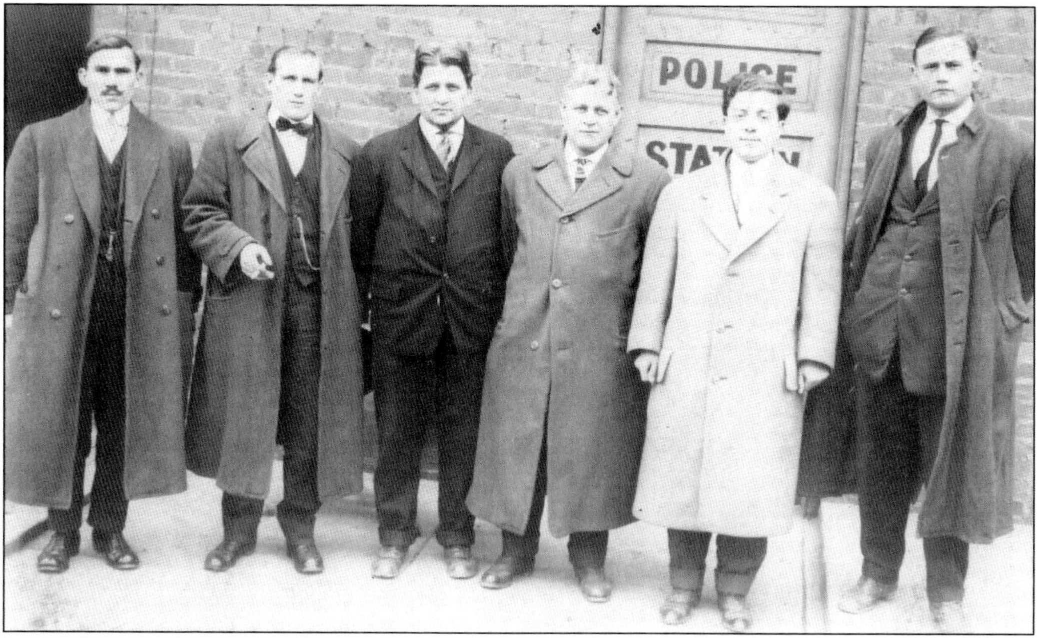

William H. Cunningham was elected as the second mayor of the village of East Youngstown and the first mayor of the city of East Youngstown. From left to right are Nick Comsia, councilman; Hugo ?; William H. Cunningham, mayor; Frank Cunningham, police chief; Gabriel Masi, treasurer; and Louis Hamrock, councilman. (Courtesy of Florence Galida.)

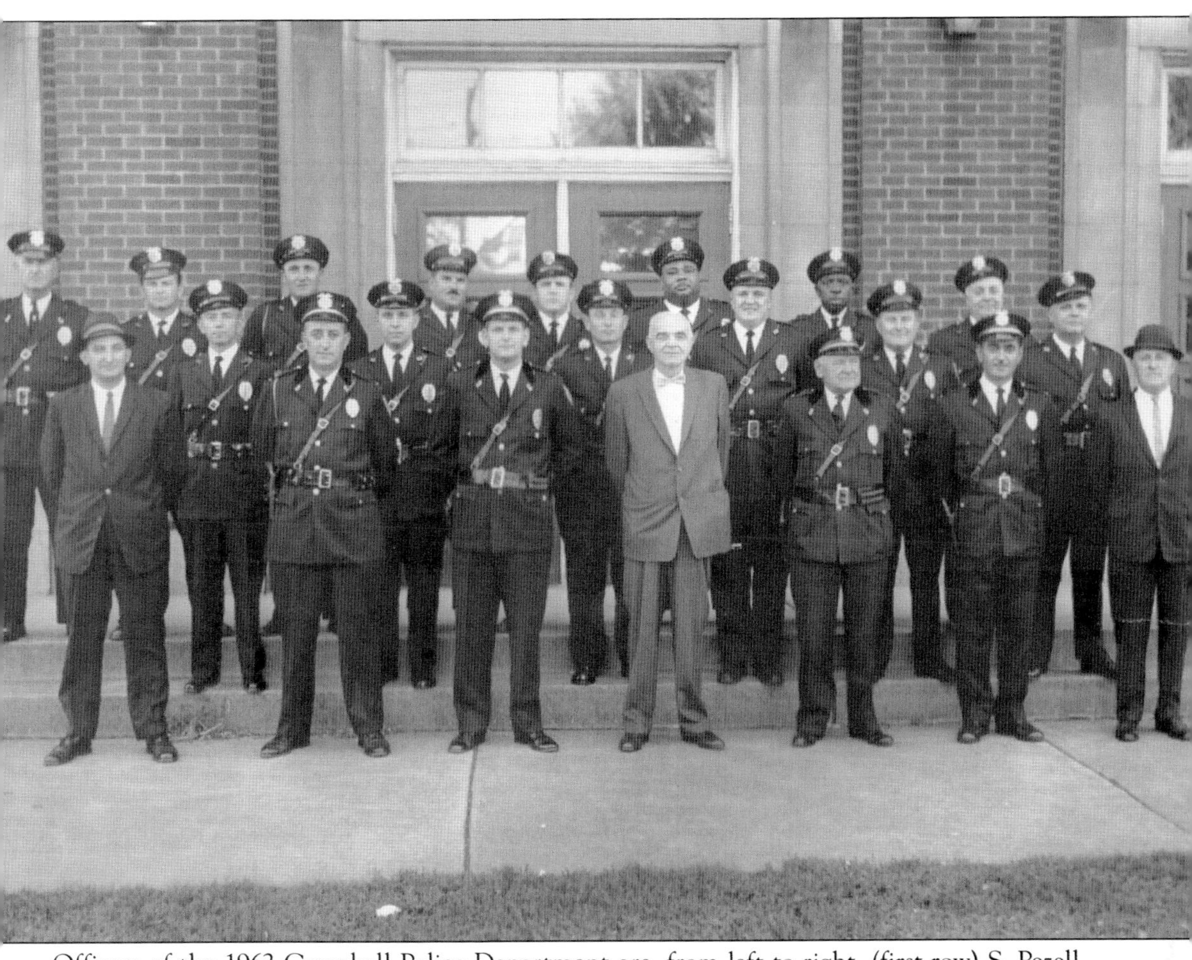

Officers of the 1962 Campbell Police Department are, from left to right, (first row) S. Pezell, C. Rich, B. Halase, Chief John Putko, J. Wasko, N. Galanses, and J. Geletka; (second row) R. Kish, P. Butchko, R. Borak, J. Mraz, J. Sajnovsky, and J. Dubyak; (third row) N. Evanoff, G. Testa, E. Franks, N. Mistovich, W. Fortner, O. Eddings, and A. Masi. (Courtesy of Joseph Pavlansky.)

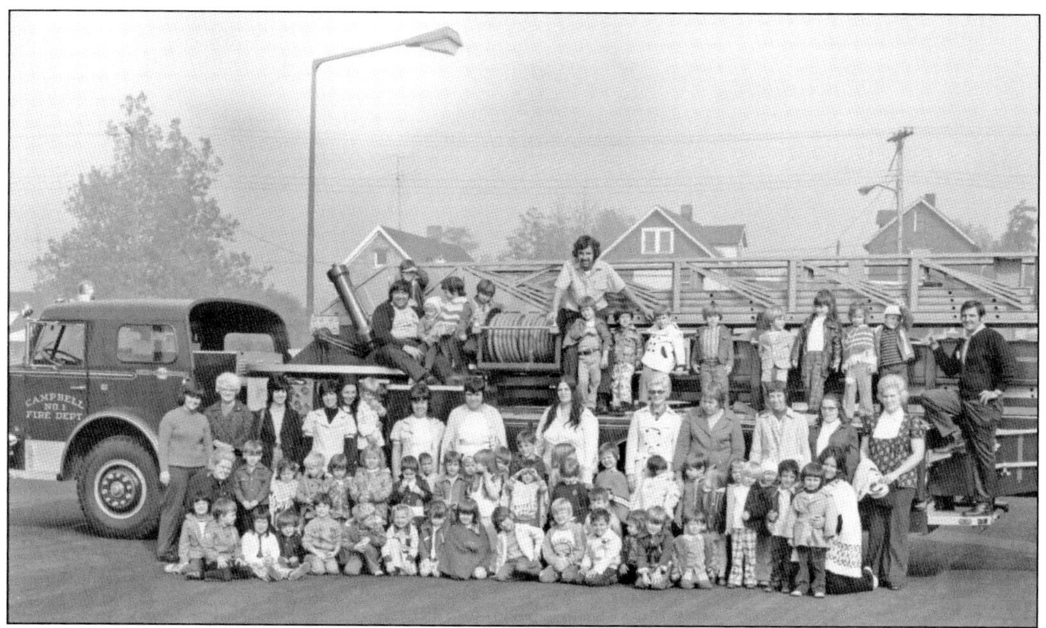

Schoolchildren and firefighters are shown posing in front of a Campbell Fire Department truck in this undated photograph. Since their inception, Campbell safety services have always provided community outreach to educate the public on their equipment and duties. (Courtesy of Florence Galida.)

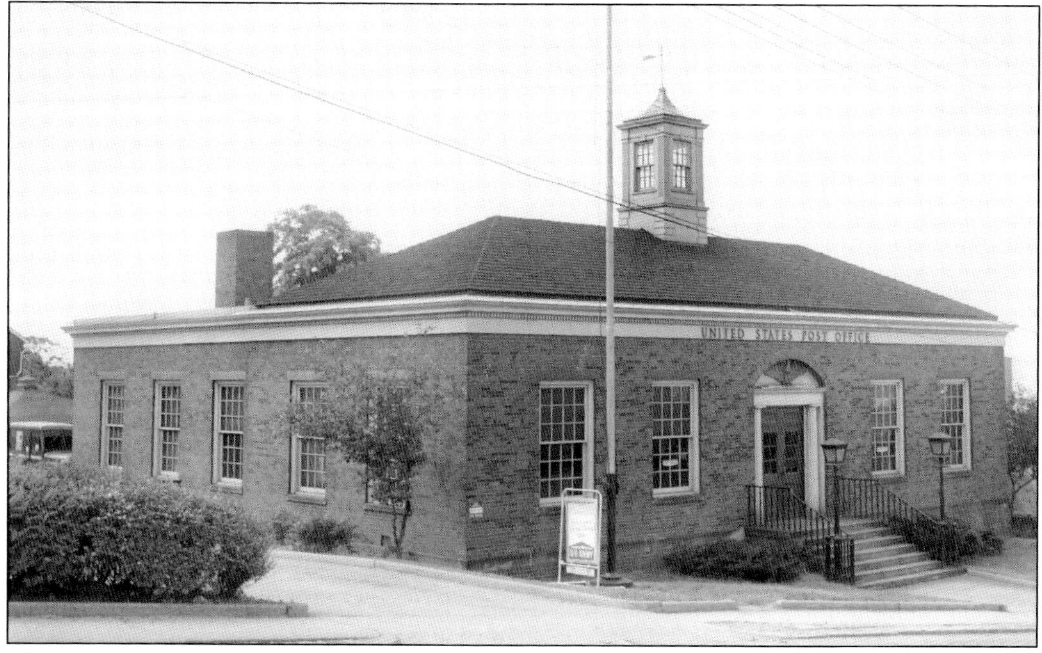

Through a resolution proposed by the city council and efforts made by Congressman Michael J. Kirwan, postmaster John Galida officially accepted the new US Post Office at 57 Robinson Road for the City of Campbell in 1939. Prior to the erection of the new post office, postal services were handled through rented buildings or storerooms, such as the James Gillette Building on Robinson Road or the T. Roy Gordon Building on Wilson Avenue. (Courtesy of Florence Galida.)

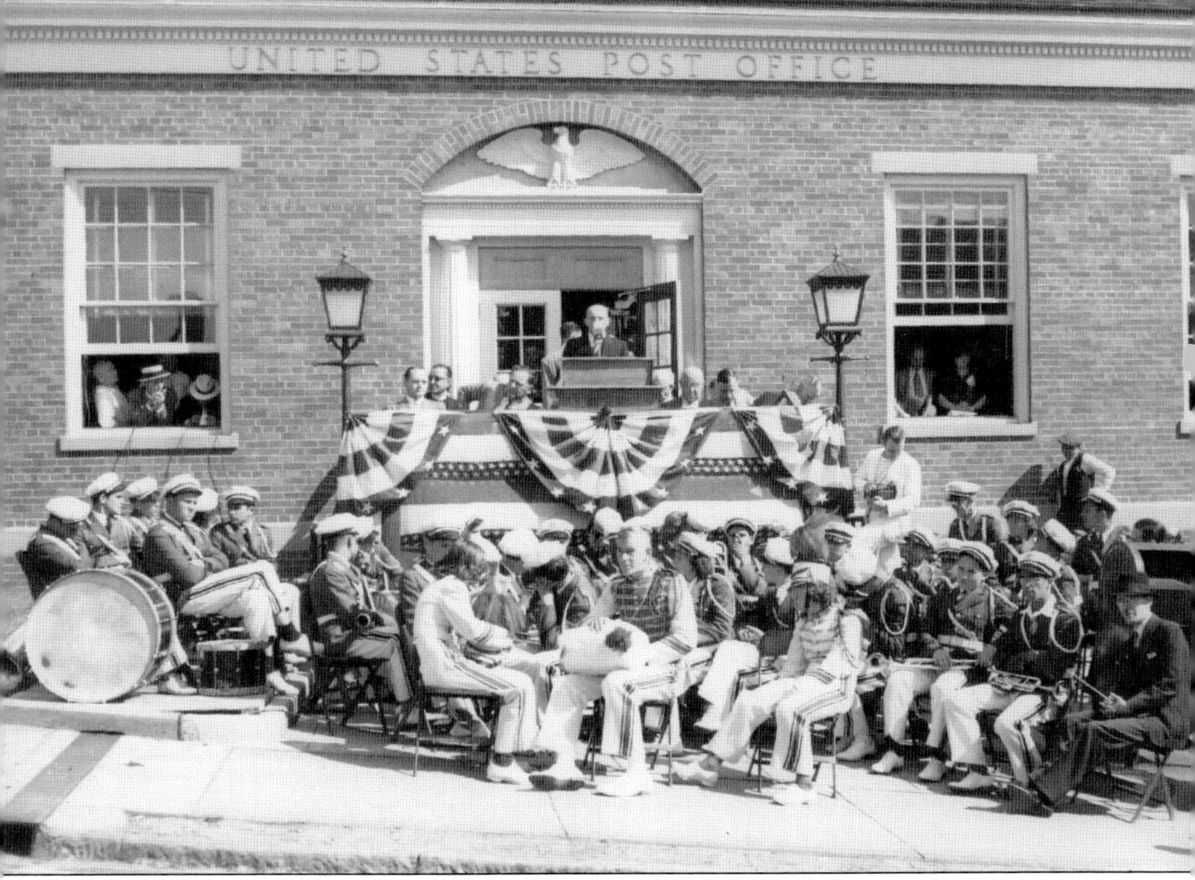

During the dedication ceremony on July 15, 1939, more than 3,000 people were there to witness the opening of the new $70,000 post office building, which postmaster John Galida had accepted on behalf of the city. The post office was the first federal building erected in Campbell. Notable people in attendance were Congressman Michael J. Kirwan, Youngstown postmaster Alvin W. Craver, and Struthers postmaster Robert C. Boylan. The post office underwent a $106,000 renovation 36 years later and remained open until a new building was erected on Twelfth Street at Devitt Avenue in 1997. (Courtesy of Florence Galida.)

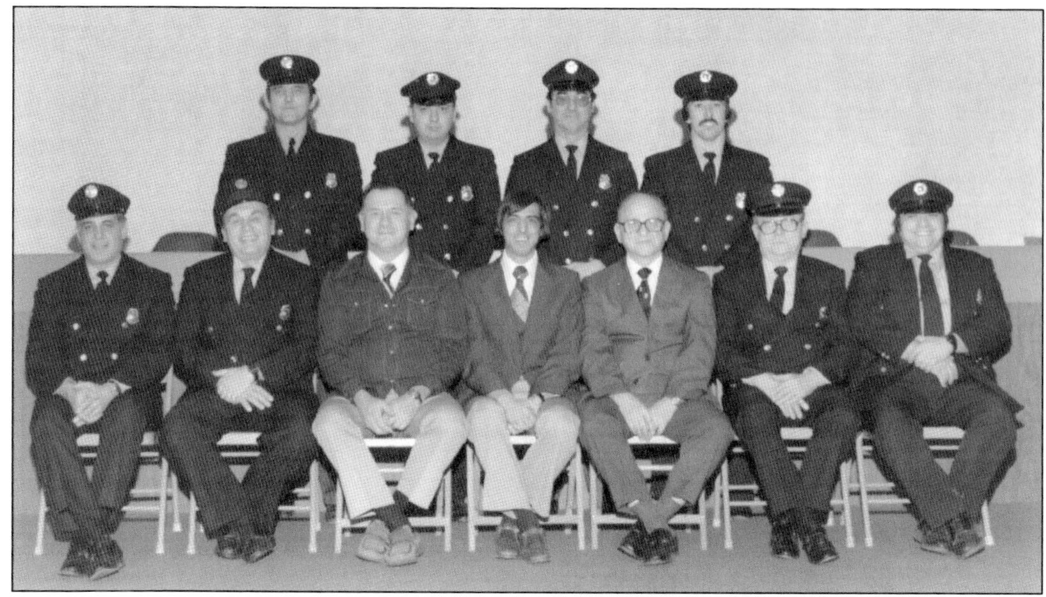

Members of the Campbell Fire Department are pictured here in 1977. From left to right are (first row) Vincent Leone, Ed Sharshan, Chief Ed Garchar, Mayor Michael J. Katula Jr., Director of Administration Mike Reichert, Paul Kuzma, and John Litch Jr.; (second row) William Vrabel, Ed Litwin, Roy Stanfar, and Ron ?. (Courtesy of Florence Galida.)

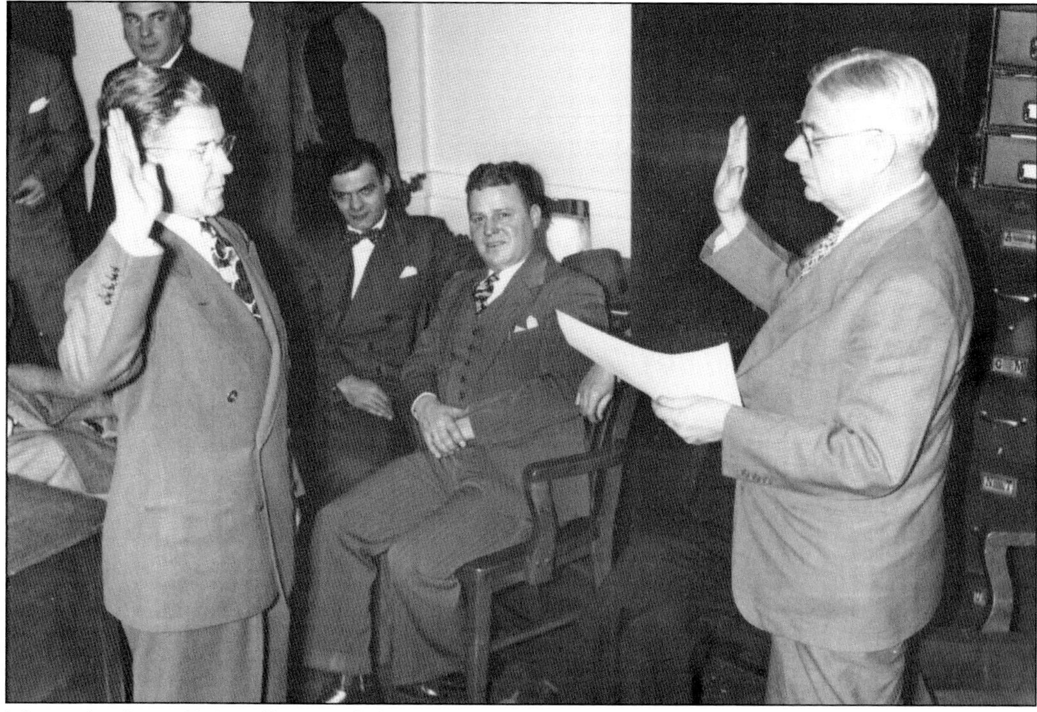

Mayor Anthony F. Pacella served the City of Campbell from 1940 to 1941 and then again from 1946 to 1949. In 1940, Pacella became the city's youngest mayor at the age of 31. Here, Pacella (standing at left) takes the oath of office for his second term as mayor beginning in 1946. (Courtesy of Florence Galida.)

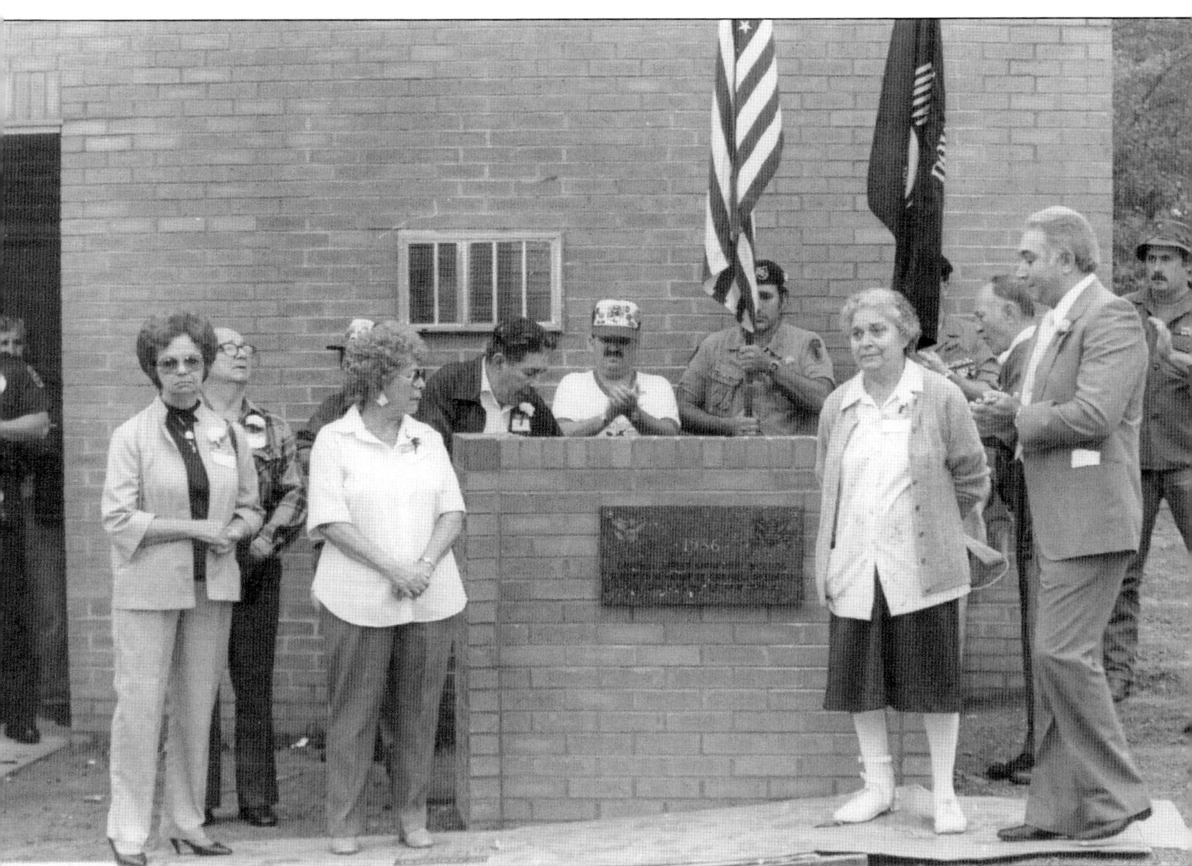

In 1986, the new Campbell Street Department building was dedicated to local residents who were killed during the Vietnam conflict. A somber look can be seen on the faces of the parents and family members who lost their loved ones in Vietnam. From its earliest beginning, Campbell residents have answered their nation's call to service and have served proudly for their country and community. From left to right are Mr. and Mrs. Carl Puskarcik, Mr. and Mrs. Holibonich, Mr. and Mrs. John Stanko, and Mayor James Vargo. (Courtesy of Florence Galida.)

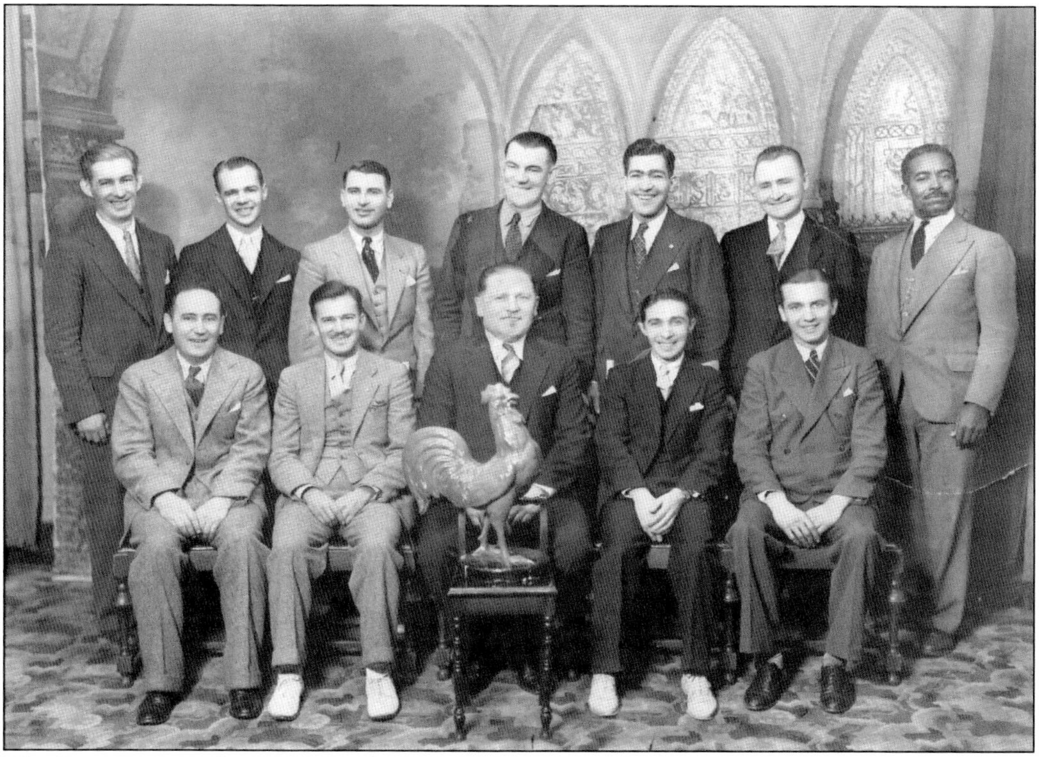

The Democratic ticket is pictured in Campbell in 1935, when the rooster ruled as the symbol of the Democratic Party. The candidates are, from left to right, (first row) Anthony Testafor for treasurer, Nicholas Petica for solicitor, John Borak for mayor, John Demart for president of council, and Michael Kovach for auditor; (second row) Michael Martinko, John Lawrence Lysowski, and Julius Fabian for councilman-at-large; Joseph Fabian for Fourth Ward; Frank DiTommaso for Third Ward; Alexander Miller for Second Ward; and Charles W. Nelson for First Ward. John J. Borak would go on to win the position of Campbell mayor and later have a road named after him in Roosevelt Park. (Courtesy of Florence Galida.)

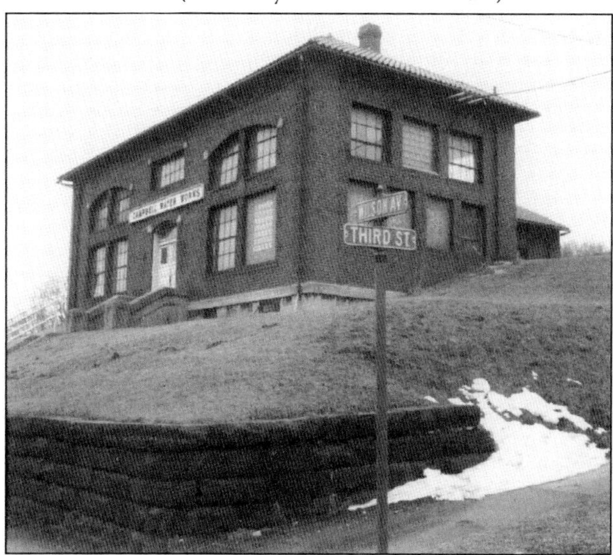

Many of the original buildings from the East Youngstown days are no longer standing within the city. Several sites have been reclaimed by Mother Nature, while others have been built over by newer businesses or houses. The southern portions (between Murray Avenue and Wilson Avenue) of Washington Street, Jefferson Avenue, Murray Avenue, and Monroe Street have been closed down and are currently being used by private businesses. This photograph depicts the Campbell water plant in the early 1930s. (Courtesy of Lynette Hardman.)

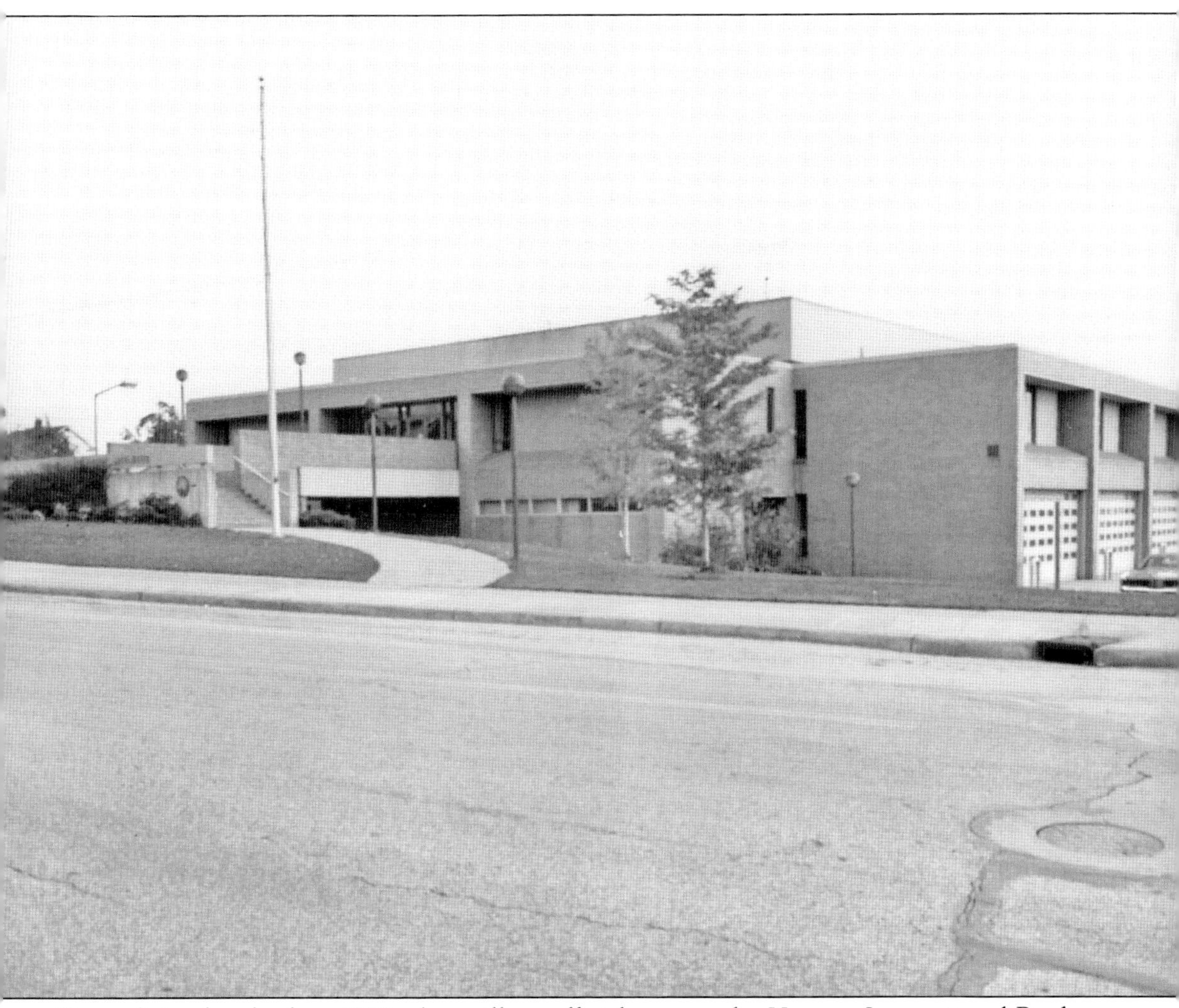

City politics date back to 1909 when village officials met at the Hamory International Bank building. After land was purchased from Thomas and Althea McVey, a village hall was constructed on Wilson Avenue between Warhurst Road and Eighth Street. In need of a more centralized location to better promote public relations with city officials, the current municipal building was constructed on the grounds of the old Gordon Park in 1972. (Courtesy of Florence Galida.)

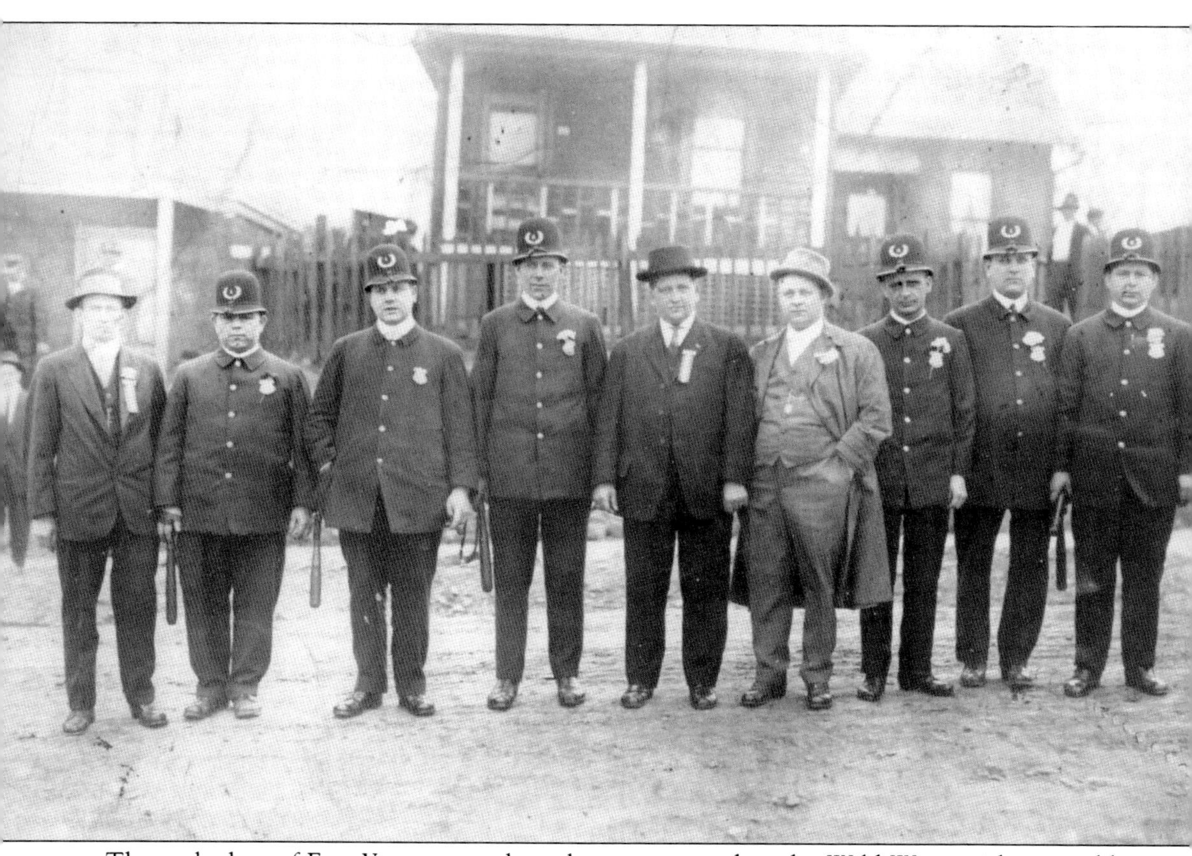

The early days of East Youngstown have been compared to the Wild West, with constables keeping order until 1909, when a police force was finally created. As a police force gradually formed, people respected the men willing to battle the troublemakers, and soon, the village found relative peace. The East Youngstown (Campbell) Police Department is pictured here in 1919. From left to right are Det. Nick Gorcheff, Joe Ruby, Nick LaRocco, unidentified, Mayor Clifford Cunningham, Chief Frank Cunningham, Jack Kenney, George Bender, and George Datko. (Courtesy of Florence Galida.)

During World War II, savings bonds could be purchased at local banks or post offices to support the war effort. Postmaster John Galida (left) and Mayor Anthony Pacella (right) stage a photograph in 1941 to show the city's cooperation with the war overseas. Mayor Pacella had purchased the first war bond sold in the city. (Courtesy of Florence Galida.)

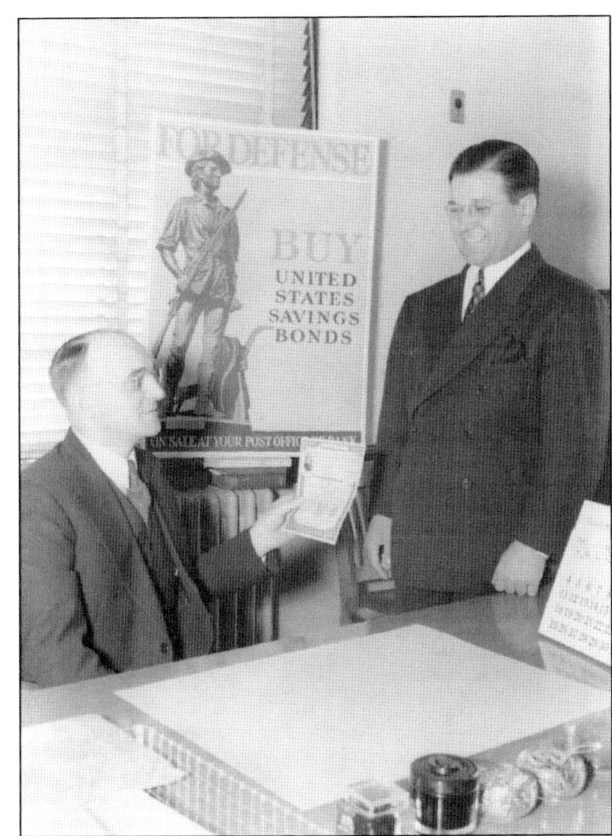

This photograph was taken from Robinson Road at Twelfth Street, looking down toward Wilson Avenue. Many of the buildings on the right, and even those tucked away behind the post office, are no longer standing or are in a very dilapidated condition. Once the steel mills began to close in 1977, many people moved from the area or no longer had the means to maintain their establishments. (Courtesy of Florence Galida.)

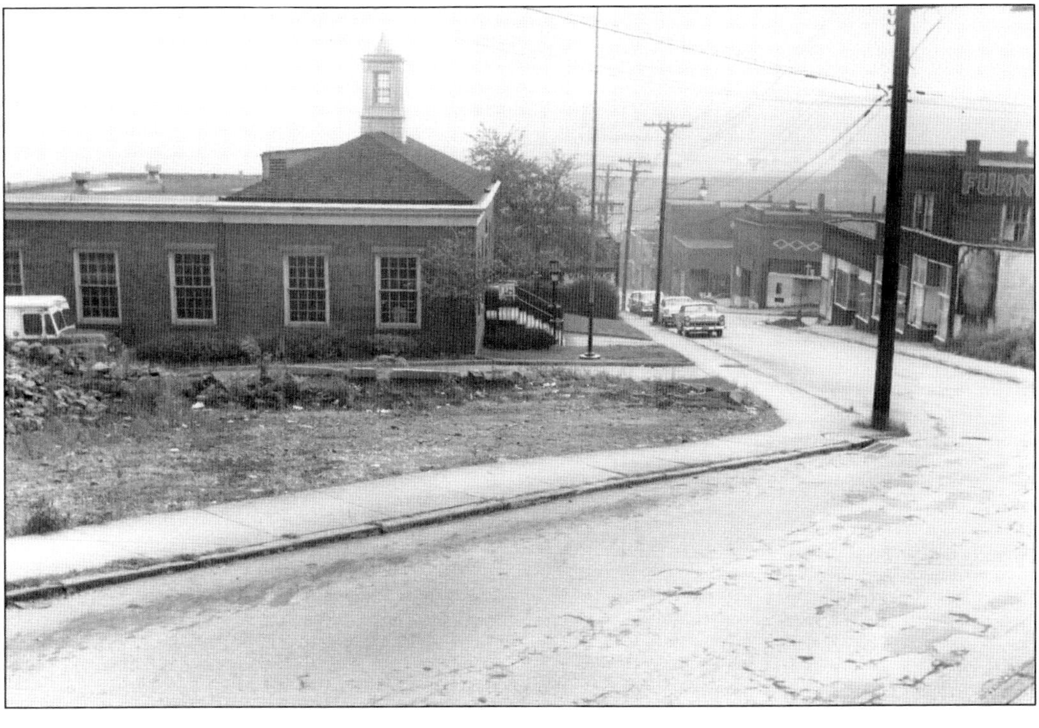

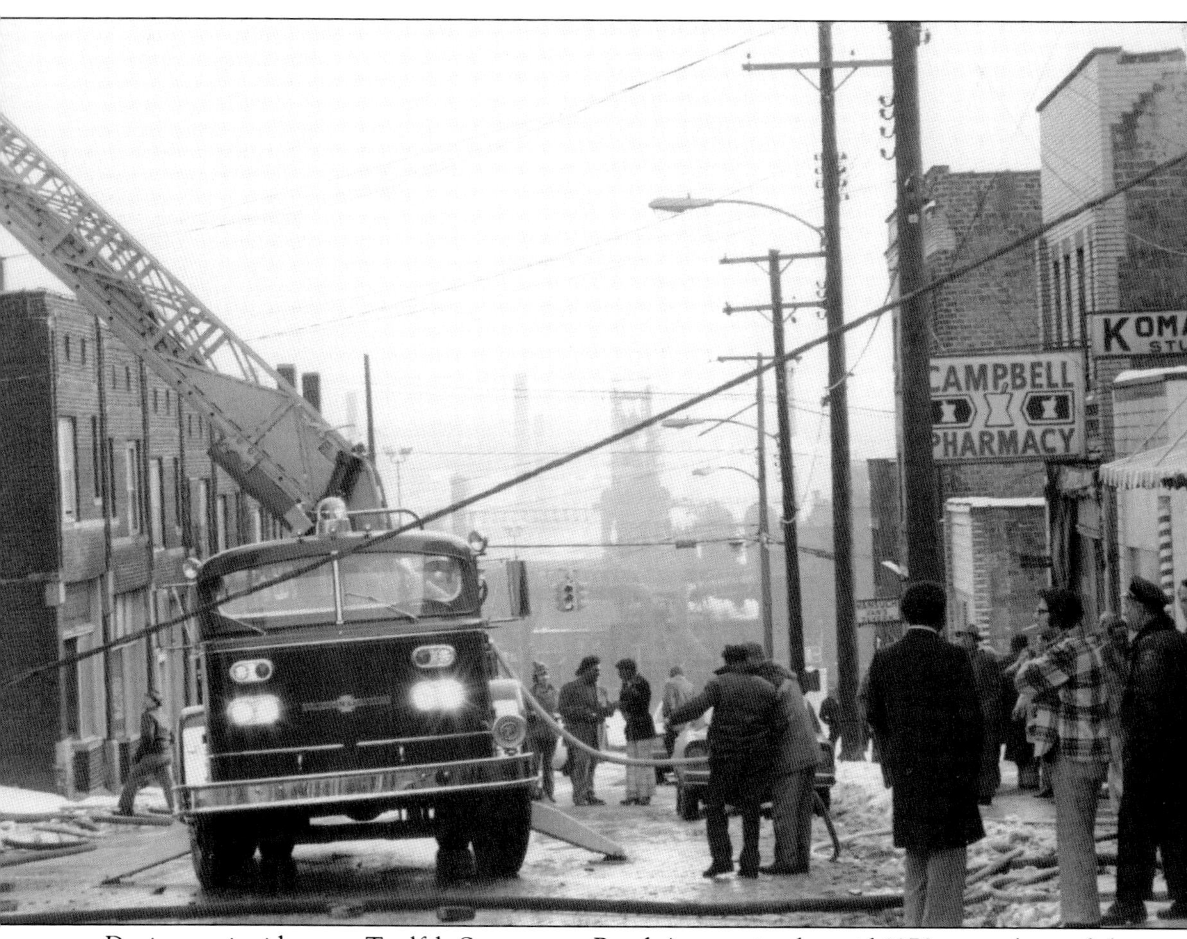

During an incident on Twelfth Street near Reed Avenue in the mid-1970s, members of the Campbell Fire Department battle a raging inferno as citizens look on. Having started as an all-volunteer force in 1910, the department emerged as a recognized and integral part of the safety services when East Youngstown became a city in 1922. George Matthews, the first fire chief, quickly worked to organize the department into an efficient full-time firefighting unit. (Courtesy of Florence Galida.)

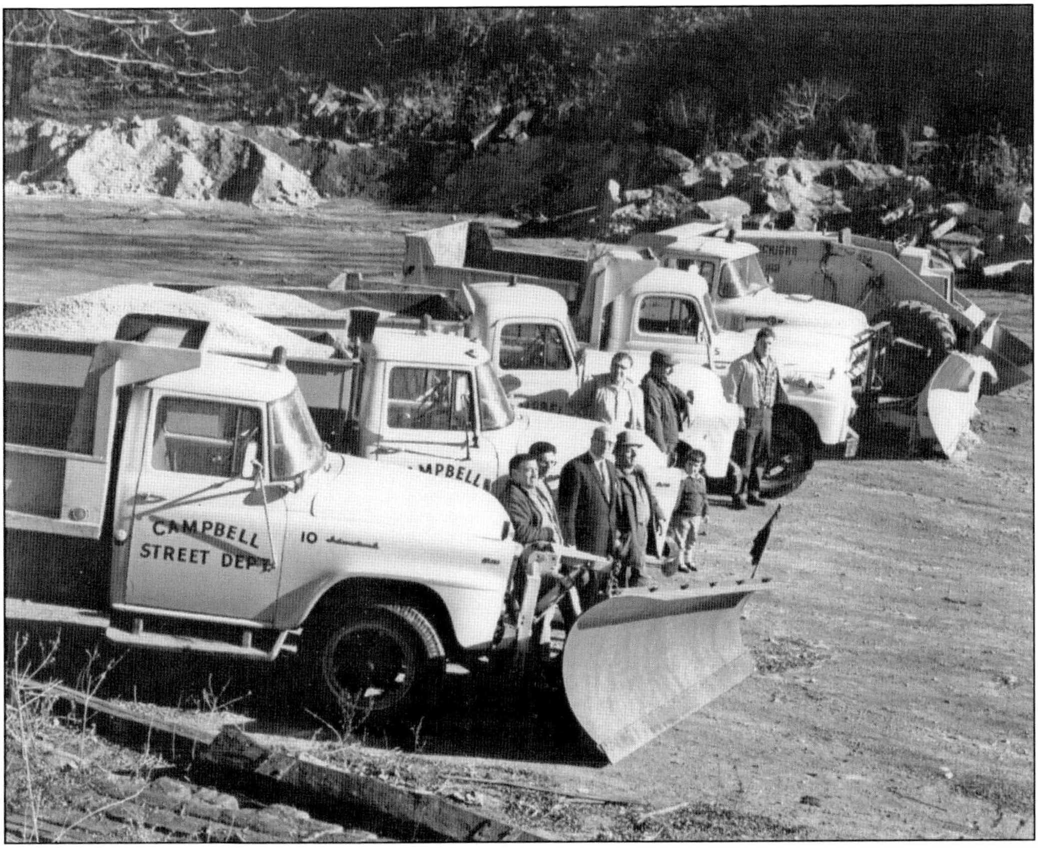

The Campbell Street Department's trucks and equipment are ready for inspection by Mayor Joseph Vrabel in the early 1960s. When the city hall building on Wilson Avenue was vacated in 1972, the property was turned over to the Street Department for its use. (Courtesy of Florence Galida.)

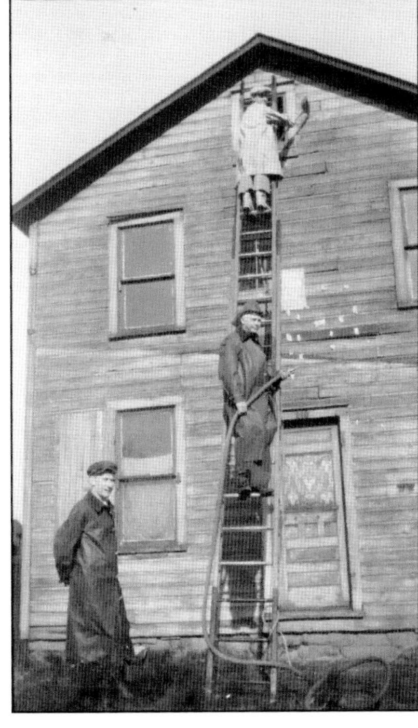

During the 1950s, many new problems arose as the population of Campbell continued to grow and spread throughout the city. One of the issues plaguing city officials was how to deal with the hill district and its fire safety needs. These city firefighters are practicing on a vacant home in the 1920s. (Courtesy of Florence Galida.)

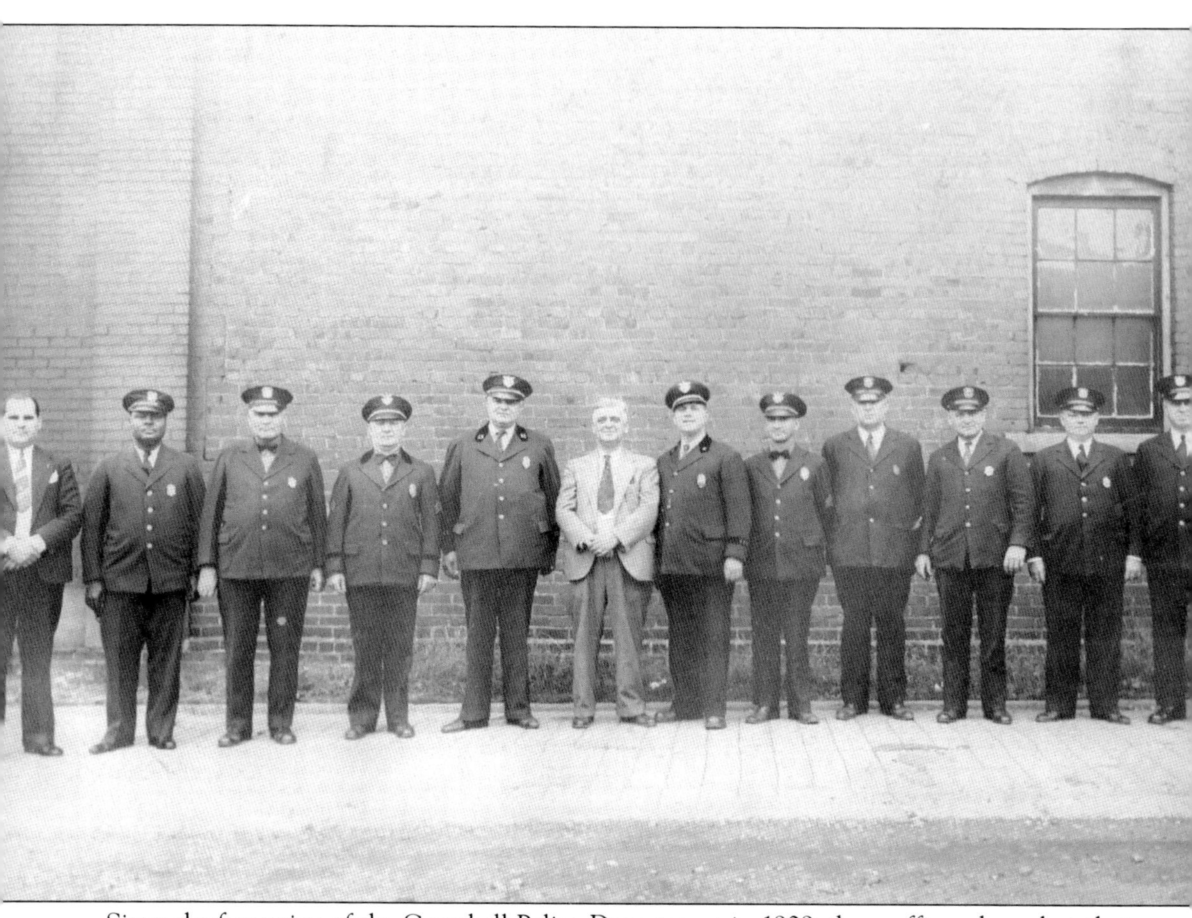

Since the formation of the Campbell Police Department in 1909, three officers have lost their lives in the line of duty: John Costantino, May 11, 1920; Capt. Joseph Ruby, November 11, 1923; and Lt. Albert Masi, February 12, 1973. Even with such a dangerous job, police officers still stand proud to serve their community, as seen here in the 1930s. From left to right are Steve Buckus, Daries Coles, Mike Yurko, Joe Yousko, John Putko, Chief Frank Cunningham, Nick Larocco, Jack Kinney, George Bender, John Wasko, John Oshelski, and Mike Dutko. (Courtesy of Florence Galida.)

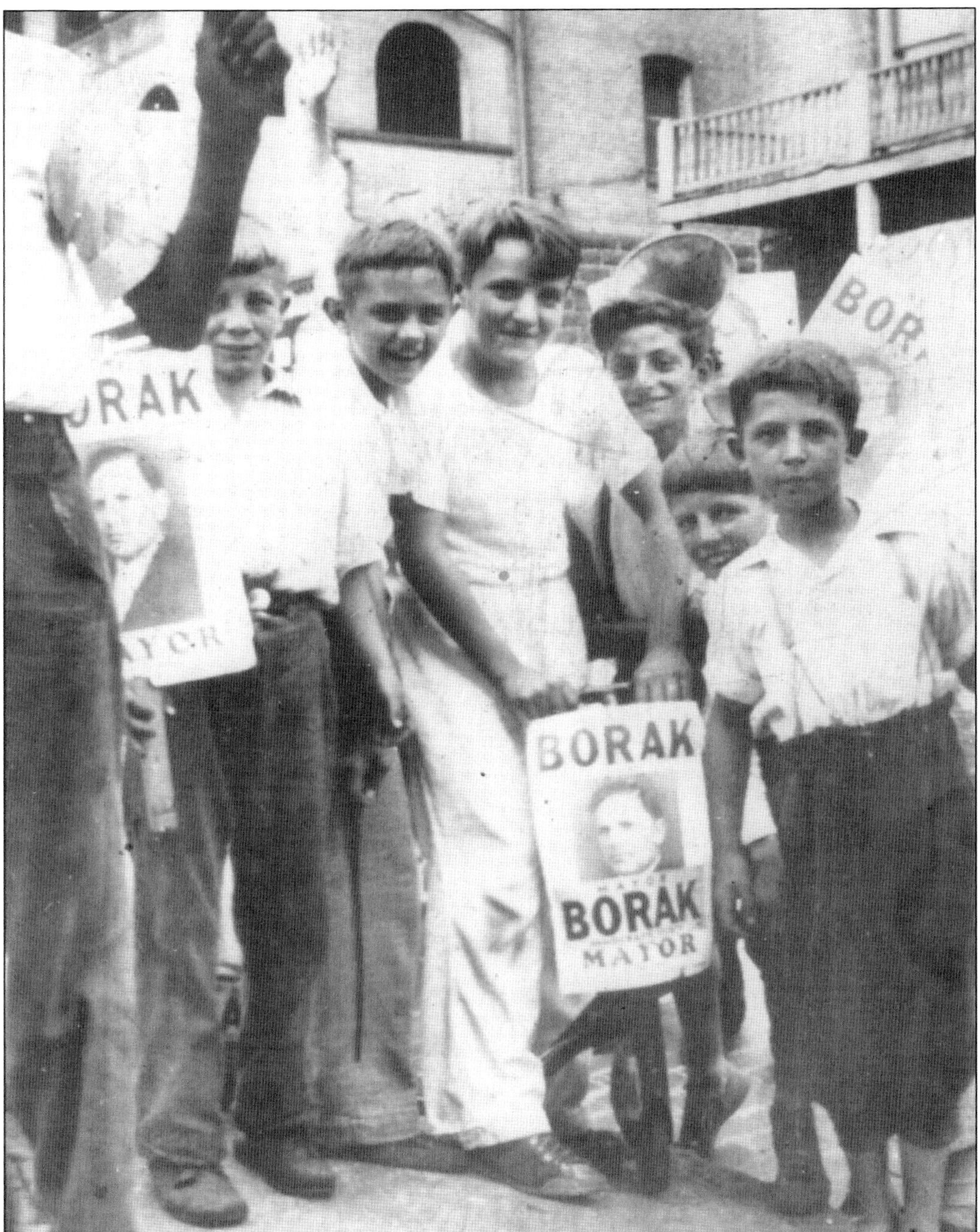

Born on April 4, 1893, in Sharpsville, Pennsylvania, John J. Borak and his family moved to East Youngstown in 1909. At the age of 16, John entered the Marine Corps and served in World War I before returning to East Youngstown, where he operated the Borak Pharmacy on Twelfth Street. In 1935, John J. Borak defeated Roy T. Gordon for the mayoral seat and subsequently served the City of Campbell from 1936 to 1939. During his time in office, Mayor Borak purchased the Gluck Farm and began the long road to creating Roosevelt Park. After leaving city politics, Borak continued as a businessman within the city, as well as a building inspector. (Courtesy of Florence Galida.)

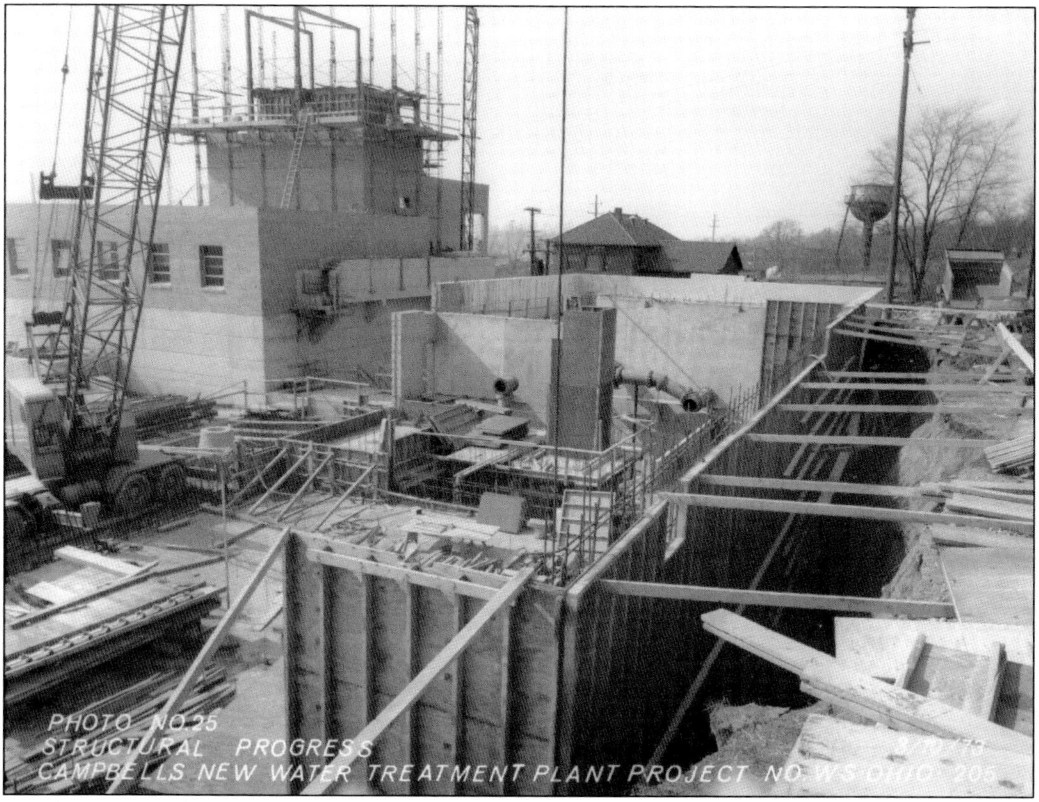

Until a waterworks was established on Third Street at Wilson Avenue in 1917, the people of East Youngstown obtained their water from a pump that was commonly located in their backyard. In 1957, the city determined that a new water treatment plant needed to be constructed. After a rejected proposal for a new plant in 1964, the city came to terms and finished construction on the new plant in 1973, which cost approximately $2.6 million. (Courtesy of Florence Galida.)

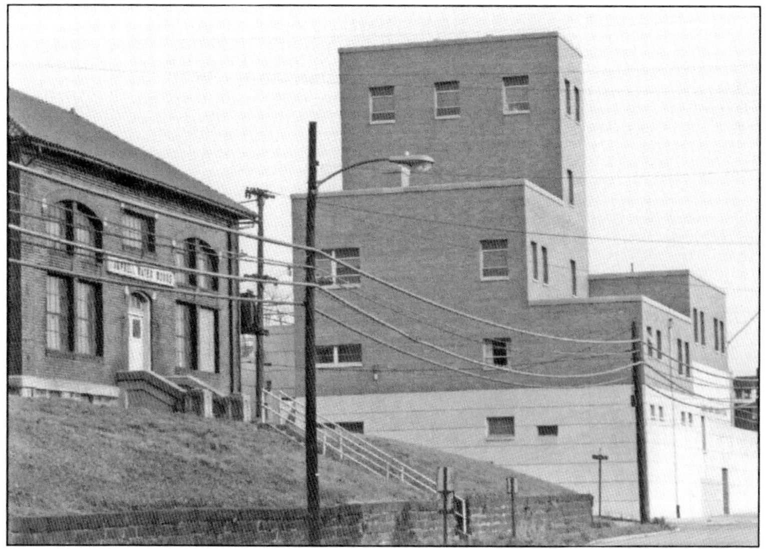

Located on Wilson Avenue at Third Street, the new Campbell Waterworks building (right) and the original (left) are pictured together as they appeared around 1973. The original Campbell Waterworks facility was built in 1917 to phase out residential water pumps. Today, all that remains of the original site is the brick wall. (Courtesy of Florence Galida.)

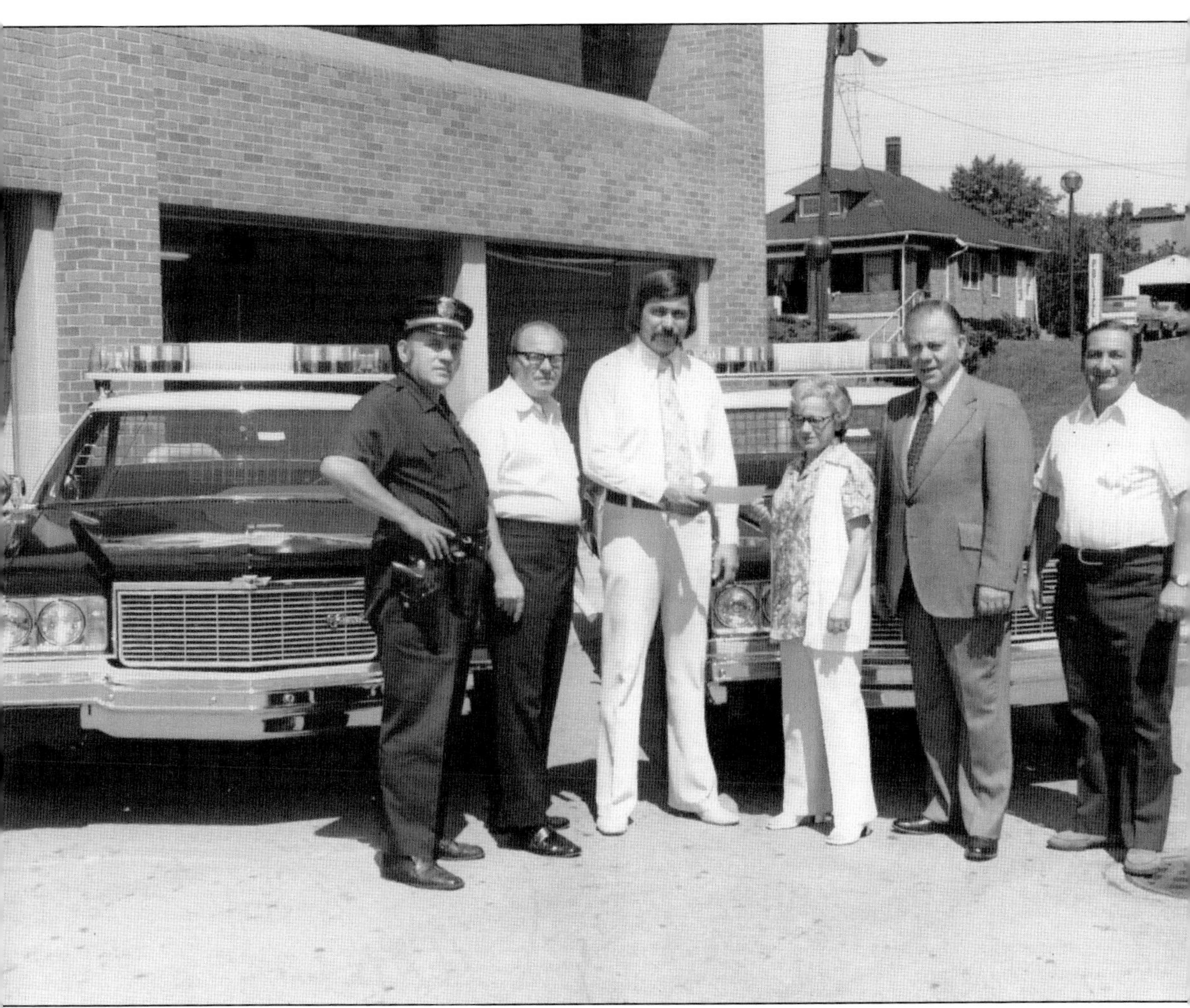

The first police force began in 1909 when the village of East Youngstown was incorporated. Prior to the department's organization, constables and justices of the peace kept law and order. The Campbell Police Department is shown receiving two new cruisers to add to their fleet. From left to right are officer Nick Mistovich, Fourth Ward councilman Edward Bayus, unidentified, Pauline Clement, Mayor Rocco Mico, and Third Ward councilman Steve Sofocleus Jr. (Courtesy of Florence Galida.)

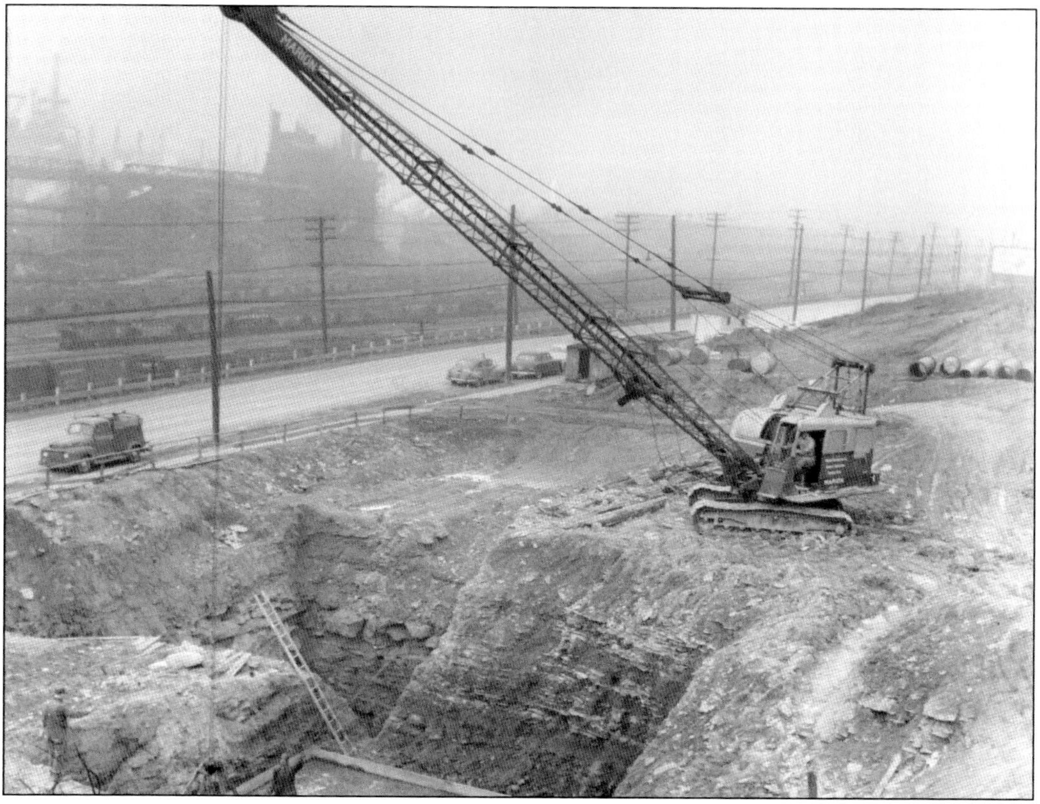

In 1957, Campbell became the first city along the Mahoning River to build a wastewater treatment plant, thanks to the passing of an income tax levy. By 1958, the facility had been completed, and it would continue under the supervision of James Armaline for the next 16 years. This was the first step taken in Campbell to combat pollution in and around the Mahoning River. The strategic placement of this plant in the southeast corner of Campbell takes advantage of the naturally sloping terrain for better drainage. These photographs show early construction of the property along Wilson Avenue at Jackson Street. New renovations have recently begun on the plant, as well as the addition of an access road through the now vacant Jackson Park. (Both, courtesy of Florence Galida.)

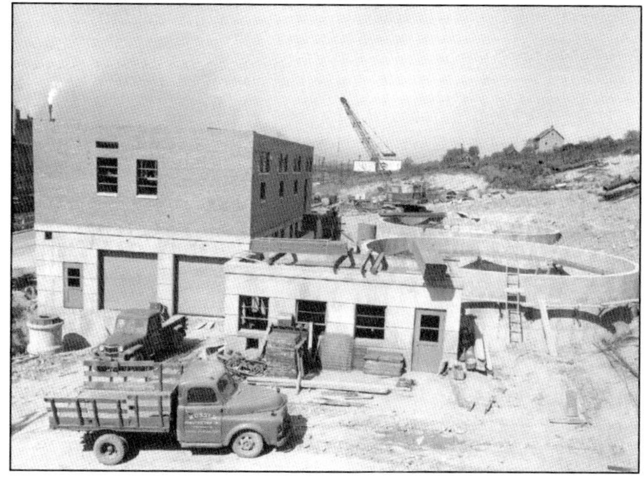

Seven

The Bicentennial and Beyond

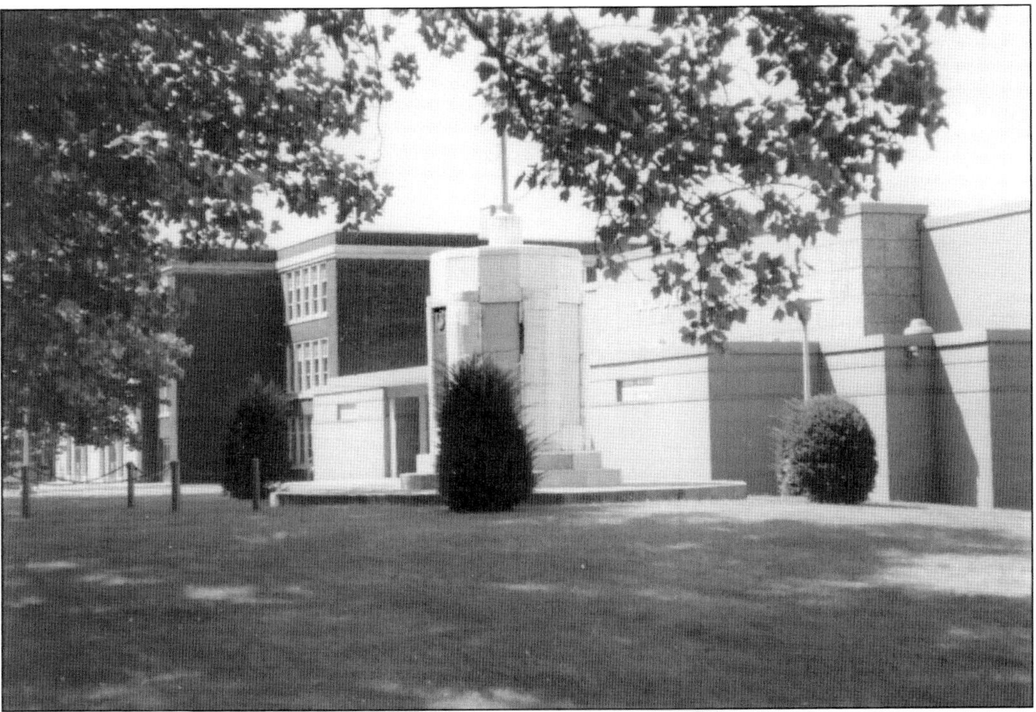

The original war monument, pictured here, stood on the northern end of Memorial High School. After 43 years of weathering, it was demolished on August 30, 1987. The new monument was proudly erected on the southern end of the new high school on November 11, 1987. Each Memorial Day, citizens gather together at the monument to pay their respects by way of guest speakers, prayers, and a celebration of America. (Courtesy of Florence Galida.)

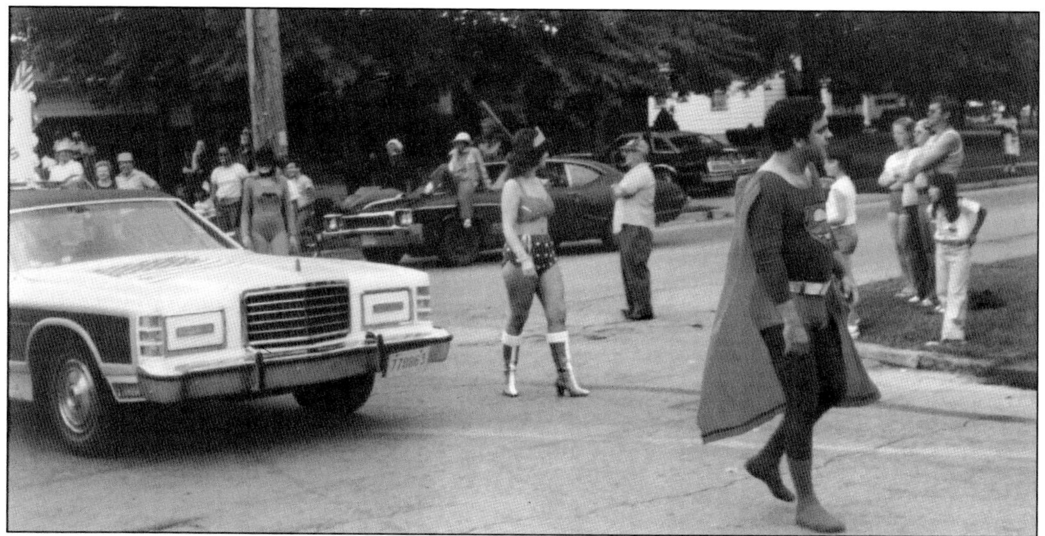

Many participants of the second-annual Campbell Festival parade dressed in their favorite superhero outfits, much to the delight of kids and adults alike. Politicians, churches, sports teams, and schools were all represented in the parade, which contained approximately 70 units. (Courtesy of Florence Galida.)

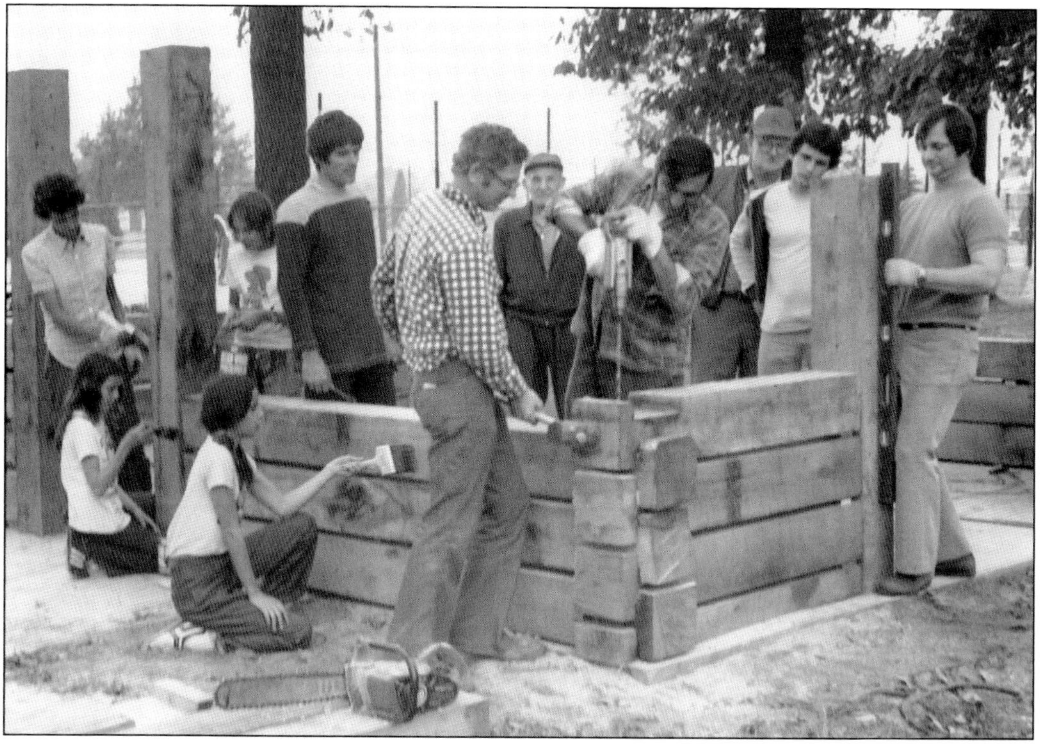

As an early winter set in and lasted longer than expected, bicentennial celebrations ventured well into 1977. Construction on the log cabin at Roosevelt Park began in the fall of 1976 but could not be completed until July 1977 due to poor weather conditions. Along with cabin designer Leonard Summers, several volunteers and full-time workers partnered with various craftsmen to finish the job. (Courtesy of Florence Galida.)

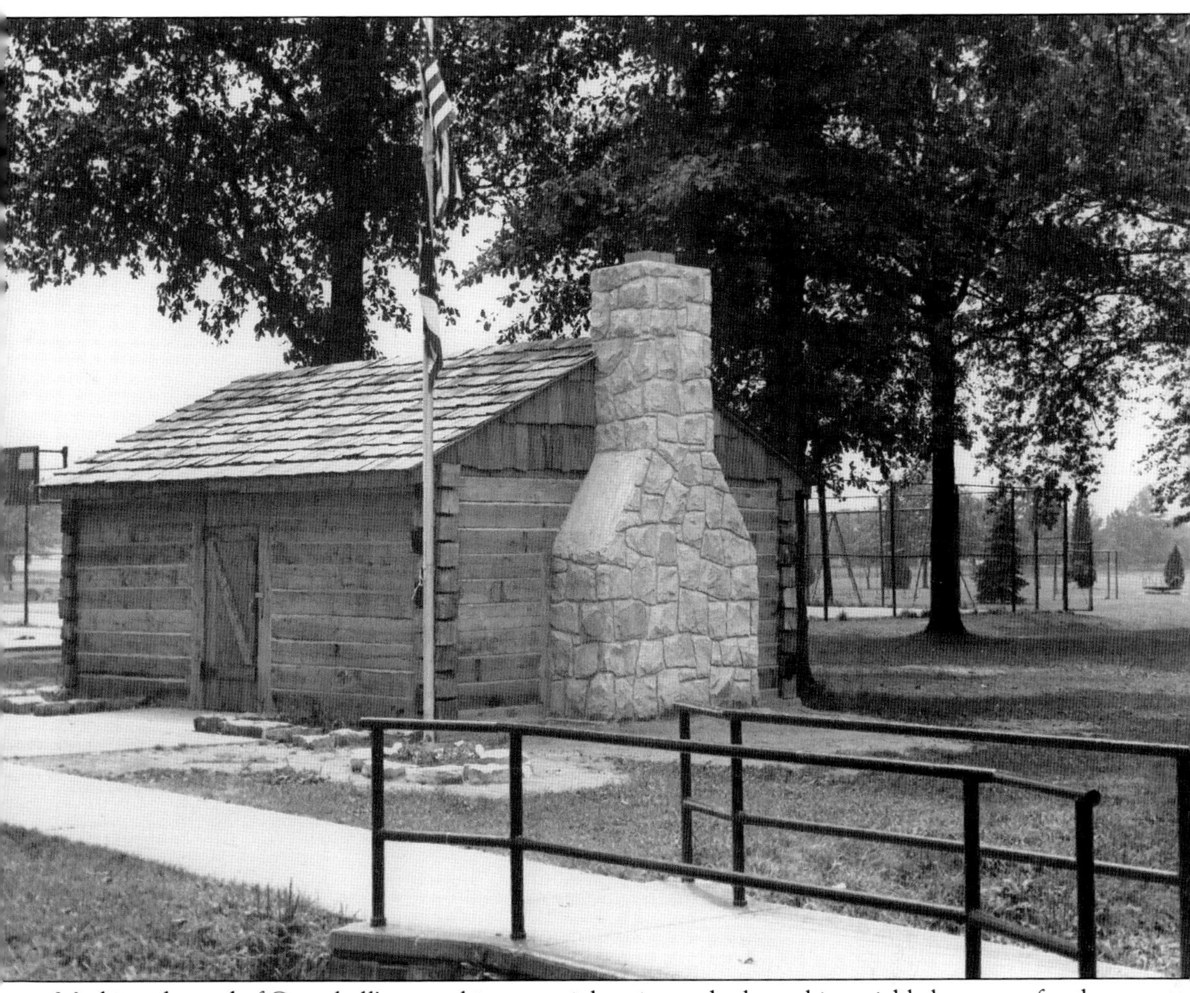

Marking the end of Campbell's seven bicentennial projects, the log cabin quickly became a focal point of Roosevelt Park. During the cold winter months, the basketball courts would be turned into an ice-skating rink. The log cabin played host to cold patrons who wanted hot chocolate and a warm fire before going back out into the bitter weather. The Calex Corporation graciously donated the flagpole, while state representative George D. Tablack presented the Ohio flag. (Courtesy of Florence Galida.)

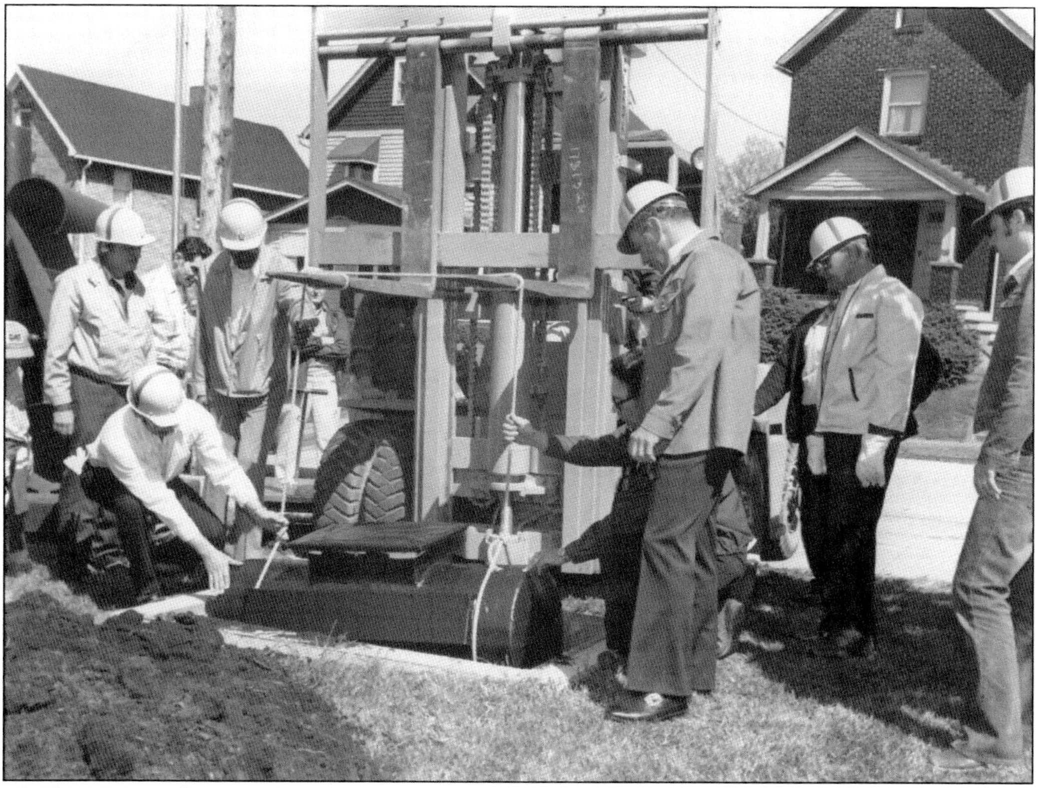

The bicentennial time capsule was originally scheduled to be buried in December 1976, but bad weather postponed the sealing of the capsule until May 7, 1977. City residents were encouraged to submit photographs of relatives, family trees, and letters to future descendants. Other objects included within the capsule were a 1976 telephone book, sports programs, articles on local history, newspapers, coins, a hard hat, and much more. Due to be opened in 2076, the time capsule vault still stands in front of the current municipal building on Tenney Avenue. (Courtesy of Florence Galida.)

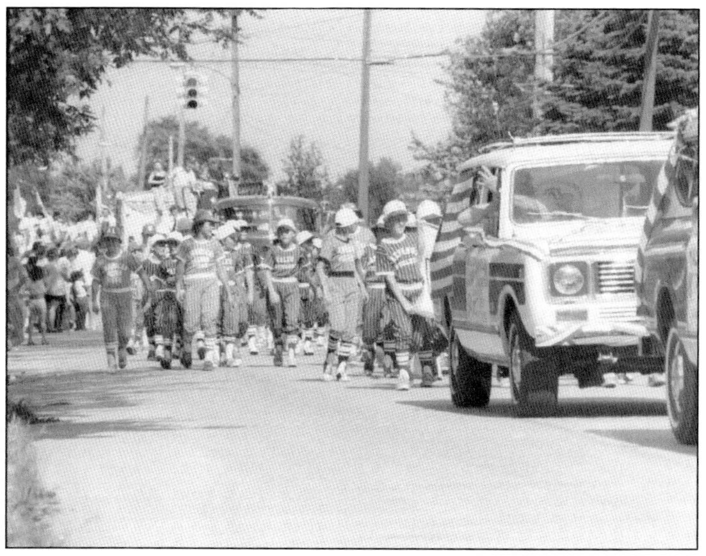

On July 2, 1976, the entire city came together to celebrate the bicentennial of the United States. Police officers, firefighters, politicians, and business owners participated in the parade alongside children from various local sports teams, churches, and schools. This was a great time in the city with many activities planned to encourage patriotism and fellowship. (Courtesy of Florence Galida.)

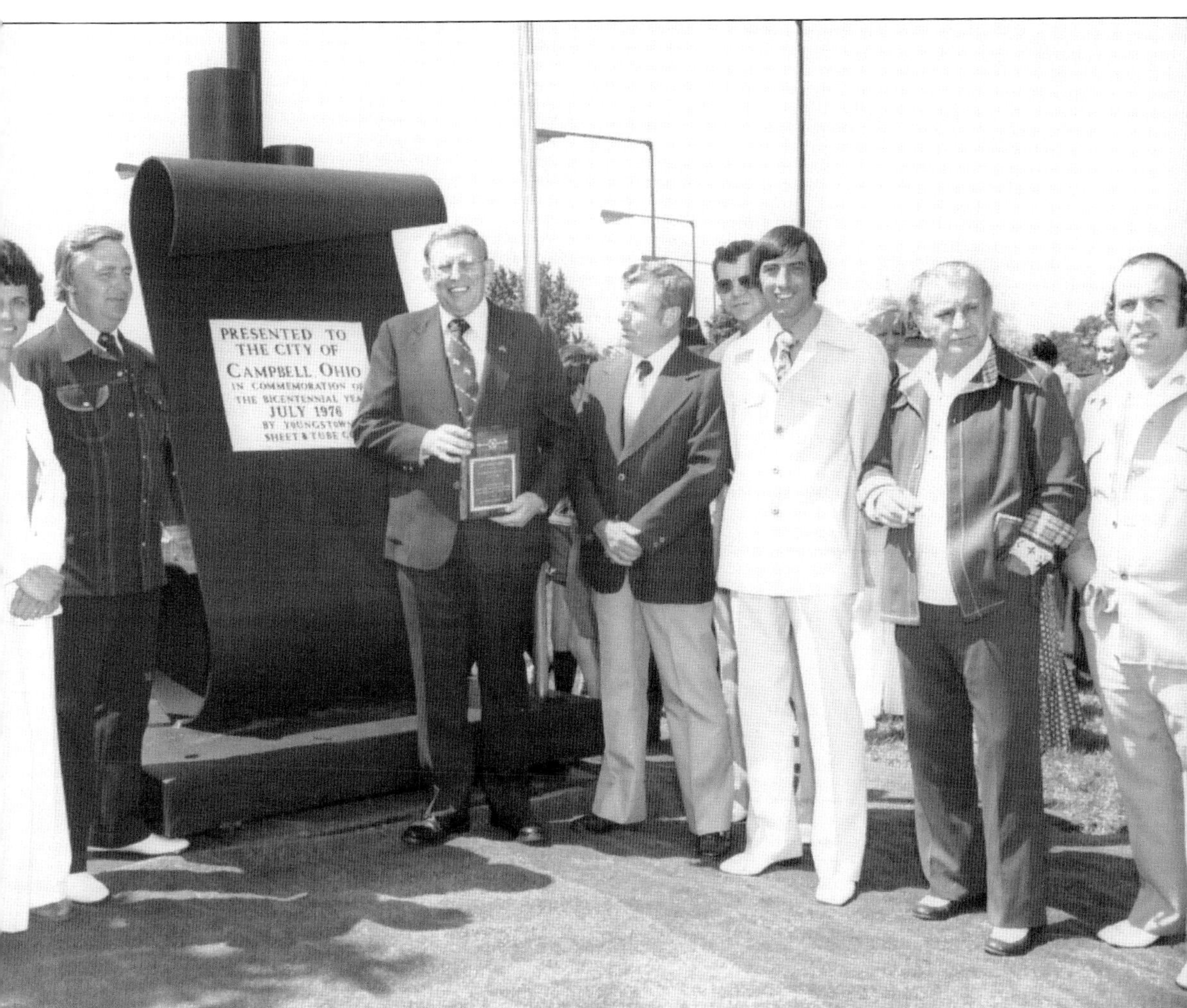

On July 2, 1976, this monument was donated to the city with the following inscription: "Presented to the City of Campbell, Ohio, in commemoration of the bicentennial year July 1976 by Youngstown Sheet & Tube Company." From left to right are Florence Galida, cochairman of the Campbell Bicentennial Committee; Jim Bowman of Youngstown Sheet and Tube Company; Ronald Towns, district manager of Youngstown Sheet and Tube Company; Jim Walker, designer of monument from Youngstown Sheet and Tube Company; Mike Kushma, cochairman of the Campbell Bicentennial Committee; Michael J. Katula Jr., mayor of Campbell; Frank Leseganich, director of United Steelworkers, District 26; and Jim Sferra, president of Local 1418. (Courtesy of Florence Galida.)

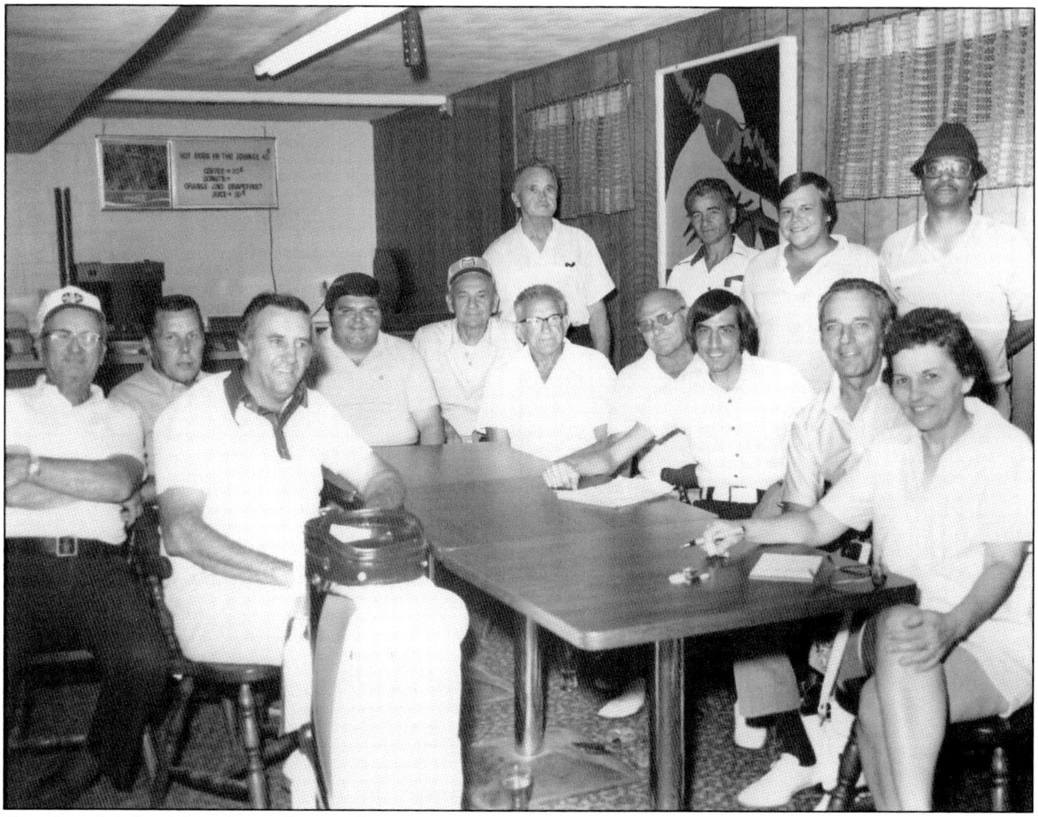

On April 26, 1926, the village of East Youngstown changed its name to the city of Campbell. To commemorate this notable event in the city's history, several residents organized a golf tournament held at the Countryside Golf Course on Sunday, September 5, 1976. Here, members of the committee, chaired by Mayor Michael J. Katula Jr., pause for a photograph while discussing details of the event. (Courtesy of Florence Galida.)

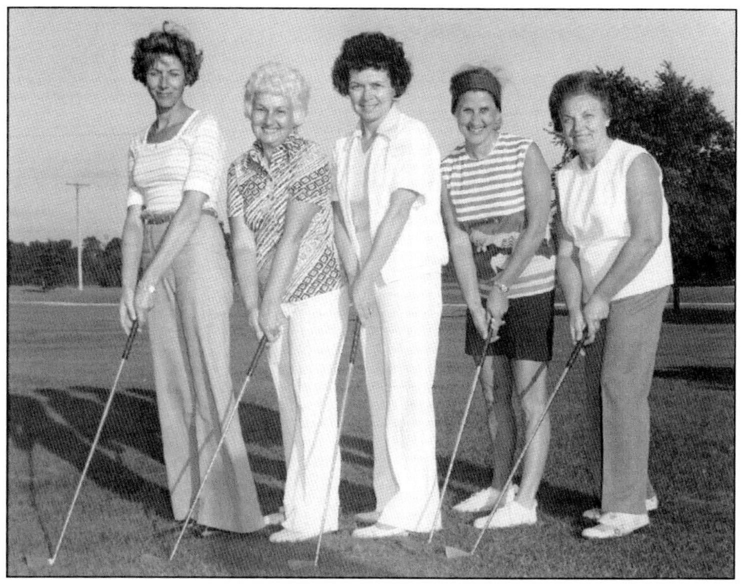

The winners of the women's competition during the first-annual Campbell Open are pictured here in 1976. From left to right are Gloria Katula, Stasia Sertich, Dorothy Korchnak, Natalie Vetresin, and Sue Reichert. (Courtesy of Florence Galida.)

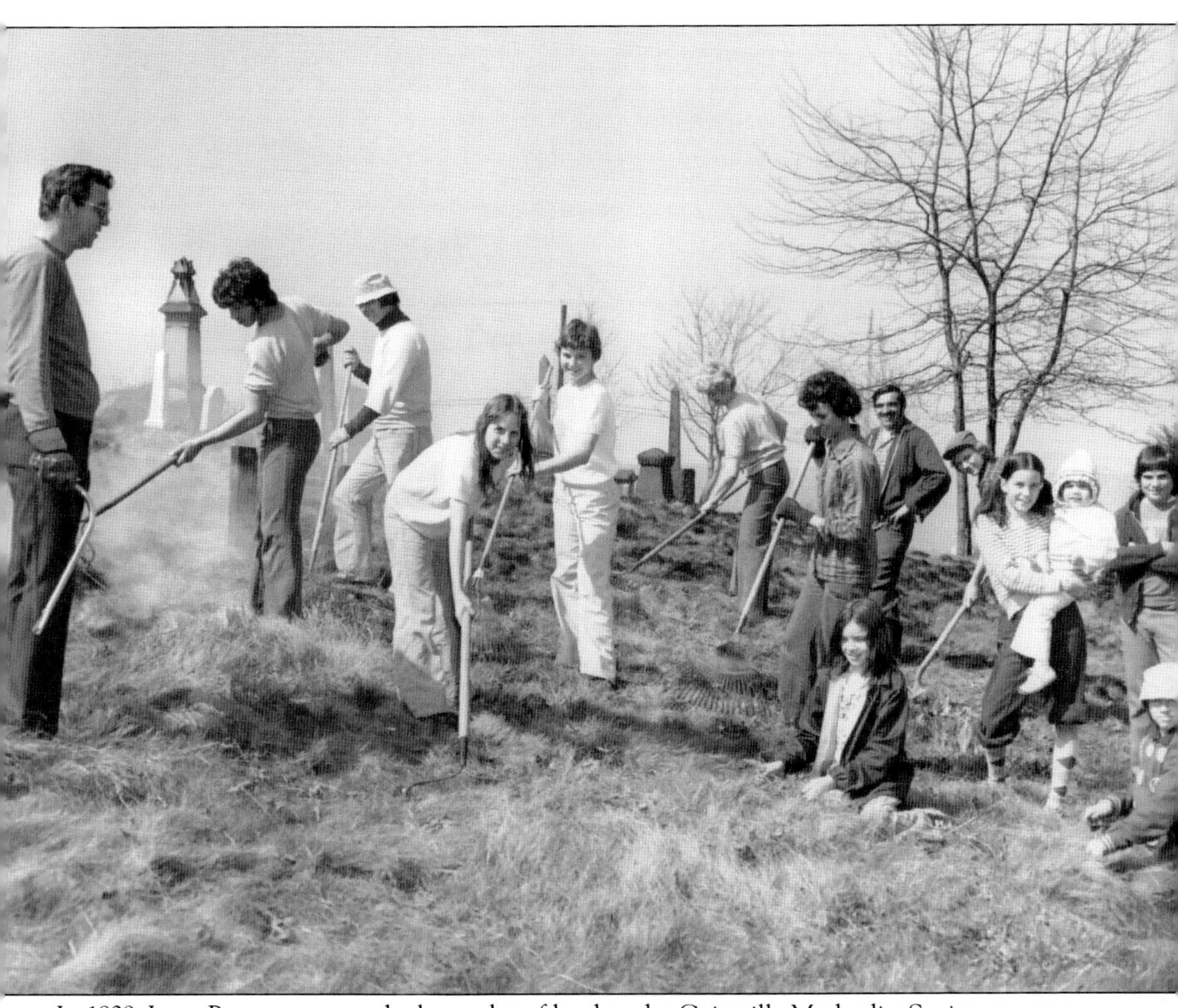

In 1839, Isaac Powers presented a large plot of land to the Coitsville Methodist Society to erect a church and cemetery, the first in Coitsville Township. The Pioneer Methodist Cemetery is seen as it appeared in 1976 during the early stages of its restoration. Located on the corner of Struthers-Liberty and McCartney Roads (formerly Youngstown-Bedford and Poland Roads, respectively), the cemetery contains the remains of some of the area's earliest settlers. (Courtesy of Florence Galida.)

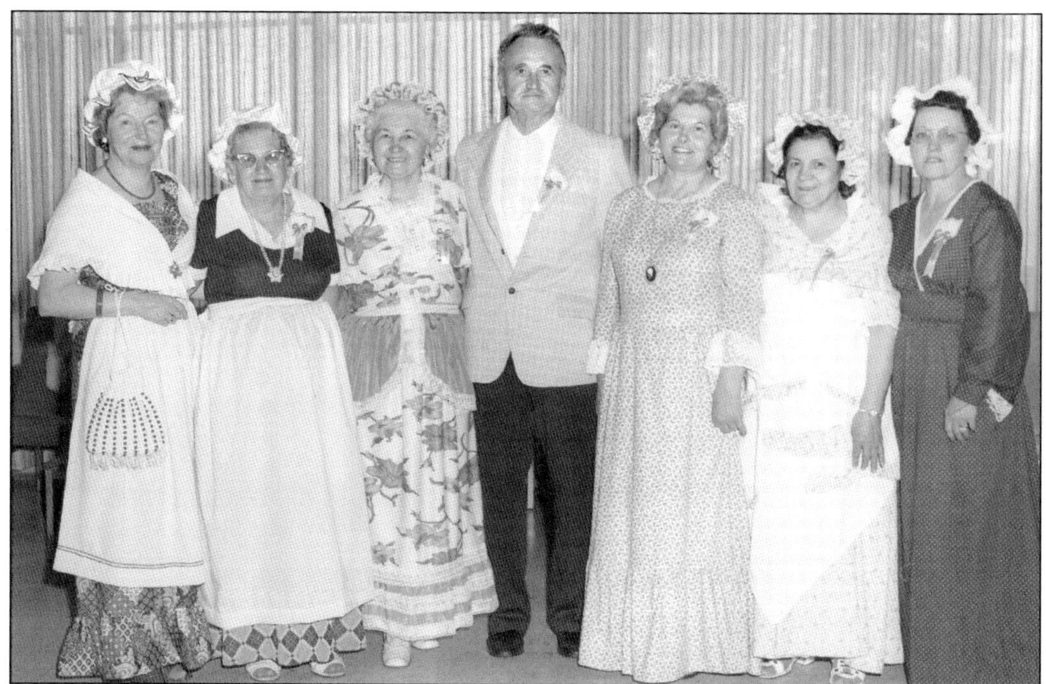

Celebrations continued during the Bicentennial Ball held at the Archangel Michael Hall on April 30, 1976. Not only did participants celebrate the nation's birthday, they also commemorated the 50th anniversary of the changing of East Youngstown to the city of Campbell. (Courtesy of Florence Galida.)

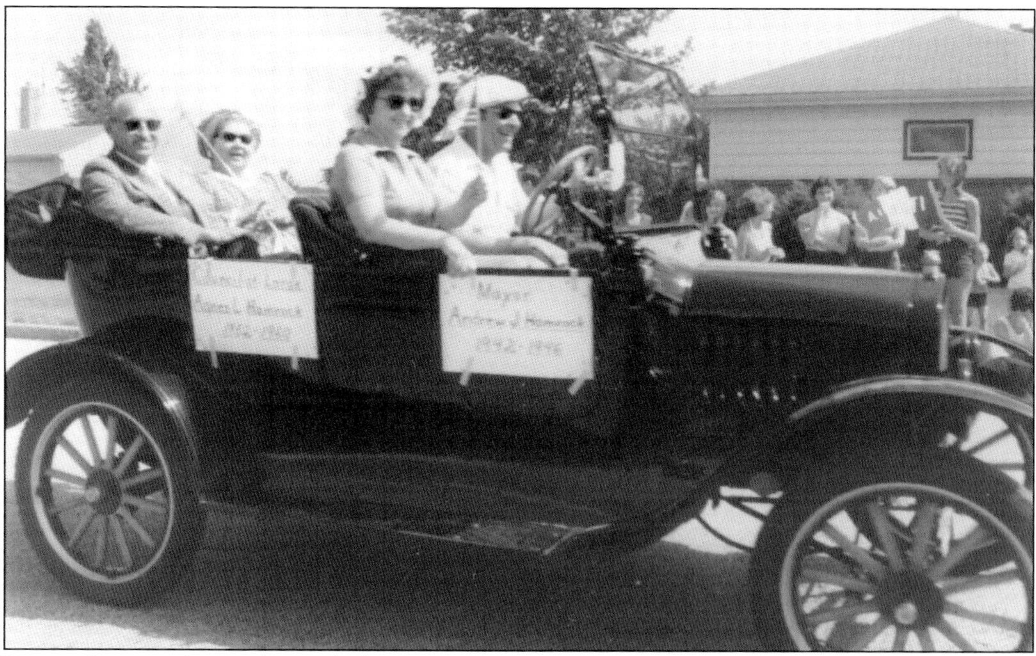

During the second-annual Campbell Festival in 1977, many former and current politicians participated to show off their city pride. Seen in the rear of the vehicle are former mayor Andrew J. Hamrock and his wife, former councilwoman-at-large Agnes L. Hamrock. (Courtesy of Florence Galida.)

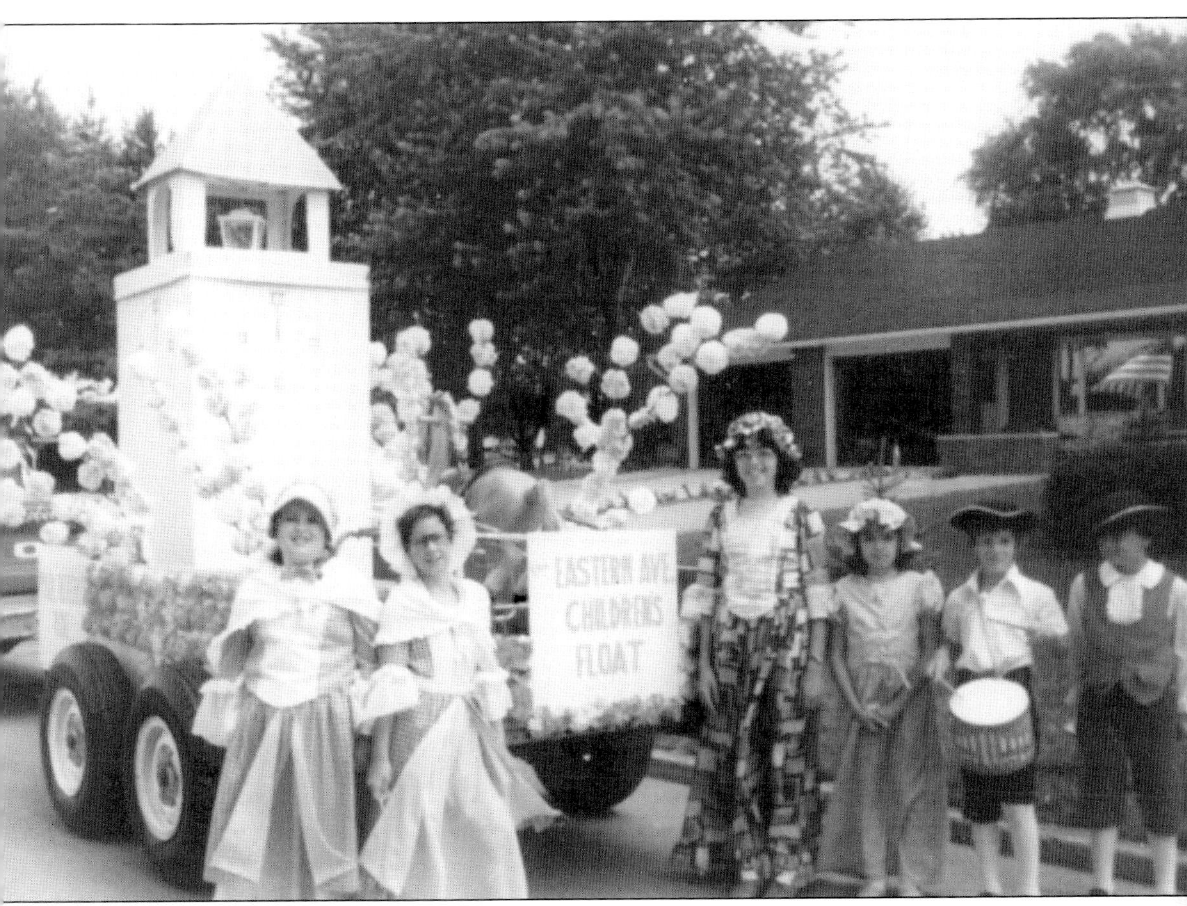

Children from Eastern Avenue are pictured during the 1976 bicentennial parade. These kids worked together to create an astonishingly awesome float to show their American spirit. (Courtesy of Florence Galida.)

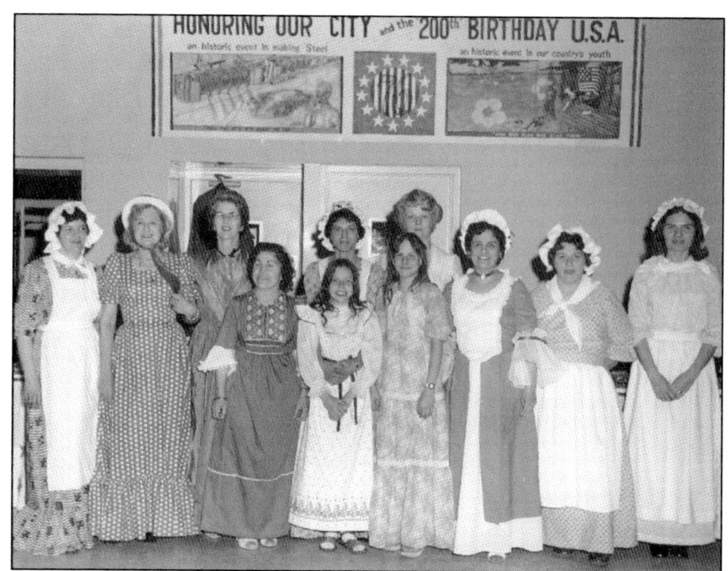

At the 1776 Bicentennial Ball at the Archangel Michael Hall, women wore Colonial dresses and danced to traditional music. From left to right are (first row) Toni Mafrica, Joan Galida, and Gale Galida; (second row) Matilda Marino, Kaye Travers, Peg Kornick, Florence Galida, Susan Summers, Carmel Malmer, Rosalee DeTunno, and Edwina Minnie. (Courtesy of Florence Galida.)

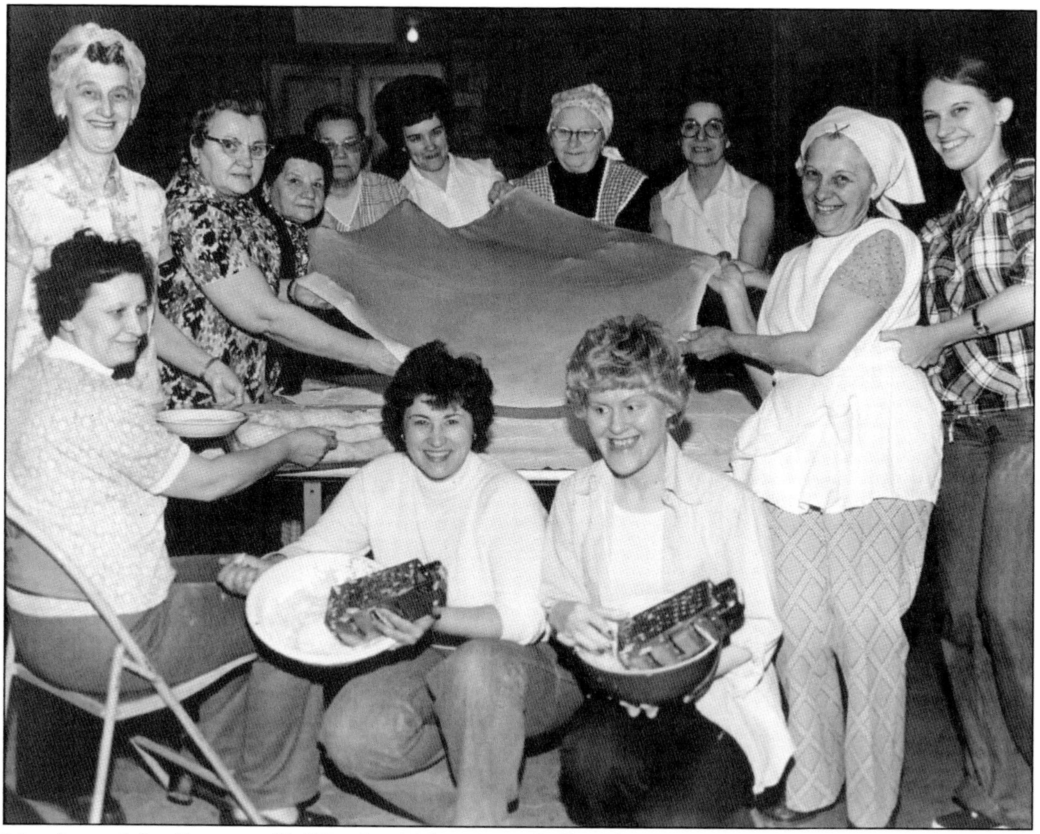

Members of the Croatian Hall Lodge 185 in Campbell make a tasty strudel treat for an upcoming lamb roast. From left to right are (first row) Antonietta Tomich, JoAnn Borak, Theresa Rabovsky, Helen Chapella, and Rosemary Olsavsky; (second row) Marie Tekac, Marie Blazo, Daisy Litch, Mary Stankich, Helen Urichich, Mitzi Kolmacic, and Josephine Kolmacic. (Courtesy of Florence Galida.)

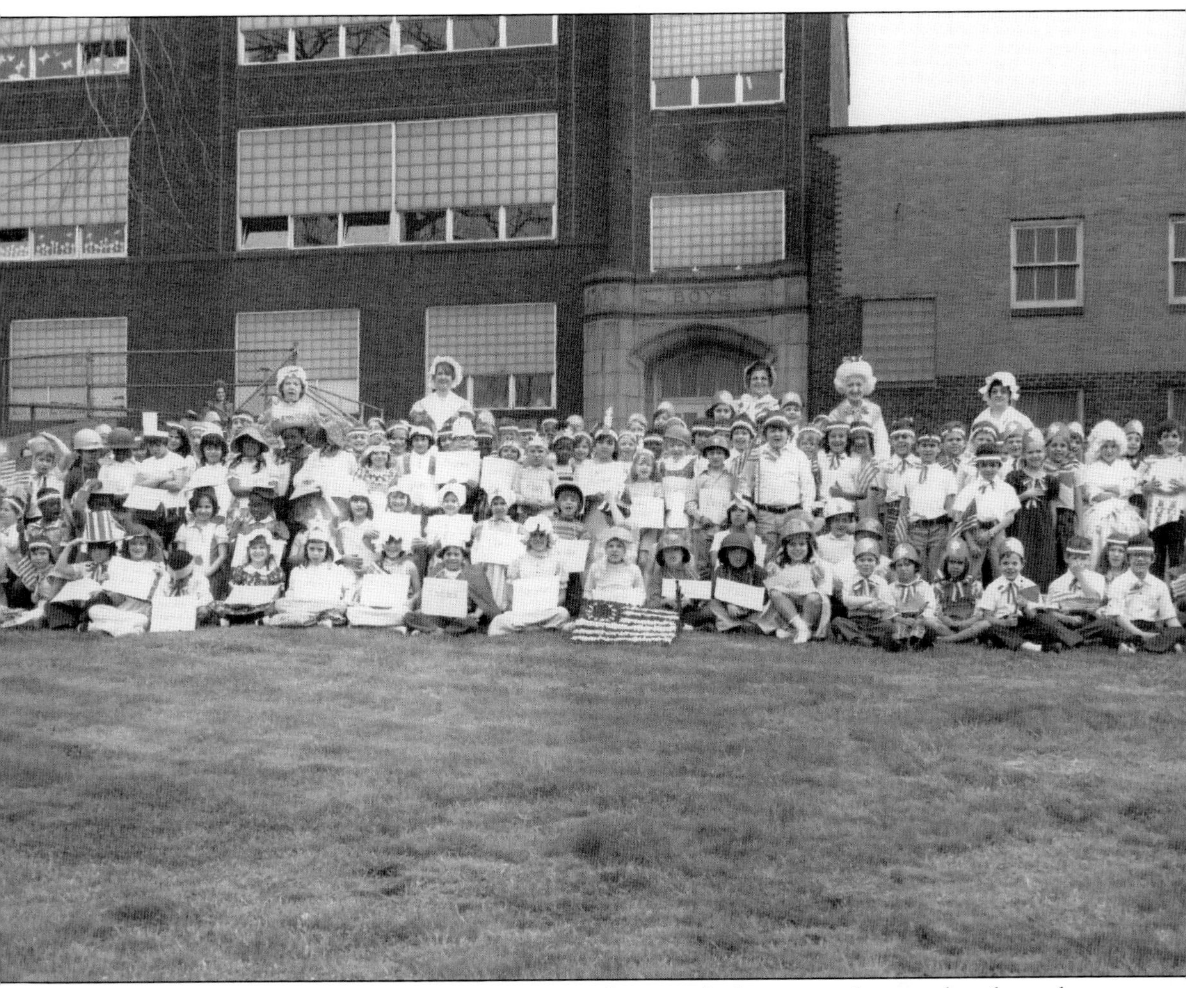

In support of the 1976 bicentennial activities and city-wide festivities, first graders from the Penhale School dressed in Colonial outfits and accessories made in their classroom. Teachers in particular loved these events because they were able to educate the students, all while having fun. Participation did not stop in the classroom. Students, teachers, and family members were also known to donate their time to make the festivities a joyous occasion for the entire city. (Courtesy of Florence Galida.)

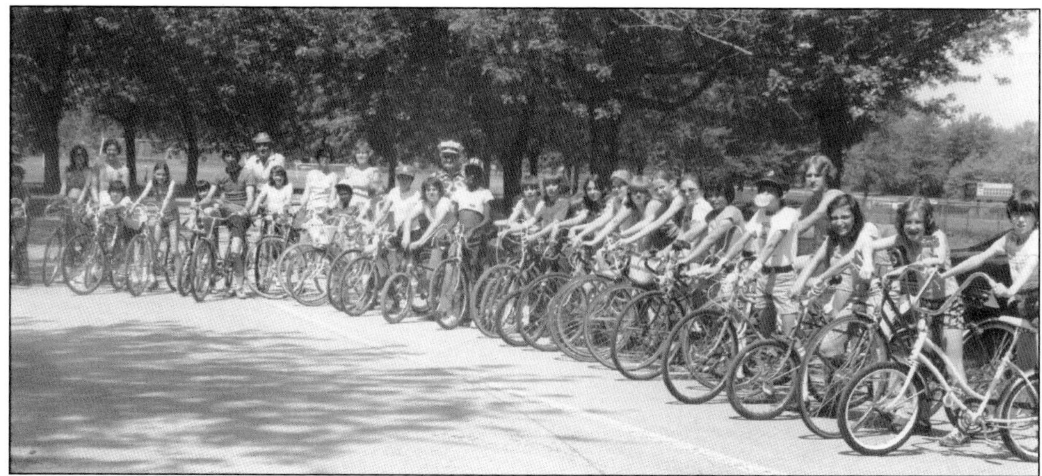

Ready to enjoy the summer weather, Campbell kids of all ages line up with their bicycles for a photograph in Roosevelt Park. Currently, there are five baseball diamonds, a large field used for soccer and flag football, multiple playgrounds and pavilions, and a beautiful community center with a gazebo. The modernization of park facilities and roads is a far cry from the swamp that encompassed the land prior to 1937. (Courtesy of Florence Galida.)

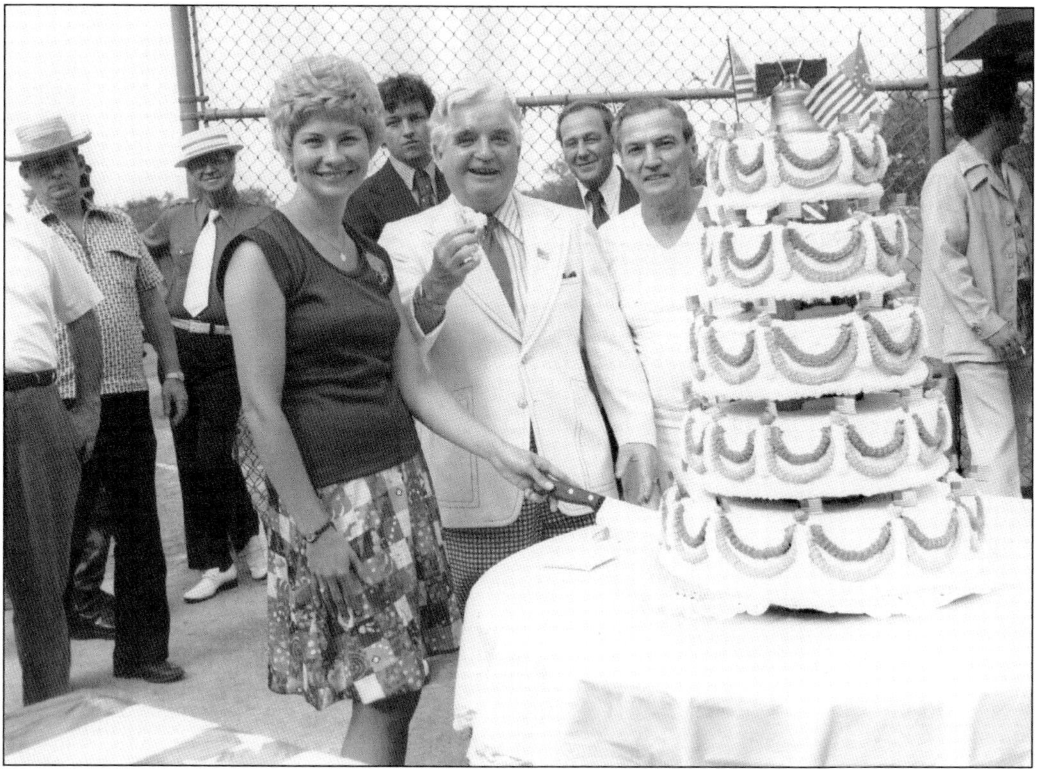

The 1976 bicentennial parade began on Tenney Avenue at Struthers-Liberty Road and continued to its final destination at the Campbell Athletic Club field in Roosevelt Park. Christy's Pastry Shoppe donated this red, white, and blue cake, baked to feed over a 1,000 people. From left to right around the table are Marian Katula, Congressman Charles J. Carney, and cake creator John Kristian. (Courtesy of Florence Galida.)

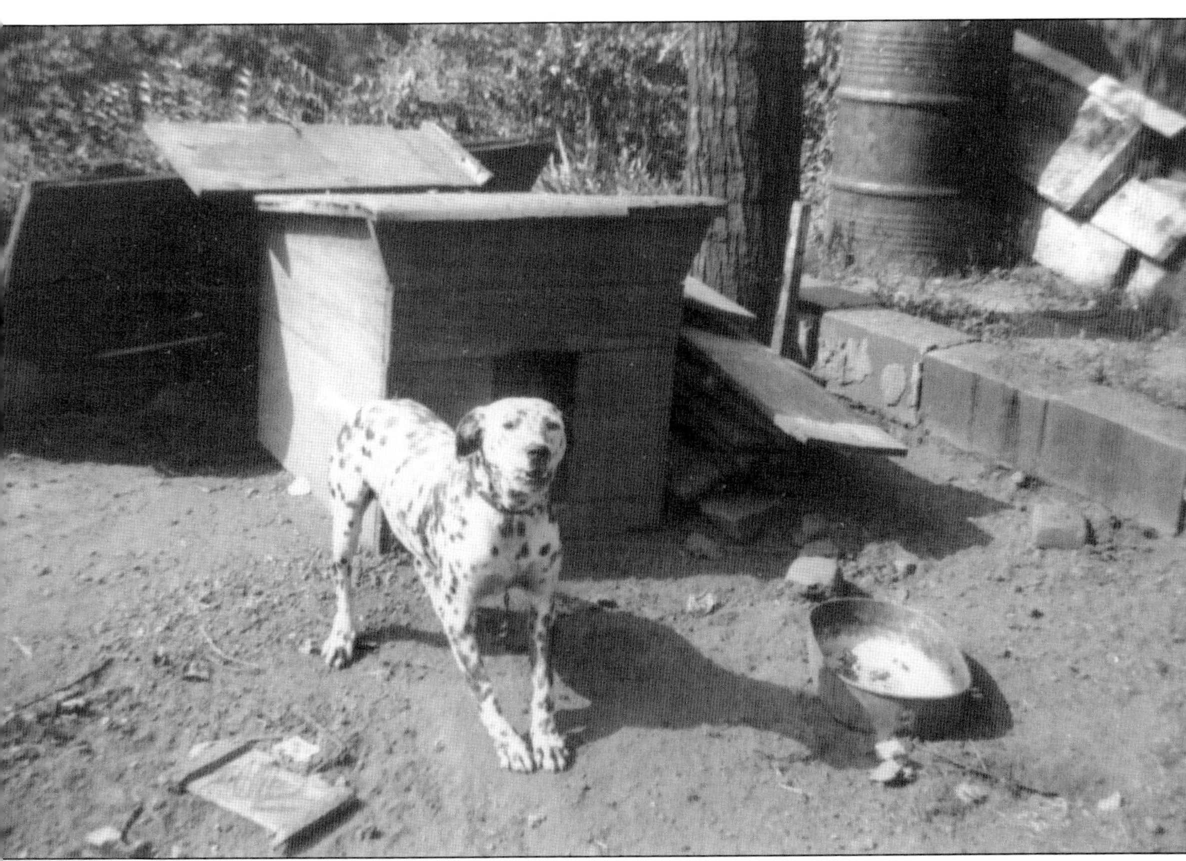

The city of Campbell was born from the needs of the Youngstown Sheet and Tube Company Campbell Works. Through hard work, dedication, and love, the people of this proud community continue on the traditions and cultures of past generations for the betterment of their future. Today, several Campbell organizations have been established to preserve history, beautify the city, and provide an overall positive experience that only a small community could. Bambi the dalmatian of Gary Zayac is pictured in the backyard of a Tremble Avenue residence on July 2, 1951. (Courtesy of Edward Zamets.)

Discover Thousands of Local History Books Featuring Millions of Vintage Images

Arcadia Publishing, the leading local history publisher in the United States, is committed to making history accessible and meaningful through publishing books that celebrate and preserve the heritage of America's people and places.

Find more books like this at
www.arcadiapublishing.com

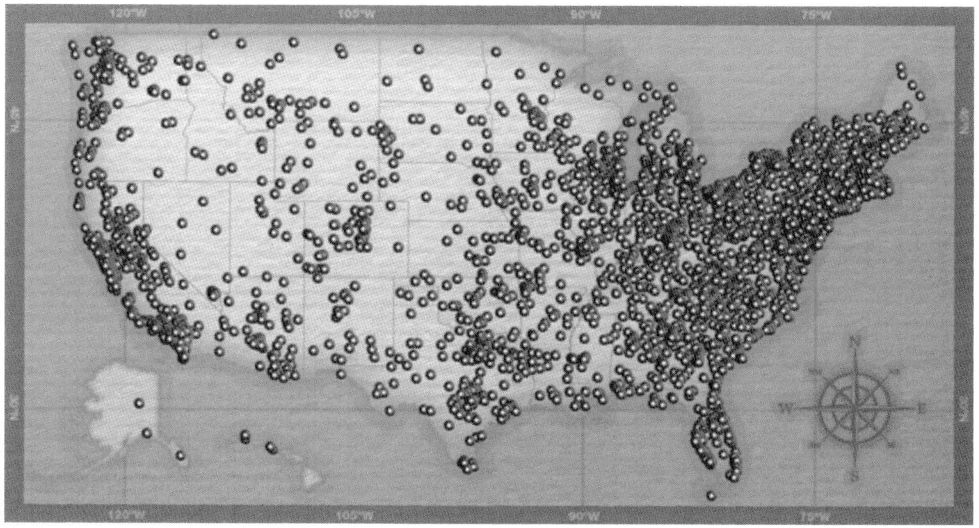

Search for your hometown history, your old stomping grounds, and even your favorite sports team.

Consistent with our mission to preserve history on a local level, this book was printed in South Carolina on American-made paper and manufactured entirely in the United States. Products carrying the accredited Forest Stewardship Council (FSC) label are printed on 100 percent FSC-certified paper.

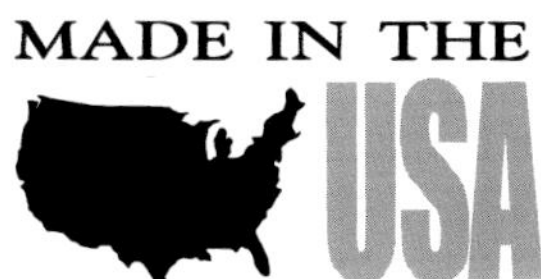